Epochal Crisis

In a groundbreaking new study, acclaimed scholar of global capitalism William I. Robinson presents a bold, original, and timely "big picture" analysis of the unprecedented global crisis. Robinson synthesizes the different economic, social, political, military, and ecological dimensions of the crisis, applying his theory of global capitalism to elucidate these multidimensional and interconnected aspects. Addressing urgent issues such as economic stagnation, runaway financial speculation, unprecedented social inequalities, political conflict, expanding wars, and the threat to the biosphere, he illustrates how these different dimensions relate to one another and stem from the underlying contradictions of a global system spiralling out of control. This is a significant theoretical contribution to the study of globalization and capitalist crisis, in which Robinson concludes that the conditions for global capitalist renewal are becoming exhausted.

WILLIAM I. ROBINSON is Distinguished Professor of Sociology, and Global and International Studies at the University of California at Santa Barbara. He is the acclaimed author of numerous award-winning books, including *Global Capitalism and the Crisis of Humanity* (Cambridge, 2014), and is a frequent speaker on a wide range of current topics, among them global politics and economics, capitalist crises, and resistance movements. His theory of global capitalism has been hailed as a theoretical milestone in understanding the dynamics of the contemporary global order.

Epochal Crisis

The Exhaustion of Global Capitalism

WILLIAM I. ROBINSON
University of California

CAMBRIDGE
UNIVERSITY PRESS

Shaftesbury Road, Cambridge CB2 8EA, United Kingdom

One Liberty Plaza, 20th Floor, New York, NY 10006, USA

477 Williamstown Road, Port Melbourne, VIC 3207, Australia

314–321, 3rd Floor, Plot 3, Splendor Forum, Jasola District Centre, New Delhi – 110025, India

103 Penang Road, #05–06/07, Visioncrest Commercial, Singapore 238467

Cambridge University Press is part of Cambridge University Press & Assessment, a department of the University of Cambridge.

We share the University's mission to contribute to society through the pursuit of education, learning and research at the highest international levels of excellence.

www.cambridge.org
Information on this title: www.cambridge.org/9781009670494

DOI: 10.1017/9781009670517

© William I. Robinson 2025

This publication is in copyright. Subject to statutory exception and to the provisions of relevant collective licensing agreements, no reproduction of any part may take place without the written permission of Cambridge University Press & Assessment.

When citing this work, please include a reference to the DOI 10.1017/9781009670517

First published 2025

Cover image: Planet Earth – Getty Images

A catalogue record for this publication is available from the British Library

A Cataloging-in-Publication data record for this book is available from the Library of Congress

ISBN 978-1-009-67053-1 Hardback
ISBN 978-1-009-67049-4 Paperback

Cambridge University Press & Assessment has no responsibility for the persistence or accuracy of URLs for external or third-party internet websites referred to in this publication and does not guarantee that any content on such websites is, or will remain, accurate or appropriate.

For EU product safety concerns, contact us at Calle de José Abascal, 56, 1°, 28003 Madrid, Spain, or email eugpsr@cambridge.org

Contents

Acknowledgments		*page* vi
	Introduction: Toward a Theory of Global Capitalist Exhaustion	1
1	Structural Crisis: Overaccumulation	12
2	Crisis of Social Reproduction	54
3	Legitimacy Crisis, Geopolitical Conflict, and Global Police State	103
4	Collapse of the Biosphere	143
5	Into the Vortex	180
Select Bibliography		215
Index		218

Acknowledgments

Although the name that appears on the cover of a book gets the credit for writing it, any such endeavor is a collective product of social labor. One can only engage in intellectual labor because many other people cannot. Millions of people worked to produce the food and other essentials I needed to get by while researching and writing this book. My own ideas and insights build on those of countless others whom I have learned from and whose ideas I have studied and absorbed throughout my life. The list of people who have contributed to my own intellectual and political development, which in turn placed me in a position to write this book, is too vast to mention. The many talks I have been invited to give over the years that I have been engaged with the topic of the crisis of global capitalism have given me the opportunity to dialogue with a great many people and to develop the ideas put forth in this book. The best I can do here is mention some of the people who made a more direct contribution to this book. Many thanks, in alphabetical order, to: the late Mario Barrera, Christopher Chase-Dunn, Michael Gordy, Jerry Harris, Marek Hrubec, Rueben Kadushin, Zhandarka Kurti, Rosemary Lee, Joshua Martínez, Chris Meghen, Steven Miller, Jason W. Moore, Peter Phillips, Salvador Rangel, Ryan "Flaco" Rising, Manuel Rozental, Oscar Soto, Manfred Steger, Rodolfo D. Torres, and Hilbourne Watson. Many thanks to Barbara Foley and other comrades from the journal *Science & Society*, in particular, for the symposium in that journal on imperialism and anti-imperialism that helped me debate and clarify my own ideas. A special thanks to: Juan Manuel Sandoval of the Seminario Permanente de Estudios Chicanos y de Fronteras of the Mexican National Institute of Anthropology and History; to my colleagues at the Borders, Regionalization, and Globalization section of the Latin American Social Science Council (CLACSO), among them Marcela Orozco and Thiago Aguiar; to Phil Hearse and Fred Laped at the UK-based Anti-Capitalist Resistance and Resistance Books; to Andy Willis and comrades from Poor People's Army; to Haki, Ali, and their comrades from faraway; to Fred Fuentes of the *LINKS Journal of Socialist Renewal*; and to compañeras and compañeros from Nicaragua and Venezuela who must remain anonymous and whose struggles have helped me better understand the nature of global capitalism, as it touches down in distinct forms in their lands and of resistance to it. I would be remiss not to give a special thanks and acknowledgment to Hoai-An Nguyen, Gursan Senalp, Esra Sengor-Senalp, and Venus Leung for the very many conversations we have had into the wee hours of the morning around the dining room table, at restaurants, bars, and social outings, on many of the topics discussed in this study. I greatly appreciate the invaluable suggestions provided by two anonymous reviewers on an earlier draft of the manuscript. Many thanks to my editors at Cambridge University Press, John Haslam and Carrie Parkinson. My apologies to those whom I may have inadvertently left out. As a matter of course, I am wholly responsible for the many shortcomings of this study.

Introduction
Toward a Theory of Global Capitalist Exhaustion

As any dialectician would tell us, the only thing permanent in the universe is change itself. Everything is in a process of emergence, development, transformation, and ultimately transcendence into something qualitatively new. Capitalism is no exception. The current moment in world capitalism is defined by three key developments. First, the system has become universal through globalization processes that date to the late twentieth century. Second, the system is undergoing a new round of restructuring and transformation based on a much more advanced digitalization and financialization of the entire global economy and society. And third, the system faces an unprecedented and multidimensional crisis that points to the impending exhaustion of global capitalism's capacity for renewal.

If the conquest of the Americas from 1492 and on marked the bloody birth of the world capitalist system, a letter written almost 500 years later, on August 23, 1971, may be as good a date as any to start this story of globalization and civilizational crisis. On that day, soon-to-be U.S. Supreme Court Justice Lewis Powell wrote a confidential memorandum to the U.S. Chamber of Commerce warning that opposition to the capitalist system was becoming widespread. "The sources are varied and diffuse. They include, not unexpectedly, the Communists, New Leftists and other revolutionaries who would destroy the entire system, both political and economic," wrote Powell. However, he continued, "the most disquieting voices joining the chorus of criticism come from perfectly respectable elements of society: from the college campus, the pulpit, the media, the intellectual and literary journals, the arts and sciences, and from politicians."[1]

---

[1] For discussion on the Powell Memorandum and its political context, see Jacob S. Hacker and Paul Pierson, *Winner-Take-All Politics: How Washington Made the Rich Richer – And Turned its Back on the Middle Class* (New York: Simon

The memorandum was a call for the ruling classes to push back against the mounting crisis of capitalist hegemony. The problem was not just political. As states faced a loss of legitimacy, great tremors were also being felt in the world economy. Just a week before the memorandum was drafted, U.S. President Richard Nixon had taken the United States off the gold standard, signaling the start of a deep structural crisis of world capitalism. To retain power, Powell called for the political mobilization of the capitalist class. The ruling groups had to launch a vast counteroffensive, concerted action to restore the freedom of capital to accumulate unconstrained by the working classes and by state regulatory powers. The universities, the mass media, the courts, and politics – all were to become battlefields in the campaign to reconstruct the hegemony of capital. "Business must learn the lesson that political power is necessary; that such power must be assiduously [sic] cultivated; and that when necessary, it must be used aggressively and with determination — without embarrassment and without the reluctance." Nothing less than a call to class warfare from above, it concluded: "There should not be the slightest hesitation to press vigorously in all political arenas for support of the enterprise system. Nor should there be reluctance to penalize politically those who oppose it."

The 1960s and early 1970s were a time of escalating labor militancy, radical social movements, anti-colonial and national liberation struggles, and widespread social unrest. These mass struggles from below were forcing states to impose regulations on the market and reign in on the freedom of capital to accumulate without restraint. The worldwide correlation of class and social forces was shifting in favor of the working and popular classes. Revolution was in the air. If the Powell memorandum's call to class warfare was to have success, the capitalist class would have to exercise a more direct, instrumental control over the state in order to crush the growing power of labor and social movements, to roll back state regulatory powers, and to restore profit-making. Capitalists in the United States mobilized rapidly to meet the challenge.[2] A decisive

---

& Shuster, 2011). For a pdf of the memorandum, see here: www.greenpeace.org/usa/wp-content/uploads/2021/08/PowellMemorandumTypescript.pdf.

[2] The political mobilization of the capitalist class in the United States was swift. The number of corporations with public affairs offices in Washington jumped from 100 in 1968 to over 500 in 1978. In 1971, only 175 firms had registered lobbyists in Washington, but by 1982, nearly 2,500 did. The number of corporate Political Action Committees increased from under 300 in 1976 to

turning point came in 1980, when Federal Reserve Chair Paul Volcker increased interest rates, provoking the worst recession since the Great Depression of the 1930s and breaking the stalemate among contending class forces that had persisted through the 1970s.

If the Volker shocks, as they came to be known, were a critical salvo against labor in the United States, they also marked the onset of a sweeping restructuring and transformation of the world economy. The increase in interest rates thrust the former Third World into an unprecedented debt crisis that undermined attempts to loosen the grip of world capitalist control, bringing an end to calls for a New International Economic Order, and paving the way for austerity and structural adjustment programs. While Powell was referring specifically to the United States, ruling classes around the world heeded the call. An emerging transnational elite organized to regain control. Two years after Powell's memorandum, in July 1973, David Rockefeller convened the political and economic elite from North America, Western Europe, and Japan to form the Trilateral Commission as a top-level multilateral forum for transnational policy coordination and economic globalization.[3] Only two years prior, the CEOs of the top 1,000 transnational corporations, representatives from 100 of the most influential media groups worldwide, key policymakers from national governments and international organizations, and select academics and experts from political, economic, scientific, social, and technological fields established the World Economic Forum (WEF). In the following years, the WEF became the premier clearinghouse and planning body for an emerging transnational capitalist class (TCC) and its political allies – a true international of capital.

The crisis that began in the 1970s was a turning point for world capitalism. The emerging transnational elite set about to beat back the threat from below and restore the power of capital by launching what came to be known as globalization. Realms have been written about the process, much of it focused on the rise of a new global economy. Its quintessence, however, was and is political: Violent class warfare by capital against the global working and popular classes. The

---

over 1,200 by the middle of 1980. See Hacker and Person, *Winner-Take-All*, for these details.

[3] The best account of the rise of Trilateralism remains Stephen Gill, *American Hegemony and the Trilateral Commission* (Cambridge: Cambridge University Press, 1992). Although writing in 1992, Gill foresaw that the establishment of the Commission was bound up with the rise of transnational capital.

ruling groups went global to break free from nation-state constraints to accumulation. Transnationally oriented fractions among them vied for and, in many countries, won state power in the 1980s and 1990s. The TCC and its agents in these capitalist states undertook a vast new round of restructuring and expansion of the world economy, putting into place a globally integrated production, financial, and service system into which every country has become inserted.

The TCC, as the hegemonic fraction of capital on a world scale, reconstituted the power of capital through new worldwide circuits of accumulation. Globalization has often been referred to as a vast expansion of markets around the world. But more than market integration, it involved the transnationalization of the production process itself, an organic integration of the worldwide circuits of capital. The inverse of the fragmentation and decentralization of production across the planet has been an unprecedented concentration and centralization of capital on a world scale. In 2018, just seventeen global financial conglomerates collectively managed $41.1 trillion dollars, more than half the GDP of the entire planet. These conglomerates are so transnationally entangled among themselves that separating them out into national boxes or into clearly delineated companies, much less countries, is simply impossible – they constitute a self-invested network of interlocking capital that spans the globe.[4]

I have been researching and writing since the 1990s about these worldwide transformations.[5] Global capitalism as a qualitatively

---

[4] Peter Phillips, *Giants: The Global Power Elite* (New York: Seven Stories Press, 2018), p. 35. In 2016 the inward stock of FDI totaled $27 trillion, foreign affiliates of TNCs registered total assets of $113 trillion, and sales of $38 trillion. See Jerry R. Harris, "Who Leads Global Capitalism? The Unlikely Rise of China," *Class, Race and Corporate Power*, 6(1), 2018, https://digitalcommons.fiu.edu/cgi/viewcontent.cgi?article=1119&context=classracecorporatepower, pp. 8–10.

[5] In Chapter 1 I will recap my theory of global capitalism but will not flesh out the argument already developed in earlier works. I refer readers, inter-alia, to William I. Robinson: *Promoting Polyarchy: Globalization, U.S. Intervention, Hegemony* (Cambridge: Cambridge University Press, 1996); *Transnational Conflicts: Central America, Social Change, and Globalization* (London: Verso, 2003); *A Theory of Global Capitalism* (Baltimore: Johns Hopkins University Press, 2004); *Latin America and Global Capitalism* (Baltimore: Johns Hopkins University Press, 2008); *Global Capitalism and the Crisis of Humanity* (New York: Cambridge University Press, 2014); *The Global Police State* (London: Pluto Press, 2020).

new epoch in this ongoing and open-ended evolution of world capitalism preceded three earlier ones – mercantilism, competitive or classical industrial capitalism, and national corporate or "monopoly" capitalism. Each of these long waves in the system's development involved a series of minor crises that eventually culminated in major system-wide structural crises that were resolved through radical restructuring and expansion of the system, in the midst of economic turbulence, social and political upheavals, wars and revolutions that brought about new class relations, technologies, and patterns of capital accumulation.

Ernest Mandel published his noted study, *Late Capitalism*, in 1972, just at the end of the long wave of post-WWII capitalist expansion and the onset of the structural crisis of the 1970s. He attempted to theorize the post-WWII development of world capitalism and come to grips with the incipient transformations that would lead to the epoch of globalization, including the increasing international expansion of capital. He claimed, however, that "late capitalism" was not a new epoch in the ongoing development of world capitalism but "merely a further development of the imperialist, monopoly-capitalist epoch."[6] Yet there can be no "late capitalism," only continuously "la*ter* capitalism" with moments in which quantitative changes give way to qualitatively new forms.

Half a century after Mandel published his book and with the benefit of hindsight, we can show how global capitalism is a qualitatively new epoch in this open-ended history, and we can explore how the crisis of the 1970s unfolded. That crisis marked a transition to the new epoch of global capitalism that resolved, for the time being, the system-wide structural crisis to which the Powell Memorandum referred. The ruling groups pushed back the tide of revolution in the former Third World. The Soviet bloc disintegrated as both it and China reintegrated into world capitalism. Social democracy gave way to a savage neoliberalism that disorganized working classes around the world. The global economy experienced a boom in the 1990s. Profit rates and the power of capital were restored. As the left retreated into liberal reformism and identitarian politics, the ruling classes, giddy with excess amidst escalating inequalities and mass discontent, celebrated the "end of history."

---

[6] Ernest Mandel, *Late Capitalism* (London: Verso, 1975 [1972]), p. 9.

But the halcyon days of globalization came to an end with the global financial collapse of 2008. World trade contracted for the first time in several decades in the wake of that collapse, while populists and political demagogues, mostly from the far-right, put forth a protectionist and anti-globalization discourse as they stoked the fans of xenophobia and nationalism. The 2008 Great Recession signaled the onset of a new system-wide crisis. It is a structural crisis of overaccumulation and chronic stagnation. The TCC has accumulated obscene amounts of wealth, well beyond what it can reinvest. The problem of surplus capital has never been greater. The wave of expansion launched with globalization has become exhausted. The TCC and its agents in states are in an incessant and increasingly desperate search for new outlets to invest overaccumulated capital. This leads the system to become even more violent, predatory, and reckless.

But the crisis is much more than just economic. It is a crisis of social reproduction. Billions of people cannot survive as social disintegration spreads. Whole regions and countries are collapsing. Hundreds of millions are being displaced by climate change, conflict, and persecution. The ruling groups face a political crisis of state legitimacy, capitalist hegemony, and geopolitical confrontation. Rising inequality, impoverishment, and insecurity for working and popular classes after decades of social decay wrought by neoliberalism are throwing states into crises of legitimacy, destabilizing national political systems, and jeopardizing elite control. The Ukraine and Gaza wars, along with the New Cold War between Washington and Beijing, are accelerating the violent crackup of the post-WWII international system. The planetary ecosystem on which human civilization is based is breaking down under the impact of unrestrained global capital accumulation. The ecological dimension of the crisis makes it existential.

As global corporate and political elites woke up from a drunkard's hangover after the world capitalist boom of the late twentieth and early twenty-first centuries, they have had to acknowledge that the crisis is out of control. In its 2023 Global Risk Report, the WEF warned that the world confronts a "polycrisis" involving escalating economic, political, social, and climactic impacts that "are converging to shape a unique, uncertain and turbulent decade to come."[7] Just two years

---

[7] World Economic Forum, "The Global Risks Report 2023," Geneva, 2023, www3.weforum.org/docs/WEF_Global_Risks_Report_2023.pdf.

earlier, in 2021, a U.S. government intelligence report warned that the world "will face more intense and cascading global challenges" in the coming years, including "climate change, disease, financial crises, and technological disruptions" that "are likely to manifest more frequently and intensely in almost every region and country" and that "produce widespread strains on states and societies as well as shocks that could be catastrophic."[8] The TCC's drive to expand at all costs the endless accumulation of capital makes it impossible for the global ruling class to offer viable solutions to the epochal crisis. The Davos elite may be clueless as to how to resolve the crisis, but other factions of the ruling groups are experimenting with how to mold interminable political chaos and financial instability into a new and more deadly phase of global capitalism. As the crisis progresses, it is cracking up political systems and undermining stability everywhere. The center collapses. Consensual mechanisms of domination are breaking down as the ruling groups turn toward authoritarianism, dictatorship, and fascism.

Capitalism has managed to weather one crisis after another in its centuries-long existence, proving more resilient than its doomsday forecaster. But the current crisis is like no other. We appear to be arriving at the historic exhaustion of the conditions for capitalist renewal. An epochal crisis signals the irreversible decline in capitalism's capacity to reproduce itself through time and space. New digital technologies coupled with major reforms may lead to a renewed lease of life for global capitalism, but only for a time, giving a last gasp to an historic system that is reaching the end of its ability to reproduce itself for reasons this book explores. The time frame for such an exhaustion is not years but decades. Reform of a more radical nature may prolong the life of the system for decades. But the system *must* expand constantly. The type of statis we would need to avert a collapse of the biosphere is not an option for capitalism. At some point in the coming decades, the self-expansion of capitalism must cease in order for us to survive.

These are, of course, bold claims. Marxists have debated for many decades the nature of capitalist crises, whether the system will inevitably collapse, and if such a collapse would result in a superior form of social organization or in a degeneration of civilization. We shall

---

[8] National Intelligence Council, "Global Trends 2040: A More Contested World," March 2021, www.dni.gov/files/ODNI/documents/assessments/GlobalTrends_2040.pdf.

explore these matters in the chapters to follow. Theories of capitalism were historically also theories of crisis. Much crisis theory, however, deals with cyclical crises, whereas I am concerned here with structural crisis and, beyond that, a more general systemic crisis. The crisis of the 1970s contributed to a revival of Marxist crisis theories, whereas that of 2008 sparked widespread discussion and conjunctural analysis but little if any new theoretical work.[9] This work attempts to point us in the direction of a theory of capitalist exhaustion by identifying and analyzing the epochal crisis that is before us.

The different dimensions of crisis – economic, social, political, and ecological – constitute a single historic process of capitalist exhaustion. The separation of the different dimensions of global capitalist crisis as laid out in this book is for methodological purposes only. Capitalism is not just an economic system. It is a social order. What breaks down with capitalist crisis is capitalist civilization itself. It is not that distinct crises – economic, social, political, and ecological – are "converging." These are not separate crises; they are distinct moments that are mutually constitutive and form a unity, the epochal crisis of capitalist civilization. An analysis of economic (structural) crisis alone will only tell us so much, insofar as economic crisis is itself a consequence of class struggle and is conditioned by other dimensions of crisis, such as those of social reproduction, political legitimation, and ecological breakdown that I discuss in the chapters to follow. The movement as a whole must be grasped, the dynamic interplay of its varied moments and mediations.

Because this epochal crisis is existential, it constitutes a crisis of humanity, and for that matter, for much life on the planet. All historical systems have genesis, lifespans in which they develop, decay or entropy, and are eventually superseded. What supersedes a system remains an open and contingent question. We must make sure that capitalism does not do away with humanity in the process of its own demise. Peering into the future to analyze possible scenarios from the perspective of the twenty-first into the twenty-second century involves advancing propositions that cannot be proven at this time, on top of

---

[9] On theorizing crisis in the 1970s, see, inter-alia, *Late Capitalism*. It is not entirely true to say that there has been no theoretical work on capitalist crisis since 2008. See, for example, David Harvey, *Seventeen Contradictions and the End of Capitalism* (Oxford: Oxford University Press, 2014).

which we must recall that how the coming decades will play out will be fundamentally shaped by collective human agency and contingent developments that by definition make prediction risky. Nonetheless, I anticipate, for reasons developed in the pages to follow, that global capitalism cannot survive into the twenty-second century. We are not in the end game of capitalism if we take a short-term perspective of the next few years and even decades. However, in the perspective of the next century or so, we enter the dusk of world capitalism.

The Tool of Radical Political Economy

We can never hope to attain the "big picture" of global capitalism and crisis with anything but radical political economy. "Radical" means to get to the roots of something. The art of radical social science lies in identifying the dialectics of change, what is new and emergent, no matter how the old forms and the ideas that correspond to them appear as strong and stable. Perhaps above all, radical social science is premised on identifying contradictions. Global capitalism is driven by contradictions. The crisis is driven by contradictions. Whatever future awaits us will be determined by how contradictions at the systemic level play out. We see things as contradictory because they *are* contradictory. If in our analyses we do not uncover contradictions, then our analyses are flawed. But identifying contradictions is only half the task: The dialectical approach searches for the *inner connection* between *apparently* contradictory phenomena. Political economy does not separate economics from political, social, cultural, and ideological processes. Our task is to grasp the inner connection among these processes.

The type of radical political economy I pursue here seeks out multiple determinations, the starting point for which are class and social forces in struggle. There are no monocausal explanations for the epochal crisis; the economic or material base of society is always mediated by many layers that form a complex unity, but it does ultimately exert a causal influence on historic development. Radical political economy, informed by historical materialism, starts with the totality, that is, the understanding that everything is connected to everything else, everything is interpenetrated and exists only in relation to everything else and to the totality of all relations. We want to avoid three fallacies that often violate the rules of critical social science. First is the failure to distinguish surface appearance from the underlying essence of the phenomena we are observing. Surface appearance must not be taken at face value.[10] Intermediary links or mediations must be studied in order for surface appearance and underlying essence to be unified. Second is the failure to see contradictions not as anomalies that undermine an argument but as intrinsic aspect of reality. They are internal to the phenomena we are studying and drive their development. Third, data and counter-data must be presented in developing an argument, but facts must be interpreted at all times. The interpretation of facts is, as a rule, equal to if not more important than the facts themselves. In turn, these interpretations are organized according to theories that are not neutral with regard to the class and social interests bound up with the phenomena that concern us.

Our theories always lag behind reality because the latter is in a constant state of flux and change – change whose tempo is accelerating in the epoch of global capitalism. As Faulkner notes, "theory is grey and the tree of life is green. Theory is compelled to lag behind, seeking to define being when in fact there is only becoming, seeking to define what is when it has already become something else." Our theoretical reflections on reality must at all times remain in contact with the actual movement of history. As that movement is continuous and never ending, so too our theoretical reflection must be brought up to date on an ongoing basis with that actual movement. I concur with Faulkner that Marxism "comes closest to comprehending holistically the fluid, shape-shifting, eternally evolving nature of social reality in all its complexity, is contradictory interconnectedness, its dynamism."[11] The most complex problems in Marxist theory are those that involve the relationship between the general laws of motion of the capitalist system and the concrete history of that system. It is this relationship that is my object of inquiry. The crisis has sparked renewed interest in Marxism and in socialism. In preparation for this book, I reread in its entirely Marx's three-volume magnum opus, *Capital*. More so than when I first read it several decades ago, I found Marx's theory and analysis of the dynamics of capitalism and its crises to be a precision scalpel in dissecting the horrible mess that humanity is in, and as such

---

[10] "All science would be superfluous if the form of appearance of things directly coincided with their essence," observed Karl Marx in Capital, Vol. III (London: Penguin, 1981), p. 956.

[11] Neil Faulkner, *Alienation, Spectacle & Revolution: A Critical Marxist Essay* (London: Resistance Books, 2021), pp. 23–24.

I draw on it liberally throughout the book, particularly in Chapter 1 and Chapter 2 (recall: A scalpel does not perform the operation; it simply gives you the tool to do so).

Radical political economy and political sociology are powerful tools in our effort to understand the momentous changes underway around the world, to grasp the nature of the existential crisis, and to predict where we may be headed. Employ it we must, though Marxist political economy can be daunting. I will strive to take the reader step by step through the most difficult passages that follow. Chapter 1 takes up the structural crisis of overaccumulation within the framework of my theory of global capitalism. I start the chapter by reviewing the essential tenets of Marxist political economy and crisis theory for those not yet familiar with this theory. Chapter 2 focuses on the crisis of social reproduction, Chapter 3 on the political dimensions of the crisis, and Chapter 4 on the ecological dimensions. Throughout, I am centrally concerned with the causal role played by class struggle in historic waves of crisis and transformation in the world capitalist system. I will show how globalization and the epochal crisis that we now face spring from the contradictions of earlier moments and crises, with particular attention to how the imperative of expansion has played out in recent decades, emphasizing the triple processes of globalization, financialization, and digitalization. Chapter 5 is a brief and open-ended reflection on some of the matters we must consider in thinking about the current global conjuncture and alternative futures.

Needless to say, anything that we attempt to explain about the world, or for that matter, about the universe, is necessarily a simplification of reality. The topics taken up by any one of the chapters here could and rightly should constitute a book in itself. Some of my arguments are propositional, meaning that they are working hypotheses that require further investigation and elaboration elsewhere. The best scholarship is that which raises as many questions as it attempts to answer and inspires further exploration while generating new ideas in the academic and political endeavor.

1 | *Structural Crisis*
Overaccumulation

The Vocabulary of Capitalism and Its Crises

"The history of all hitherto existing societies is the history of class struggle," famously declared Karl Marx and Frederick Engels in *The Communist Manifesto*. The process of capitalist globalization that we shall explore in this book is the outcome of worldwide class struggle. The crisis of global capitalism that is the principal focus is also the outcome of worldwide class struggle. In this chapter I will unpack these bold assertions. Let us start with the basic vocabulary of capitalism and its crises.

As mainstream economists and pundits would tell it, capitalist crises come about because of some unwanted exogenous event that occurs by chance or because of errors in human behavior. But crises are as intrinsic as they are endemic to capitalism. They cannot be avoided. They may be triggered by precipitating events such as stock market crashes, political turmoil, and wars. But they originate in the inner workings of capitalism, in contradictions internal to the system. Accumulation crises of two types have been recurrent in capitalism's centuries-long existence. The first are cyclical, what mainstream economists call the business cycle, or the industrial cycle, and appear typically about once a decade as recessions. The second are structural and occur approximately every forty to fifty years. We may refer to these as restructuring crises because the resolution of these types of crises involves sweeping restructuring of the way in which capitalism is organized and permutation in the social, political, cultural, and ideological fabric of capitalist society. Cyclical crises may affect only certain countries or regions, whereas structural crises generally affect the entire world economy. Each major episode of structural crisis in the world capitalist system has involved the breakdown of state legitimacy, escalating class and social struggles, and military conflicts through which restructuring takes place, resulting eventually in a restabilization of the system and renewed capitalist expansion. There were structural crises in the 1830s, the 1870s, and the 1930s. We are concerned here, in particular, with the two most recent structural crises, that of the 1970s, which was "resolved" through globalization, and that which began with the global financial collapse of 2008 and to date remains unresolved.[1]

Structural crises have their origin in the emergence of obstacles to the ongoing process of accumulation, that is, to profit-making. Ironically, as we shall see, these accumulation crises are actually the result of *too much* accumulation; they are *overaccumulation* crises, or the overproduction of capital. This refers to a situation in which enormous amounts of capital (profits) are built up, but this capital cannot find productive outlets for reinvestment. Capital grows more rapidly than its opportunities for valorization and is thus in a constant search for where to expand. When it cannot find new opportunities for expansion, it becomes stagnant, as capitalists hold on to their accumulated profits rather than productively reinvesting them, throwing the system into crisis. This problem of surplus capital – of overaccumulation, or the overproduction of capital – is internal to the very nature of the capitalist system. We start the inquiry into accumulation crisis with the concepts of the circuit of capital, reproduction, accumulation, surplus, exploitation, surplus value, and capitalist expansion.

Capital has but one objective: to *accumulate*, or to make profit, that is, to self-expand. Marx laid out the formula for the expanded reproduction of capital as such: M-C-P-C'-M'. This is known as the circuit of capitalist production. M as money starts the process. The capitalist uses the money to purchase two commodities, represented in the formula as C: means of production in the form of machinery, physical plant, technology, and raw materials; and labor power. These are mixed together in the process of production, represented as P. Out of this production come new commodities, or C'. The value of these commodities, C', must be greater than the value of the commodities, C, that went into the production process. Otherwise, the capitalist would have gained nothing, as his profit derives from the difference between the value of the commodities that went into the process, C, and their value coming out, C'. However, before

---

[1] Seen as a cyclical crisis, the 2008 Great Recession was resolved in the 2010s. Seen as a structural crisis, as I discuss here, it remains unresolved in the 2020s.

the profit is realized, there is a final step in the circuit of capital. The commodities must actually be sold in the market so that the capitalist recovers the initial outlay, M, plus also makes a profit by getting more money than that with which he started the process, represented as M'. The movement from M to M' is the self-expansion of capital in its universal money form, referred to as the expanded reproduction of capital.

Let us say an investor has $100 million. His *sole* concern as an investor (capitalist) is to throw the $100 million into the circuit of capital outlined above and have it come back to him with greater value, say, as $110 million. This is the movement of M-M', or $100 million invested and $110 million returned, with $10 million in profit, in this case, with a rate of profit (simplified here) of 10 percent. But appropriating that extra $10 million is *not* the end goal, as the only goal in capitalism is to sustain the endless expansion of value. In fact, as Marx put it, "the process of production appears merely as an unavoidable intermediate link, as a necessary evil for the sake of money-making."[2] Therefore, the investor now throws out the $110 million to a renewed circuit of production, and it comes back as $121 million, for a profit now of $11 million, assuming the same rate of profit of 10 percent. This expanded reproduction, referred to as the valorization of capital, is what makes capitalism such a dynamic system, in distinction to what is referred to as simple reproduction, such as in a feudal or foraging society, whereby what is produced is consumed without a significant surplus remaining to be reinvested for further expansion. In simplified form, serfs under feudalism produce grains. They consume a portion of what they produce, with which they reproduce themselves. And they turn over a portion of what they have produced to the lord and other members of the ruling class in feudal society, who do not actually participate in producing the grains but nonetheless consume those grains whereby they reproduce themselves. The system does not generate a surplus beyond what the members of society – laboring and nonlaboring – consume for the reproduction of that society.

Surplus refers to what is left over after the members of society consume what is produced in order to subsist, or reproduce themselves,

---

[2] Karl Max, *Capital*, Vol. II (New York: International Publishers, 1967 [1893]), p. 58.

from one day to the next, one year to the next, one generation to the next. Significant surpluses first appeared in human society at the dawn of civilization thousands of years ago. The production of a surplus allowed for some members of society to withdraw from direct participation in the social labor process. These individuals would now be able to live off of the labor of others. They would constitute the first ruling classes. They required political power over the laboring masses in order to assure that these new social arrangements of exploitation were defended and reproduced, through force, when necessary, as well as through ideologies that legitimated their newfound domination. The rise of a significant surplus in human society thus marked the division of society into antagonistic social classes – of exploited and exploiter – and of the state as an instrument of class rule.

Exploitation refers to the appropriation of wealth from those who produced it by those who do not produce it, such as the transfer of grains from the peasant to the feudal lord and the clergy, or the transfer of value in the form of surplus value, later to be realized as profits, from the worker to the capitalist. Capitalist crises can be understood in the first instance as the outcome of obstacles to the ongoing process of exploitation. That is, an accumulation crisis presents itself when the process of ongoing accumulation is obstructed. Exploitation and oppression must remain conceptually and analytically distinct; the former refers to this appropriation and transfer of wealth, and the latter to all those social, cultural, political, legal, military or coercive, and ideological mechanisms that facilitate the production. Racial oppression, for instance, was created by capitalism (as was the fiction of "race" itself) in order to differentiate certain sectors of the toiling masses from others and to apply special controls and conditions of exploitation on those racialized, as well as a mechanism to keep these exploited classes divided. The history of class society is the history of how the ruling classes extract surplus from the toiling masses and how those masses have struggled against such exploitation and oppression.

Surplus value refers to the specific capitalistic form of exploitation, whereby workers are paid a wage for their labor power. That labor power produces value above what the workers are paid, wages being the cost of reproducing that labor power – that is, wages from which the worker must acquire the necessities of life in order for her to continue working for capital. Later on, we shall see how globalization dramatically lowered the cost of labor power for the Transnational Capitalist Class (TCC) – or to say this another way, how it allowed the TCC to intensify exploitation around the world. We will also explore the contradictions of this intensified exploitation, namely how it has paradoxically contributed to the global crisis. As we saw in the hypothetical above, the capitalist pumped out surplus value that resulted in a profit of $10 million in the first sequence and then $11 million in the second, and so on. We note that this passage from $100 million to $110 million to $121 million is an *expansion*. Capitalism, by its very nature, is an expansionary system. Money that remains idle is not capital, as its value does not expand. Capitalism that is not expanding is capitalism that is stagnant. Stasis *is* a state of crisis for capitalism. Capitalism can only reproduce itself through an endless process of expansion, for this is the law of capital accumulation that drives the system, the law of the expanded reproduction of capital.

Capitalism expands through cycles of growth and crisis, but it also experiences secular or cumulative expansion insofar as the value relation incorporates more and more of humanity and extra-human nature. This process may come to a violent end either by the collapse or the overthrow of global capitalism. There are, in short, two interwoven forms of capitalist expansion, what I refer to as *extensive* enlargement and *intensive* enlargement. (In fact, these two forms of expansion are part of a single historical dynamic; their separation is for methodological purposes only.) Capitalism expands by *commodifying* social relations, a process that takes place through both forms of enlargement. Extensive enlargement refers to the historic process of the system's outward expansion and the incorporation of more and more peoples and territories into it. For five centuries the system has gone through prolonged waves of geographic expansion from its birthplace in Western Europe involving colonialism and imperialism as violent and bloody mechanisms of enlargement. The last great waves of outward expansion of capitalism came with the globalization boom of the late twentieth and early twenty-first centuries. During these decades, the former Soviet-bloc countries and China became (re)incorporated into world capitalism, while the neoliberal counteroffensive that I will refer to below tore down barriers to a more far-reaching penetration of transnational capital in the former Third World. Globalization signals the near culmination of this centuries-long process of the spread of capitalist production relations around the world and its displacement of precapitalist relations.[3] By the turn of the century there were no longer any countries or regions in the world that remained outside of world capitalism, and there were no longer any pre- or noncapitalist modes of production on a significant scale, thus bringing to a close one historic phase in its ongoing and open-ended evolution of world capitalism and opening up another, the epoch of global capitalism.

Intensive enlargement refers to the constant deepening of commodification by subordinating more and more spheres of society to the logic of accumulation. This means that human activities that previously remained outside of the logic of capitalist production are brought into this logic. For example, when small farmers must sell their produce in the capitalist market – rather than consume it themselves or barter it – that produce becomes commodities. At this point we can say that the farmer experiences *formal* subsumption by capital. Later on, if these same small farmers lose their land and must then work for large landowners or agribusiness, or must migrate to cities to seek employment, they become workers and the labor power they must sell itself becomes a commodity. This is the *real* subsumption by capital.

In this epoch of global capitalism, a major mechanism for intensive expansion has been the ever-increasing privatization of the commons, or of cultural and natural resources accessible to all members of society, and of public sectors, or parts of the economy held by governments in the name of public rather than private interests. Public health care, education, or water supply, for instance, are provided not in order for capitalists to make profit but in order to meet social needs. But when health care, education, and water are privatized – that is, turned over to capitalist investors who now own them – these services are provided in order to generate profit. Those who cannot afford water or private medical care must do without, even when life itself depends on such resources. In recent decades capitalism's intensive expansion has involved ongoing campaigns to privatize around the world everything from public industry, infrastructure, utilities, prisons, education and health care systems, and more recently, even space exploration, nature reserves, the oceans, and government itself. This drumbeat of commodification is ongoing, although intensive expansion too is finite and

---

[3] Note that precapitalist and noncapitalist are not identical, although I defer such discussion for elsewhere.

eventually runs up against limitations. When everything in society has been commodified, how can the system continue intensive expansion?

Thus, there are limits to capitalist expansion through both intensive and extensive enlargement. However, in the big picture, the most fundamental limit to this expansion – and hence the most fundamental cause of *stasis and crisis* – is capital itself, that is, the "normal" process of capitalist production. As Marx famously put it, "The *real barrier* of capitalist production is *capital itself*" (emphasis in original).[4] At the core of the capitalist system there are two moments in the generation of crises. The first is a decline in the rate of profit, or more generally, low levels of profitability. The second is the inability to actually sell commodities in the market due to a lack of effective demand, or what is known as overproduction and underconsumption. Marxists have debated for decades whether capitalist crises are caused by the decline in the rate of profit or by the lack of effective market demand. In my view, these two causes are far from mutually exclusive; the cause of the decline in profitability is simultaneously the cause of the lack of market demand. The two expressions of crisis may appear as sequential insofar as crisis originates in the first instance in the circuit of production as low levels of profitability and then becomes manifest in the sphere of circulation, or in the market, as a lack of effective demand. However, to ask which one accounts for the crisis is to misframe the question. Production and circulation form a dialectical unity.

Globalization, Crisis Theory, and Absolute and Relative Surplus Value

Luxemburg and Grossman

The Polish-German revolutionary socialist Rosa Luxemburg argued in her classic 1913 study, *The Accumulation of Capital*, that capitalism needs to constantly expand into noncapitalist areas through imperialism in order to access new sources of raw material, markets, and reservoirs of labor and to unload surplus capital. The market within the fully developed capitalist system, she argued, could not absorb output because workers could not afford to purchase the commodities

---

[4] Karl Max, *Capital*, Vol. III, Penguin ed. (London: Penguin, 1981), p. 358.

they produced, and therefore capitalists could not realize their profits. For this reason, capitalism could not survive indefinitely into the future: The system would collapse once there were no longer noncapitalist areas that could be conquered. Her study established one pole in the debate among Marxists on the origins of crisis that focuses on the sphere of circulation, namely the overproduction of commodities, which is to say the underconsumption of these commodities, or in more technical terms, a crisis of realization. As I will discuss further, realization refers to the conversion of surplus value into profit in the market.[5] Her focus on the process of capitalist expansion, as we shall see, is essential to understanding globalization as a response to crisis.

A decade later, in 1923, the Polish economist Henryk Grossman argued in *The Law of Accumulation and the Breakdown of the Capitalist System* that capitalism was doomed to collapse not because it could no longer expand into noncapitalist areas but because capitalism's capacity for its own internal reproduction breaks down. "Under capitalism the entire mechanism of the productive process is ruled by the law of value," he argued, "and just as its dynamic and tendencies are only comprehensible in terms of this law its final end, the breakdown, is likewise only explicable in terms of it."[6] The organic composition of capital refers to the ratio of constant to variable capital, as I will discuss further. Grossman focused on how this composition will tend to rise, and as a result, the rate of profit will fall. He was the first Marxist to systematically explore, after Marx himself, this tendency for the organic composition to rise on the basis of the law of the tendency for the rate of profit to fall (often abbreviated as TRPF) that Marx introduced in Volumes I and III of *Capital*. Capitalist crises are crises of valorization, that is, crises of the production of surplus value and its realization as profit. In this theoretical approach, what breaks down, it must be stressed, is capitalism's capacity for its own reproduction. Grossman's work established the other pole in the debate among Marxists that focuses on the sphere of production.

While I cannot visit here the fierce debates around Luxemburg's work, the so-called "collapse controversy," or the ongoing debates on

---

[5] Rosa Luxemburg, *The Accumulation of Capital* (Eastford: Martino Fine Books, 2015 [1913]).
[6] Henryk Grossmann, *The Law of Accumulation and Breakdown of the Capitalist System* (London: Pluto Press, 1992 [1929]), p. 38.

the nature of capitalist crises,[7] I believe it was Grossman's (and others') mistake to counterpose his theory of capitalist breakdown to that of Luxemburg rather than see them as two complementary dimensions in our understanding of crisis, as two moments in a unitary process of capitalist reproduction. I agree with Ernest Mandel that a focus on the sphere of production alone as the cause of crises "assumes tacitly that there is no specific problem of value realization, only one of surplus value production." This in turn assumes "that what we have under capitalism is production for barter, not production for sale; and that somehow, at least at a macro-economic level, all value produced is automatically realized."[8] As Marx insisted, the conditions for immediate exploitation (which takes place in production) and for the realization of that exploitation (which takes place in circulation) are not identical. It is not just that these two approaches are compatible. Rather, we cannot understand crises or the possibility of their resolution without combining them, nay, without seeing them as two moments of a unity. The two moments – production and circulation, or the rate and the realization of profit – have an inner connection. Let us unpack further.

As opportunities become exhausted for the system to resolve crises by new waves of outward expansion or by extensive enlargement, it must seek to expand from within. This "inner expansion" involves the intensive enlargement I already discussed, the commodification of more and more spheres of social existence. But more important for the discussion here, it involves a further increase in the organic composition of capital (more on this momentarily). The debate over the origin of capitalist crises too often fails to see production and circulation in their unity, with the separation of the capital accumulation process into its two spheres, production and circulation, as a methodology of analysis and nothing more. "The total process [of capitalist

---

[7] A good introduction to Marxist approaches to crises is James O'Connor, *The Meaning of Crisis: A Theoretical Introduction* (New York: Basil Blackwell, 1987). While written over three decades ago, the essential discussion is not outdated. See also David Harvey, *The Limits of Capital* (London: Verso, 2006, updated ed.).

[8] Ernest Mandel, "Introduction," in Karl Marx, *Capital*, Vol. III, Penguin ed. (London: Penguin, 1981), pp. 38–39. Mandel continues: "This critique of the mechanical and one-sided explanation of crises of overproduction by the falling rate of profit alone can be extended, in a more general way, into a critique of *any* monocausal explanation of crises" (p. 42, emphasis in original).

production] presents itself as the unity of the processes of production and circulation," observes Marx. "The process of production becomes the mediator of the process of circulation and vice versa."[9] A capitalist will not invest if he doesn't believe there will be a sufficient market. Corporations generally undertake extensive market studies before making major investments. But why would there not be a market? Because there is insufficient effective demand (underconsumption). But why would there be underconsumption? Because in the circuit of production of surplus value is extracted from the worker so that she is paid less than the value her labor produces.

Capitalists do not make a profit until they are able to actually sell, or "unload" on the market, the products of their factories, farms, mines, and service complexes. If capital in the first instance must assure the extraction of surplus value in production, it must also assure that this surplus value is then converted into profit in the market. Converting the value embodied in the commodities produced into actual profit thus confronts capitalists as a realization problem. In Volume II of *Capital*, dedicated to the process of circulation, Marx discusses the three forms, or circuits, of capital: the money form, the industrial form, and the commodity form, the second pertaining to production and the third to circulation.[10] We can observe the unity as follows: in the equation M-C-P-C'-M', if in the first portion, M-C-P, profitability is low, then the circuit will be interrupted in the phase of production; in the second, C-M', if surplus value is not realized in the market as profit, the circuit is interrupted in the phase of circulation and is not renewed. The transformation of money capital into means of production and labor is the first site of potential crisis. What comes out of the

---

[9] Marx, *Capital*, Vol. II, p. 103.
[10] The third form is distinguished from the first two by the fact that it is only in this circuit that the self-expanded capital value – and not the original one, the capital value that must still produce surplus-value – appears as the starting point of its self-expansion. C as a capital relation is here the starting point and as such relation has a determining influence on the entire circuit because it included the circuit of the capital-value as well as that of the surplus-value already in its first phase, and because the surplus-value must at least in the average, if not in every single circuit, be expended partly as revenue, go through the circulation c-m-c [representing the surplus-value portion of C' and M'] and must partly perform the function of than element of capital accumulation.

Karl Marx, *Capital*, Vol. III, pp. 95–96.

production phase is only, in Marx's words, commodities "pregnant with surplus value." Pregnancy has to give way to birth if surplus valued is to be realized as profit. The transformation of C' into M' is the second site of potential crisis. "Every stagnation in one stage [e.g., exchange] causes more or less stagnation in the entire circuit of not only the stagnant part of the capital but also of the total individual capital."[11] Marx continues:

> A fall in the profit rate, and accelerated accumulation, are simply different expressions of the same process, in so far as both express the development of productivity....In view of the fact that the rate at which the total capital is valorized, i.e., the rate of profit, is the spur to capitalist production, a fall in this rate appears as a threat to the development of the capitalist process; it promotes overproduction, speculation and crises.[12]

Crises, we shall see, can only be overcome if there occurs simultaneously a rise in the production of surplus value and an expansion of the market. Globalization in recent decades made possible the simultaneous occurrence of both of these. It involved a vast expansion of capitalism around the world in the sense analyzed by Luxemburg precisely as a countertendency to capitalist breakdown discussed by Grossman. Let us unpack these two Marxist approaches to capitalist crisis in relation to globalization.

Absolute and Relative Surplus Value

Capitalists seek to maximize profit by lowering production costs, in particular, lowering the wage bill, and therefore increasing the extraction of surplus value from labor. Lowering production costs also allows capitalists to sell commodities for less than their competitors and therefore to outcompete them in the market. Marx referred to two ways in which capital can increase the rate of exploitation. The first he termed *absolute surplus value*, which involves squeezing out more surplus value from the worker by increasing the number of hours worked without increasing the wage rate, by a more intense exploitation through speed-ups (acceleration of turnover time), or by replacing more expensive labor with cheaper labor. A major part of the story of globalization

---

[11] Marx, *Capital*, Vol. II, p. 106.
[12] As quoted in Joseph Choonara, *Unravelling Capitalism*, p. 66.

has been the drive by transnational capitalists to tap new reservoirs of cheap, exploitable workers around the world by relocating production from higher to lower-wage zones. By going global, the TCC was able to tap into vast reserves of such labor made available to it as countries in the former Third World, including China, opened up and integrated into the new globalized circuits of accumulation. The global wage labor force doubled from some 1.5 billion in 1980 to some three billion in 2006, as workers from China, India, and the former Soviet bloc entered the global labor pool,[13] and then increased by another 500 million by 2018, the largest size of the global labor force in recorded history.[14]

The quintessential images of this worldwide search for cheap labor are the "global assembly line," involving deindustrialization and the decay of urban industrial centers in the former First World, and its flip side in the former Third World, the employment of armies of young, mostly female workers intensely exploited and tightly controlled in corporate sweatshops and export-processing zones throughout the global supply chain. Globalization has facilitated a vast expansion in the prospects worldwide for the valorization of capital. Although capital has never been valorized in a single country, globalization has brought about the transnationalization of the entire circuit of capital. Historically, the first portion of the circuit, M-C-P, occurred in particular countries, while the second portion, C'-M', occurred in the world market, at the level of the international circulation of commodities and money. Through globalization, the first portion of the circuit, M-C-P, has transnationalized as production itself has become globally fragmented and decentralized. Vast production chains now crisscross the planet. Valorization is categorically *not* a national affair; it is unquestionably global. Capital valorizes in the globally integrated

---

[13] Richard Freeman, "The Great Doubling: The Challenge of the New Global Labor Market," *The Globalist*, March 5, 2010, www.theglobalist.com/StoryId.aspx?StoryId=4542. The ILO placed the global working class in 2017 at 3.2 billion. International Labor Organization, *World Employment and Social Outlook 2017: Sustainable Enterprises and Jobs: Formal Enterprises and Decent Work* (Geneva: ILO, 2017), https://ilo.org/wcmsp5/groups/public/---dgreports/---dcomm/---publ/documents/publication/wcms_579893.pdf.

[14] International Labor Organization, *World Employment and Social Outlook: Trends 2019* (Geneva: ILO, 2019), p. 5, www.ilo.org/wcmsp5/groups/public/---dgreports/---dcomm/---publ/documents/publication/wcms_670542.pdf.

production, financial, and service system that has come about since the late 1970s through globalization.

The French philosopher and sociologist Henri Lefebvre observed in his milestone study, *The Production of Space*, that capital *produces* space and that social relations *are* spatial relations.[15] Capital constantly restructures that space. Capital turns to spatial restructuring when spatial configurations established in one historical moment become obstacles to accumulation. Globalization can be seen in this regard as an immense wave of worldwide spatial restructuring involving an acceleration in the pace of accumulation, that is, in the turnover time of capital, in time-space compression, or in what Marx referred to as the annihilation of space by time. This process has involved the transformation of local and national markets through their integration into global markets, a process that starts as market integration and proceeds to productive integration. Every country has been integrated into this system, such that "national" economies have been "disassembled" and reassembled in recent decades as constituent parts of a singular global economy. The global economy is not the mere sum of national economies; it is a unity, a global space not reducible to exchanges among national spaces. The TCC operates in this global space, transgressing national spaces and taking advantage of the uneven development of its constituent elements to organize its worldwide circuits of exploitation.

If production was the first to transnationalize, starting in the 1970s, a wave of financial deregulation in most countries around the world of national banking and financial systems led to a very rapid transnationalization of finance in the 1990s and 2000s. The transnationalization of services followed through the application of digital technologies and platforms and now appears to be the cutting edge of new waves of economic globalization. The massive transformation of services into commodity-producing activities began in the late nineteenth century and accelerated in the post-WWII period. The commodification of services provided a temporary fix for accumulation crisis by opening up new service-based outlets for overaccumulated capital. But it was not until the epoch of globalization, with computer, information, and related

---

[15] Henri Lefebvre, *The Production of Space* (Malden: Blackwell, 1991).

technologies (CIT), and now with a second wave of digital technologies (see below) do services become more fully commodified and also transnationalized. By 2017, services accounted for some 70 percent of the total gross world product.[16]

Personal services for the most part involve direct contact between the client and the provider, such as haircuts, cleaning services, child care, vehicle repair, and so on, and as such remain tied to specific places, whereas general services can be outsourced to lower-wage zones through the extension of more advanced CIT. In the early stages of globalization, industry relocated to low-wage zones. Later on, such services as data entry, accounting, and call centers were being located to lower-wage zones. More recently, through the so-called remote-work revolution, it has become possible to relocate even complex, high-skilled service work such as engineering, financial analysis, and computer programing to lower-wage zones.[17] The export of these commercial services from the six largest national economies in the former Third World grew by 16.5 percent a year from 2020 to 2023, compared to 6.5 percent in prior years.[18] The general shift toward outsourcing labor to low-wage zones around the world constitutes a new transnational putting-out system, as much commercial as industrial and in services, involving both manual and white-collar workers.

The second way that capitalists attempt to lower production costs and thereby increase profits is to replace human labor with machinery and technology in order to raise productivity while lowering the wage bill. Marx referred to this as an increase in *relative* surplus value. Over time, the principal mechanism for reducing the wage bill is to increase *relative* surplus value – that is, to raise productivity, or output

---

[16] Thomas Marois, "TiSA and the Threat to Public Banks," April 21, 2017, Transnational Institute, accessed on July 18, 2020 at www.tni.org/en/publication/tisa-and-the-threat-to-public-banks.

[17] Evidence of the outsourcing to low-wage zones of high-skilled service work is widespread, both systematic and anecdotal. In 2022, such companies as Coinbase and Shopify and a host of Silicon Valley companies undertook a wave of relocations from North America to Latin America. This outsourcing of high-skills tech work increased in late 2021 and early 2022 by 156 percent. Augusta Saraiva, "U.S. Tech Firms Hunt for Cheap Home-Based Hires in Latin America," *Bloomberg*, February 14, 2022, www.bloomberg.com/news/articles/2022-02-14/u-s-tech-firms-hunt-for-cheap-home-based-hires-in-latin-america#xj4y7vzkg.

[18] *The Economist*, "The Fuzzy Corporation," January 14, 2023, p. 55.

per worker per unit of time worked – through the introduction of new technologies and production methods, so that less workers are needed for the same output. More is produced with the same amount of labor, or alternatively, the same amount is produced with less labor – in either case, the capitalist pumps out more value per unit of labor power. The same CIT that made globalization technically possible, first as the transnationalization of production, then of finance, and later of services, also accelerated the replacement of workers with technology in high-wage zones, resulting in an expansion of relative surplus value. The labor power of workers in the former First World becomes cheapened as these workers, forced to compete with their counterparts abroad, experience rising under- and unemployment and downward pressure on their wages. The turn toward expanding absolute and relative surplus value in low- and high-wage zones was mutually reinforcing insofar as the shift in the industrial production of basic consumer goods to low-wage zones lowered their cost, which in turn lowered the cost of labor (the value of labor power) in the high-wage zones.

Ironically, this drive to lower that portion of outlays to pay labor and therefore to increase profits – whether through an expansion of absolute or relative surplus value – ends up generating crisis tendencies. To reiterate, there are two moments in the generation of crises: A decline in the rate of profit, or more generally, low levels of profitability; and the inability to actually sell commodities in the market due to a lack of demand, or overproduction/underconsumption. How did the successful effort by the emerging TCC to lower wages around the world through an expansion of both absolute and relative surplus value extraction boomerang back in the form of accumulation crisis? Marx identified two types of capital: *constant* and *variable*. Constant capital refers to the physical plant, machinery, raw materials, stock, and so on – the so-called object element of the means of production. Variable capital refers to human labor itself, as a commodity, as labor power that is sold by the worker to the capitalist for a wage – the so-called subjective element of the means of production.

The ratio of constant to variable capital is what Marx termed the organic composition of capital. According to the law of value, only living labor can generate surplus value, which, when realized, becomes profit. The profit rate is determined by the relationship of the surplus value to the total capital (constant + variable) so that an increase in the constant portion reduces the proportion of total capital that is variable. The greater the proportion of machinery and technology to living labor, that is, the greater the organic composition of capital, the less surplus value can be extracted relative to the total capital. Marx referred to this downward pressure on profitability as the tendency for the rate of profit to fall, or TRPF, the central "law of motion" of capitalism.[19] As capital accumulation proceeds, the variable portion tends to decline relative to the constant portion of total capital, leading to a tendency for the mass of surplus value to increase at a slower rate than the total capital required to generate that surplus value. It cannot be otherwise if capital is to undergo *expanded* and not mere simple reproduction.[20] To state this another way, as total capital outlays increase, the labor input per product unit – or per commodity produced – declines. The ratio of the sum total of surplus value produced during the production process divided by the sum total of capital will decrease. Hence, the long-run effect of increasing relative surplus value by replacing living labor with machinery and technology is to place downward pressure on profitability as constant capital expands more rapidly than variable capital. As I will discuss momentarily, Marx was explicit in describing the falling rate of profit as a *tendency* that can be offset by *countervailing forces*.

The decline in the average rate of profit in the post-WWII period has been broadly documented. While figures for the rate of profit tend to vary depending on who is doing the reporting and through what methodology, one report after another has confirmed this long-term secular decline in profitability, notwithstanding short-term fluctuations, and along with it, the steady decline since 1970 in the growth of the net stock of capital (a proxy for productive investment) in the rich countries of the Organization of Economic Cooperation and Development (OECD).[21] According to the *Financial Times*, it

---

[19] His detailed discussion of TRPF is to be found in Part III of Vol. III of *Capital*, "The Law of the Tendential Fall in the Rate of Profit."

[20] "The Progressive tendency for the general rate of profit to fall is thus simply *the expression, peculiar to the capitalist mode of production*, of the progressive development of the social productivity of labor" (emphasis in original). Marx, Capital, Vol. III, p. 319.

[21] Economist Michael Roberts presented a wealth of data on this decline from multiple sources in *The Long Depression: How It Happened, Why It*

stood at about 15 percent in the post-WWII period, dropped by the end of the 1980s to 10 percent and continued to decline, to 6 percent in 2017.[22] In perhaps the most comprehensive study on world profit rates to date (the weighted average of country-level profit rates), Basu and his colleagues found "an unconditional decline in the world profit rate over the past 60 years" (1960–2018) as a result in the fall in the output-capital ratio and an increase in capital's share of income[23] – that is, a combination of an increasing organic composition of capital and the relative decline in wages (presumably generating difficulties in realizing value) resulted in the fall in the rate of profit.[24]

Let us reiterate: The tendency for the rate of profit to fall results from the inner workings of capital accumulation. From the total value produced, a portion must be reinvested so that the total stock of capital measured in value must increase as long as accumulation proceeds, as Marx demonstrated in *Capital*, Vol. III.[25] As the total value of constant capital increases relative to variable capital, the less surplus value can be extracted relative to total value. The decline in the rate of profit results in stagnation that can only be overcome by further raising productivity above any increase in wages or by tapping into new sources of cheap, exploitable labor. The two drives – to seek out new reserves of cheap labor and to replace workers with machinery and technology, or, in Marx's language, to replace living with dead labor – are mutually reinforcing. Both may resolve momentarily the problem of declining profitability, but in the long run, both end up aggravating the crisis of overaccumulation by a combination

---

Happened, and What Happens Next (Chicago: Haymarket, 2016). For the decline in the growth of the net stock of capital, see the graph on p. 241.

[22] *Financial Times*, as cited by Joseph Choona, *Unravelling Capitalism* (London: Bookmarks Pubs, 2009), p. 120.

[23] Deepankar Basu, Julio Huato, Jesus Lara Jauregui and Evan Wasner (2022): World Profit Rates, 1960–2019, *Review of Political Economy*, DOI:10.1080/09538259.2022.2140007.

[24] In the United States, productivity grew by 241.8 percent from 1948 to 2016, while hourly compensation grew by only 115.14 percent during this period. In other words, workers produced much more wealth for capitalists than they got back in higher wages. However, starting in 1973, which is the year to which I date the beginning of globalization, productivity rose by 73.7 percent, while wages stagnated. As reported in Vivek Chibber, *Understanding Capitalism* (Brooklyn: Jacobin Foundation, 2022), pp. 22–23.

[25] Marx, *Capital*, Vol. III.

of a decline of profitability and of effective global demand relative to actual or potential output.

But why would capitalists increase the organic composition of capital if it results in a decline in the rate of profit? Put simply, they have no choice. First, workers struggle for higher wages and better working conditions, and in certain historical moments, even struggle to wrest control from the capitalist. Replacing workers with machinery is a weapon in the capitalists' class struggle against workers, just as is relocating to lower-wage zones. Globalization in this sense is *class warfare* by capital against the global working and popular classes. Second, competition forces each capitalist to raise productivity by investing in new machinery and technology. Doing so decreases the unit value of each product, allowing the capitalist to undersell competitors and increase market shares – at least until all capitalists come to adopt the new machinery and technologies, at which point competition then forces capitalists to seek further increases in the organic composition of capital.

However, the more the TCC has sought out through globalization to push down wages and/or to replace workers with machinery and technology, the more it has aggravated the contradiction between what the global economy can churn out and what the global market can absorb. Capital's drive to maximize the extraction of surplus value from labor results in the accumulation of wealth in one pole and the accumulation of poverty in the other pole of the antagonistic unity of capital and labor. When commodities cannot be absorbed by the market, the capitalist cannot risk further investment. In either case – if the rate of profit declines or if the output cannot be sold – capitalists will have no incentive to continue to invest in the circuit of production, and the system enters into a crisis of stagnation. The social polarization inherent to capitalism and the problem of stagnation can be offset by countervailing tendencies, such as workers' struggles for higher wages or state intervention in the economy to redistribute income. In fact, such redistribution of value back to labor, irrespective of what has brought it about, has served as a major mechanism that has historically offset polarization and renewed capitalism's lease on life *despite itself* (other mechanisms, to be discussed later, include the destruction of capital through devaluation and through wars).

By going global from the 1970s and on, capital was able to undercut mechanisms of wealth redistribution and regulation at the level of the nation-state. What has followed over the past half a century has been a dizzying process of worldwide social polarization that has been broadly documented. By 2018, just 1 percent of humanity owned over half of the world's wealth and the top 20 percent owned 94.5 percent of that wealth, while the remaining 80 percent had to make do with just 5.5 percent.[26] These expanding inequalities end up aggravating crisis tendencies since the mass of working people cannot purchase the wealth that pours out of the capitalist economy to the extent that capitalists and the well-off retain more and more of total income relative to that which goes to labor. Hence, in the long run, the flight of transnational capital from high-wage to low-wage zones, as well as the downward pressure on wages in the higher-wage zones has aggravated the crisis of overaccumulation.

Cycles of Crises as Cycles of Class Struggle

If the history of capitalist globalization is the history of class struggle, so too is it the causal starting point for dialectical analysis of the global crisis. Class struggles from below force ruling groups to modify their modalities of control and accumulation that in turn alter the terms under which the exploited and oppressed struggle. The resolution of crises through new rounds of capitalist expansion is, in fact, achieved through countervailing tendencies forced on capital by mass struggles of the working and popular classes. If we pick up the story of successive waves of class struggle and capitalist crises from the second half of the eighteenth century, a structural crisis of worldwide impact, from the late 1870s to the early 1890s, was resolved through a new wave of colonialism and imperialism that restored profits and growth in the so-called *belle époque*. But this was a time of intense class struggle and of the spread of socialist movements, especially in the historic cores of world capitalism, including the Bolshevik revolution, only to be followed by intensified inter-imperialist rivalry that spilled out into two world wars. The structural crisis of the 1930s Great Depression unleashed mass struggles all around the world that helped force on the system a new

---

[26] Oxfam (London), *Wealth: Having it all and Wanting More*, March 4, 2018 at the Oxfam website, http://policy-practice.oxfam.org.uk/publications/wealth-having-it-all-and-wanting-more-338125.

type of redistributive capitalism following World War II, referred to as the "class compromise" of Fordist-Keynesian and developmental capitalism, social democracy New Deal capitalism, and so on. Regardless of its name, the new model involved state regulation and redistribution as well as the expansion of public sectors, industrial policies, and planning that acted to counter the tendency toward breakdown so manifest in the 1930s Great Depression.

In the dialectical perspective, the resolution of one set of contradictions gives way to new contradictions. The post-WWII "golden years" of capitalist prosperity also generated a set of internal contradictions that once again exploded into the structural crisis of the 1970s in the form of stagflation (stagnation plus inflation) and declining profitability. Mass struggles by the working and popular classes, Third World anticolonial and national liberation movements, and insurgent sectoral social movements of women, students, ethnic minorities, gays, and ecologists altered the worldwide correlation of class and social forces in favor of popular majorities. These popular majorities refused to shoulder the burden of the 1970s crisis. Transnational capital emerged as a response to the world crisis of that decade. By going global, the TCC sought to break free of nation-state constraints to accumulation that the working and popular classes had been able to impose on capital at the level of the nation-state. These classes had to be redisciplined. Capitalist hegemony had to be restored and new opportunities for profit-making had to be opened up around the world. Globalization was not, therefore, a one-way accumulation strategy by capital but an outcome of the worldwide class and social struggles of the exploited and oppressed.

In the ensuing decades, the TCC and its political agents operated through national states and supranational institutions to liberate capital from national regulatory control, to bring down all barriers to the free movement of transnational capital within and across borders, to privatize public spheres and restructure public finance, to attack national working classes and throw them into competition with one another, and to open up vast new pools of labor power ripe for exploitation. Globalization thus acted as a juggernautic countertendency to the tendency toward breakdown manifest in the structural crisis of the 1970s. Transnational capital experienced a major expansion in the 1980s and 1990s, involving hyper-accumulation through new technologies, particularly computers and informatics, through neoliberal policies, and renovated modalities of mobilizing and exploiting the global labor force – including a massive new round of primitive accumulation that uprooted and displaced hundreds of millions of people, especially in the Third World countryside, a matter to which we will return in Chapter 2. The globalization boom of the 1990s restored profits and the power of capital.

But the honeymoon for the ruling classes was short lived. The global financial collapse of 2008 marked the onset of a new structural crisis and triggered new waves of mass popular struggles around the world. By the second decade of the new century, the global capitalist historic bloc that transnational elites had strived to construct in the heyday of neoliberal hegemony lay cracked and tattered. Looking at the forty-year sweep from 1980 to 2020, average annual global growth did not top 5 percent, and hovered for the decade of the 2010s at about 2 percent, whereas in-between recessionary dips it typically averaged above 5 percent in the post-WWII period.[27] Accumulation crises, as I already discussed, originate in the circuit of production and are *expressed* as a realization problem, manifest in the market as a glut or as a crisis of overproduction and underconsumption followed by stagnation. In fact, from 2008 to 2020 there was a steady rise in underutilized capacity and a slowdown in industrial production around the world, notwithstanding momentary booms.[28] The surplus of accumulated capital with nowhere to go expanded rapidly. Global net corporate profits more than tripled in real terms from 1980 to 2013, from $2 trillion annually to $7.2 trillion.[29] Average net profits experienced a 52 percent

---

[27] World Bank, "GDP Growth (annual%)," https://data.worldbank.org/indicator/NY.GDP.MKTP.KD.ZG. Note that global growth reached 6.2 percent in 2021, but this was a momentary spurt representing recovery from the severe recession caused by the COVID pandemic shutdown, which dropped global GDP by 3.1 percent. Growth for 2022 was 3.1 percent and for 2023 it was 2.9 percent.

[28] See Ronald W. Cox, "The Crisis of Capitalism Through Global Value Chains," *Class, Race and Corporate Power*, 7(1), 2019; Eric Toussaint, "No, The Coronavirus is not Responsible for the Fall in Stock Prices," *MR Online*, March 4, 2020, https://mronline.org/2020/03/04/no-the-coronavirus-is-not-responsible-for-the-fall-of-stock-prices/.

[29] Richard Dobbs, Tim Koller, Sree Ramaswamy, Jonathan Woetzel, James Manyika, Rohit Krishnan, and Nicoló Andreula, "Playing to Win: The New Global Competition for Corporate Profits," McKinsey Global Institute, September 2015, Executive Summary, file:///Users/user./Downloads/mgi%20global%20competition_executive%20summary_sep%202015.pdf. Net earnings after interest and taxes rose five-fold during this period.

increase for the three-year period from 2021 to 2023 over the average for the preceding three years.[30] While transnational corporations registered record profits during the 2010s, corporate investment declined as opportunities for profitable reinvestment dried up.[31]

Note that there is a double movement here: The rate of profit fell while the mass of profit increased. An increase in the mass of profit and an increase in the rate of profit are not one and the same. "Along with the volume [of profit]," observed Marx, "the same laws of production and accumulation increase also the value of the constant capital in a mounting progression more rapidly than that of the variable part of capital, invested as it is in living labor. Hence, the same laws produce for the social capital a growing absolute mass of profit, and a falling rate of profit."[32] Indeed, a sign of capitalist breakdown is precisely this decrease in the rate of profit *simultaneous to* an increase in the mass of profit. In effect, as the rate of profit has fallen, the total cash held in reserves of the world's 2,000 biggest nonfinancial corporations sharply increased, from $6.6 trillion in 2010 to $14.2 trillion in 2020 – considerably more than the foreign exchange reserves of the world's central governments – as the global economy stagnated and companies retained rather than reinvested their profits.[33] Since 1980, uninvested corporate cash holdings have ballooned to 10 percent of GDP in the United States, 22 percent in Western Europe, 34 percent in South Korea, and 47 percent in Japan.[34]

Capitalists will only invest in the circuits of production if they calculate a rate of profit that is higher than unproductive profit-making activities, such as investing in financial speculation, snatching up assets, or simply hoarding accumulated capital. As uninvested capital

---

[30] Rupert Neate, "World's Five Richest Men Doubled as Poorest Get Poorer," *The Guardian*, January 14, 2024, www.theguardian.com/inequality/2024/jan/15/worlds-five-richest-men-double-their-money-as-poorest-get-poorer.

[31] *The Economist*, "The Problem with Profits," March 26, 2016, www.economist.com/news/leaders/21695392-big-firms-united-states-have-never-had-it-so-good-time-more-competition-problem.

[32] Karl Max, *Capital*, Vol. III, p. 325.

[33] *The Economist*, "Hanging Together," May 16, 2020, p. 60.

[34] Richard Dobbs, Tim Koller, Sree Ramaswamy, Jonathan Woetzel, James Manyika, Rohit Krishnan, and Nicoló Andreula, "Playing to Win: The New Global Competition for Corporate Profits," McKinsey Global Institute, September 2015, Executive Summary, file:///Users/user./Downloads/mgi%20global%20competition_executive%20summary_sep%202015.pdf, p. 4.

accumulates, enormous pressures build up to find outlets for unloading the surplus. Capitalist groups pressure states to create new opportunities for profit-making and also turn to more savage forms of accumulation, from financial frauds and racketeering to predatory lending and extortion. By the turn of century, and especially since 2008, the TCC came to rely on debt-driven growth, financial speculation, the plunder of public finance, and state-organized militarized accumulation, as countervailing tendencies that helped to sustain global accumulation in the face of chronic stagnation. Wild financial speculation and escalating government, corporate, and consumer debt drove growth in the first two decades of the twenty-first century, but these were temporary solutions to long-term stagnation. Consumer, corporate, and state debt reached an all-time high of $300 trillion in 2023, or 350 percent of the total gross world product.[35] Total global liquidity, a measure of cash and credit in the world economy, rose to an all-time high of some $170 trillion in 2023, a vast pool of footloose cash that could become idle overnight should debt default spread enough to destabilize global finance.[36] Debt-driven growth is unsustainable in the absence of such structural changes as redistribution or a substantial rise in income. Public debt, moreover, must be paid back through taxes on labor and represents an enormous and still-growing claim to the current and future earnings of working classes, which in the long run only aggravates the lack of effective demand. Marx stressed the key role of credit in expanding the accumulation of capital, but only up to a certain point, beyond which it becomes a lever for speculation and overproduction.[37]

Financialization has made it possible to turn the global economy into a giant casino for transnational investors. This casino dates to the late twentieth century with the deregulation and liberalization of financial markets worldwide, along with the introduction of CIT into

---

[35] Terry Chan and Alexandra Dimitrijevic, "Global Debt Leverage: Is a Great Reset Coming?," *S&P Global*, January 13, 2023, www.spglobal.com/en/research-insights/featured/special-editorial/look-forward/global-debt-leverage-is-a-great-reset-coming.

[36] Naomi Rovnick and Harry Robertson, "Tranquility Reigns Over Markets Still Awash with Cash, For Now," *Reuters*, June 13, 2023, www.reuters.com/markets/global-markets-liquidity-2023-06-14/.

[37] "Banking and credit, however, thereby also become the most powerful means for driving capitalist production beyond its own barriers and one of the most effective vehicles for crises and swindling." Marx, *Capital*, Vol. III, p. 742.

these markets. Financialization is typically referred to in the Marxist literature as a phase of accumulation represented as M—M'. This missing intermediate phase of production is "a necessary evil for the sake of money-making," argued Marx in *Capital*. "All nations with a capitalist mode of production are therefore seized periodically by a feverish attempt to make money without the intervention of the process of production."[38] And later on:

> In M-M' we have the irrational form of capital, the misrepresentation and objectification of the relations of production, in its highest power: the interest-bearing form, the simple form of capital, in which it is taken as logically anterior to its own reproduction process; the ability of money or a commodity to valorize its own value independent of reproduction – the capital mystification in the most flagrant form.[39]

Let us return to the circuit of capital as M-C-P-C'-M'. When a point is reached in which overaccumulated capital cannot be productively reinvested, capitalists turn to investing in the circuits of financial speculation represented as M-M'. The greater amount of money at the end point of this speculation is fictitious since no new wealth has been created so long as this movement of M-M' is detached from the productive circuits. It is unsustainable and must either reattach to the productive circuit or experience violent devaluation through financial crises. Financial speculation has indeed reached unprecedented heights. As opportunities dried up to reinvest overaccumulated capital elsewhere in the global economy, the TCC turned to unloading trillions of dollars into speculation in global commodities markets, stock markets, currency markets, futures markets, leverages, every imaginable derivative and short, cryptocurrencies, land grabs, and urban real estate, among other speculative activities in the netherworld of shadow banking, as capitalists sought to capture rents rather than to create new values.

These speculative markets become outlets for global investors to "park" their overaccumulated capital. As a result, the gap between the productive economy of goods and services and fictitious capital has grown to an unfathomable chasm. Fictitious capital refers to money thrown into circulation without any base in commodities or in production. A major portion of the income generated by financial speculation is fictitious, meaning that it exists on paper or in cyberspace but does not correspond to real

---

[38] Marx, *Capital*, Vol. II, p. 58. [39] Marx, *Capital*, Vol. III, p. 516.

wealth in the world, that is, goods and services that people need and want, such as food, clothing, houses, a haircut, child care, and so on. In 2024, the gross world product, or the total value of goods and services, stood at some $100 trillion, whereas the global derivatives market – a marker of speculative activity – was estimated at a mind-boggling $1 quadrillion.[40] New wealth at some point has to be produced by labor for which this fictitious capital has a claim. Yet so great is the chasm between the "real economy" of the production of goods and services and fictitious capital that future valorization of the mass of fictitious value appears as all but impossible. The accumulation of this fictitious capital gave the illusion of recovery in the years following the Great Recession, whereas it has only served to offset the crisis temporally into the future or spatially to new digital geographies and new population groups, while in the long run it exacerbates the underlying problem of overaccumulation.[41] The

---

[40] J. B. Maverick, "How Big is the Derivatives Market," *Investopedia*, February 6, 2024, www.investopedia.com/ask/answers/052715/how-big-derivatives-market.asp. Note that Investopedia constantly updates this data. I accessed the site for the $1 quadrillion figure on July 30, 2024. For Marx, fictitious capital referred to credit issued as bank drafts or credit money that, once lent out, could be converted into productive capital. There is a world of difference between this notion and the tens of trillions of dollars now thrown into speculation unconnected to any real productive activity. In his study *Fictitious Capital*, Durand reviews the growth of fictitious capital in the form of credit to the nonfinancial private sector, public debt, and the stock market. He observes (p. 65): "The different basic forms of fictitious capital combined to ensure that, overall, this category expanded across the whole period in question, including after the 2008 crisis. In other words, over the last three decades, the quantity of value validated in anticipation of future valorization processes has constantly increased relative to the quantity of wealth actually produced."

[41] Through its quantitative easing program, the U.S. Federal Reserve undertook a whopping $16 trillion in secret bailouts to banks and corporations from around the world following the 2008 collapse General Accounting Office (GAO), "Federal Reserve System: Opportunities Exist to Strengthen Policies and Processes for Managing Emergency Assistance" (Washington, DC: GAO-11-696, July 2011). But this only tells part of the story. According to one IMF report, the total amount that states and central banks in the "advanced economies" committed to supporting the financial sector amounted to 50.4 percent of the entire world GDP. See International Monetary Fund, "Fiscal Implications of the Global Economic and Financial Crisis," IMF Staff Position Note, June 9, 2009, www.imf.org/external/pubs/ft/spn/2009/spn0913.pdf. The U.S. and EU governments then provided an additional $8 trillion handout to private corporations in the first two months of the COVID-19 pandemic alone, an amount roughly equivalent to their profits over the preceding two years. See *The Economist*, "Corporate Bail-Outs: Bottomless Pit, Inc.," April 4, 2020, p. 8.

definitive inability of this conversion of fictitious capital into new value through production is the moment when it is devalued or destroyed, that is, when it becomes worthless as the outcome of a crisis.[42]

By financialization, however, I refer beyond M-M', to a more fundamental transformation in the global political economy.[43] As national financial systems merged into an increasingly integrated global financial system, transnational finance capital emerged as the hegemonic fraction of capital on a world scale. By turning any and every asset into something that has a financial form, or fungibles that can be instantly traded and speculated on in the global market, financialization essentially completes the long historic process of making everything commodifiable, which universalizes the law of value. It represents an extreme form of commodification, a level of alienation previously unimaginable.[44] As financialization proceeds, it swallows up and dominates all commodity relations. Financialization completes the absolute annihilation of space through time in the global movement of capital. Nothing is outside of global financial markets and networks. Transnational finance capital sucks up value through its

---

[42] On these matters of fictitious capital, see discussion by Marx, see chapters 29 and 30 of *Capital*, Vol. III, "Banking Capital's Component Parts," and "Money Capital and Real Capital: I," respectively. As for the illusion, Marx observed that "business always seems almost exaggeratedly healthy immediately before a collapse" (p. 616).

[43] There is now a vast body of literature on this financialization. Some of the works I have found useful in trying to understand it are, inter-alia: Christian Marazzi, *The Violence of Financial Capital* (Bellinzona: Edizioni Casagrande, 2011); Greta R. Krippner, *Capitalizing on Crisis: The Political Origins of the Rise of Finance* (Cambridge: Harvard University Press, 2012); Cédric Durand, *Fictitious Capital: How Finance is Appropriating Our Future* (London: Verso, 2017); Nomi Prins, *Collusion* (New York: Bold Type Books, 2019); Tooze, *Crashed: How a Decade of Financial Crises Changed the World*; Wolfgang Streeck, *Buying Time: The Delayed Crisis of Democratic Capitalism* (London: Verso, 2017); William K. Tabb, *Financialization and the Future of the American Economy* (New York: Routledge, 2023). For my earlier analysis, see Robinson, *Global Capitalism and the Crisis of Humanity* (New York: Cambridge, 2014), and *Can Global Capitalism Endure?* (Atlanta: Clarity, 2022).

[44] The next phase in global financialization would likely be the ongoing introduction of digital currencies, the implications of which would be vast. See also the excellent analysis by Fabio Vighi, "Gradually, Then Suddenly? Crisis Capitalism and Its Disavowals," *The Philosophical Salon*, May 29, 2023, https://thephilosophicalsalon.com/gradually-then-suddenly-crisis-capitalism-and-its-disavowals/.

porous and frictionless movement around the world. Exercising control through the sphere of circulation over the mass of profit and over the allocation of capital in the global economy, it accrued enormous social power, including the ability to dictate through global financial markets to states and to other circuits of accumulation, to regulate the circuits of capital worldwide, in a reversal of the historic relationship in which finance serves as an adjunct to industrial capital. From its hegemonic perch at the summit of the global capitalist economy, transnational finance capital has come to exercise a structural power over the whole social process, indeed over the very life process.

A third outlet for overaccumulated capital has been a sharp expansion of investment in systems of transnational social control, repression, and warfare. As I showed in my 2020 book, *The Global Police State*, the mechanisms of *militarized accumulation* and *accumulation by repression*, beyond earlier concepts of a permanent arms economy, play a heightened role in sustaining the global economy as the system becomes ever more dependent on the development and deployment of systems of warfare, social control, and repression simply as a means of making profit and continuing to accumulate capital in the face of stagnation. The generation of conflicts and the repression of social movements and vulnerable populations around the world become a strategy that conjoins profit-making to political objectives. All wars are for the appropriation of surplus in the broadest sense; beyond outright plunder, for the creation, defense, and reproduction of the conditions under which surplus can be generated by some groups and appropriated by others. What requires analysis is the mode of this appropriation through warfare and violence and the role that it plays within the larger political economy.

Among others, Rosa Luxemburg analyzed over a century ago the centrality of violence and militarism as a "province of accumulation." While the old-style military Keynesianism of the post-WWII period is still in place, the concept of militarized accumulation points to the more expansive role that generating war, repression, and systems of transnational social control now play as they move to the very center of the global economy. The Austrian economist Joseph Schumpeter coined the term "creative destruction" in reference to how capitalism constantly "creates and destroys" in its cycles of development.[45] Now

---

[45] Joseph A. Schumpeter, *Capitalism, Socialism, and Democracy*, 3rd ed. (New York: Harper & Row, 1975 [1942]).

"creative destruction" appears to drive the logic of militarized accumulation. The circuits of militarized accumulation coercively open up opportunities for capital accumulation worldwide. Permanent war involves endless cycles of destruction and reconstruction, each phase in the cycle fueling new rounds of accumulation and also results in the ongoing enclosure of resources that become available to the TCC. As with debt and financial speculation, however, there is just so much that militarized accumulation can do to absorb overaccumulated capital and offset stagnation.[46]

The Digital Revolution: A New Round of Time and Space Restructuring

Debt, financial speculation, war, and repression have not been able to reverse stagnation. Seen as a cyclical crisis, if more severe than most, the 2008 collapse was resolved in the course of the 2010s, especially through state intervention to bailout capital in an unprecedented creation of money known as quantitative easing. Seen as a structural crisis, however, none of the underlying contradictions have been resolved, and no new basis for long-term stabilization has been established. Successive capitalist crises followed by productive reactivation on an expanded scale have historically involved the introduction of new, cutting-edge technologies, such as synthetic materials, consumer durables, automotive and petrochemicals, and military-industrial technologies that drove the post-WWII boom. Early in the twentieth century, the Soviet economist Nikolai Kondratieff noted how the world economy, driven by new cutting-edge technologies, experiences cycles of some forty to fifty years (called Kondratieff waves). In these cycles, rounds of expansion eventually become exhausted and are followed by downturns and crises, resulting in a reorganization of the system and new technologies that help launch a new cycle.[47]

---

[46] One study found an inverse relationship from 1963 and 2008 between military expenditures and profit rates. See Adem Y. Elveren and Sara Hsu, "Military Expenditures and Profit Rates: Evidence from OECD Countries," *Metroeconomica*, December 22, 2015, https://onlinelibrary.wiley.com/doi/abs/10.1111/meca.12111.

[47] Ernest Mandel reviews and critiques the extant approaches to long waves of capitalist development in his study *Late Capitalism* (London: Verso, 1975 [1972]). See chapter four, "'Long Waves' in the History of Capitalism."

If productive reactivation were to occur now, it would surely be driven by new digital technologies, about which volumes have been written. The first generation of CIT, introduced in the 1980s, provided the original technical basis for globalization. It allowed the TCC to coordinate and synchronize global production sequences and therefore to put into place the globally integrated production system that operates as a single unit in real time. It also made possible the global integration of national financial systems and new forms of money, such as hedge funds or secondary derivative markets, and looking forward, central bank digital currencies. It enabled the frictionless and instantaneous movement of value in its money form around the world, bringing about the financialization of the global economy discussed earlier. I will discuss digitalization as the cutting edge of global capitalist restructuring in this and Chapter 2, here in relation to the crisis of overaccumulation and in Chapter 2 in relation to the transformation of the labor process and the crisis of social reproduction.

A second generation of digital technologies appears poised to drive a new round of worldwide restructuring and transformation based on a much more advanced digitalization of the entire global economy and society. At the core of this new wave of technological development are so-called fourth industrial revolution technologies. The first generation of capitalist globalization from the 1980s and on was based on simple digitalization – the so-called third industrial revolution that proceeded the first such revolution, based on steam power to mechanize production, and the second, based on electrical power that led to mass production. What distinguishes the fourth from the third revolution is a fusion of the new technologies and the blurring of lines between physical, digital, and biological worlds. Led by artificial intelligence (AI) and the collection, processing, and analysis of immense amount of data ("big data"), the emerging technologies include automation and robotics, nano- and biotechnology, including synthetic biology, the Internet of Things (IoT), quantum and cloud computing, 3D printing, augmented and virtual reality, new forms of energy storage, and autonomous land, air, and sea vehicles, among others.[48]

---

[48] There is a growing body of literature on the new technologies and the social, economic, and political impacts. See inter-alia: Robinson, *Global Civil War*; Nick Srnicek, *Platform Capitalism* (London: Polity Press, 2016); Shoshona Zuboff, *The Age of Surveillance Capitalism: The Fight for a Human Future at the New Frontier of Power* (New York: Public Affairs, 2019).

Especially important for the restructuring of the capitalist production process worldwide is the coupling of generative AI with the IoT and the power of quantum computing. The IoT is likely to be the main way to collect data in the near future, through the data generated by billions of connected electronic devices. Data can be collected through connected devices such as sensors, meters, radio frequency identification, and other gadgets that may be embedded in various internet-connected objects used in everyday life. The growing use of IoT is expected to lead to an exponential increase in cross-border data flows in the future without human intervention.[49]

This evolving structure of global capital involves a disruption of existing value chains and an ongoing radical transformation in the modalities of producing and appropriating surplus value, a transformation hastened first by the 2008 crisis and then again by the COVID pandemic of 2020–2022.[50] A small number of monopolistic high-technology companies have become household names, most notably Microsoft, Apple, Amazon, Tencent, Alibaba, Google, Meta, and Baidu. These companies conjoin with industrial tech firms such as Nvidia, TSMC, and Intel, and with numerous so-called platform companies, epitomized by Uber. These tech and platform companies experienced astonishing growth in the 2010s, absorbing enormous amounts of cash from transnational investors around the world who, desperate for new investment opportunities, have poured billions of dollars into the tech and platform companies as an outlet for their surplus accumulated capital. Annual investment in CIT jumped from $17 billion in 1970 to $65 billion in 1980, then to $175 billion in 1990, $496 billion in 2000, and $654 billion in 2016, topped $800 billion in 2019, and then topped $1 trillion in 2023.[51] In mid 2024, the capitalization of the three leading bemouths, Apple, Tencent, and

---

[49] The size of the global IoT market was projected to grow from $381.30 billion in 2021 to $1.85 trillion in 2028, an annual growth rate of 25.4 percent over 2021–2028. UNCTAD Digital Economy Report 2021 (New York: United Nations Publications, 2021), p. 33. The digital effects are global in reach, with a veritable explosion of worldwide network data traffic in recent years. Mobile network data traffic increased by 50 percent just in the one year from 2019 to 2020, reaching 230 exabytes per month in 2020. This volume is expected to more than triple by 2026, to 780 exabytes per month. Ibid., p. 17.
[50] Robinson, *Will Global Capitalism Endure?*
[51] Federal Reserve Bank of St. Louis, *Economic Research*, "Private Fixed Investment in Information Processing Equipment and Software," see

Microsoft, approached $3 trillion each, while Google surpassed $2 trillion, Facebook surpassed $1 trillion, and many others capitalized in the tens and the hundreds of billions. The top technology firms are global capital hubs that perform a "system-integrator" function.[52] They and the transnational industrial and commercial capitals they bring together are in turn enmeshed with the giant global financial conglomerates that are at the very core of the global economy. These financial conglomerates own more than half of the leading tech firms. Sociologist Peter Phillips has identified 33 trillion and multitrillion-dollar capital investment management companies in 2022, up from just 17 in 2017. These "titans of capital" controlled more than $83 trillion in combined assets,[53] over four-fifths the value that year of the entire global GDP.

Marx introduced the category of surplus profit as surplus value that does not participate in the general movement of the equalization of the rate of profit, in turn a result of monopolistic control over certain sectors of the world economy. Surplus profit may shift from one to another sector of capital, such as to the global oil industry in certain historical moments, and in fact ExxonMobil registered $56 billion in profits in 2022, which constituted not just record profits for the firm but record levels of profit for any firm in the history of capitalism.[54] If the giant tech firms enjoyed surplus profits, these profits did not "rest" with them but continued to flow through the veins of the global financial system. Value does not park itself in any one place for very long. It is in constant motion, surging through these veins. As already noted, financial markets concentrate wealth by appropriating value from other circuits that have, in turn, appropriated it from global labor. I observed in a 2022 study, taking the example of Apple, that the billionaires and multimillionaires who are the public face of Apple

---

continuously updated data in graph, U.S. Bureau of Economic Analysis, https://fred.stlouisfed.org/series/A679RC1Q027SBEA.

[52] See: Ronald W. Cox, "Transnational Capital and the Politics of Global Supply Chains," *Class, Race, and Corporate Power*, 1(1), 2013; Niles Peters, "Holding the Strings: The Role of Finance in Shaping Big Tech," in *State of Power: Digital Power* (Amsterdam: Transnational Institute, 2023), p. 25.

[53] Peter Phillips, *Titans of Capital* (New York: Seven Stories Press, 2024), p. 24.

[54] Camila Domonoske, "Exxon Announced Record Earnings. It's Bound to Renew Scrutiny of Big Oil," *NPR*, January 31, 2023, www.npr.org/2023/01/31/1152776315/exxon-mobil-earnings-chevron-big-oil-biden-windfall-tax.

capitalists owned in 2021 but a few percentage points of the company. The three top individual shareholders, Arthur Levinson, Tim Cook, and Jeff Williams, together held barely more than 1 percent, whereas the three top institutional investors, Vanguard Group, BlackRock, and Berkshire Hathaway, owned more than 20 percent of the company.[55] In turn, China Investment Corporation held 2.1 percent of Blackrock shares, the Kuwait Investment Authority held 5.24 percent, Temasek Holdings Limited from China held 3.9 percent, and so on, so that Blackrock itself appeared as a holding company and clearinghouse for networks of transnational capital.[56]

A New Era of Automation?

In the capitalist era, virtually all scientific and technological breakthroughs have been propelled by the impulse to accumulate, specifically, by the drive to augment the extraction of surplus value. Marx showed that absolute and relative surplus value "had played a different and each time a decision role in the historical development of capitalist production."[57] Could we be on the threshold of a "decisive role" for relative surplus value through the digital revolution? If this were to be so, it would be because the imperative of capitalist reproduction makes it so, because the resolution of contradictions and obstacles to this reproduction, at this time, compels it. The TCC, recall, can increase profits by lowering wages *or* by raising productivity (or a mix of the two, of course). Digitalization may lower capital's wage bill in three ways. First, the restructuring it brings about involves breaking down complex labor processes into more simple operations that reduce higher-priced skilled labor to lower-priced unskilled labor. Second, it involves replacing workers altogether with technology. And third, in doing so, it expands the ranks of those that are unemployed and underemployed. A mass of unemployed and underemployed workers disciplines those who remain employed and places downward pressure on their wages.

---

[55] Nathan Reiff, "Top Apple Shareholders," *Investopedia*, February 6, 2021, accessed on November 29, 2021 at www.investopedia.com/articles/markets/120115/top-5-apple-shareholders.asp.
[56] This data is from MarketScreener, accessed on November 29, 2021 at www.marketscreener.com/quote/stock/BLACKROCK-INC-11862/company/.
[57] Frederick Engels, "Preface," in Marx, *Capital*, Vol. II, p. 17.

Since 2008, and especially in the aftermath of the COVID-19 pandemic, which turbo-charged the introduction of the new technologies, realms have been written about the potential for automation to eliminate millions of jobs.[58] The new technologies have the capability to take automation to a qualitatively new level. If, in industry prior to machine production, the laborer produced with tools in hand, once "machine-facture," as Marx referred to it, became established, the worker operated machines that in turn produced commodities. "The machine proper is therefore a mechanism that, after being set in motion, performs with its tools the same operations that were formerly done by the workman with similar tools."[59] The next level in automation, the elimination of the machine operator herself, was already anticipated by Marx in *The Grundrisse*. "Labor no longer appears so much to be included within the production process," he said. "Rather, the human being comes to relate more as watchman and regulator to the production process itself."[60] Adorno and Horkheimer observed in their classic 1944 study, *Dialectic of Enlightenment*, that "thinking objectifies itself to become an automatic, self-activating process, an impersonation of the machine that it produces itself so that ultimately the machine can replace it."[61] In the 1950s, Friedrich Pollock defined automation as "a technique of industrial production [in which] machines are 'controlled' by machines."[62]

Such earlier theories of automation, as insightful and prescient as they were, could not have anticipated the idea of generative AI, which places the discussion in a whole new ballpark, so to say. If automation pushes the machine operator further back in the process, to computer screens that in turn control machinery, digitalization makes possible another level of separation of the worker from her tools. The potential for computers operating through AI to run machinery and also

---

[58] For a summary and analysis, see William I. Robinson, *Global Civil War: Capitalism Post-Pandemic* (Oakland: PM Press, 2022).

[59] Marx, *Capital*, Vol. I (New York: International Publishers, 1967 [1867]), p. 353.

[60] Karl Marx, *Grundrisse* (London: Penguin Books, 1973), p. 705.

[61] Theodor W. Adorno and Max Horkheimer, *Dialectic of Enlightenment* (London: Verso, 1997), p. 25.

[62] Friedrich Pollock, Automation: A Study of the Economic and Social Consequences (1956), as cited in Jason E. Smith, *Smart Machines and Service Work: Automation in the Age of Stagnation* (London: Reaktion Books, 2020), p. 23.

to replace human supervisory and decision-making functions has not been realized to date in all but the most advanced plants in certain industries. In these industries there is a centralized automated control of the entire factory complex.[63] We could anticipate a revolution in automation and attendant productivity should AI be applied to such "flow production," in which the product is assembled entirely without the interference of human beings.

Earlier industrial disruptions, such as the transition from horse-drawn transportation to transportation systems based on electricity and the combustion engine, averted mass unemployment. Later on, in the latter decades of the twentieth century, the massive expansion of services absorbed those released from industry due to technological changes or to deindustrialization in the former core countries of the world capitalist system, especially as services became commodified. AI involves machine learning (specifically, a type of machine learning driven by generative AI known as "deep learning"[64]), complex communication, independent algorithmic production, and pattern recognition and could, in theory, replace the computer operator entirely so that production is self-sustaining. It may also involve the automation of many general and even some personal services. Recall that digital technology is dead labor (constant capital), but with novel characteristics, insofar as machine learning can potentially create new constant capital (e.g., new digital realms), so that it is not, paradoxically speaking, dead labor, even if it can be traced back at some point to living labor.

This is to say that the new technologies, insofar as they are digital means of production, have the potential to produce on their own new means of production, new constant capital. This prospect may fire the imagination. The introduction in late 2022 of an AI chatbot, ChatGPT, seemed to suggest that such a scenario could be at hand in the coming years. Any such revolution in the nature of the production process would involve as well profound transformations in the labor

---

[63] See, inter-alia, Jason E. Smith, *Smart Machines and Service Work: Automation in the Age of Stagnation* (London: Reaktion Books, 2020), p. 25.

[64] Deep learning is a type of machine learning based on a stack of sequentially connected artificial "neural networks" that filters data for pattern recognition, classification, stylized description, and prediction, patterned on the very structure and functions of animal brains. See discussion in Julio Huato, "The Political Economy of Digital Technology," *Science & Society*, 88(2), 2024, 212–249.

process and class relations and massive social and political disruptions. Indeed, such impacts are already being felt around the world. Yet assessing and predicting the impact of generative AI is difficult because the technology is developing at exponential speed. ChatGPT was released in November 2022. Four months later, OpenAI released a new large language model, or LLM, called GPT-4 with substantially improved capabilities. Then just four months after that Anthropic's generative AI, Claude, was able to process 100,000 tokens of text, equal to about 75,000 words in a minute – the length of the average novel – compared with roughly 9,000 tokens when it was introduced in March 2023, according to a report by McKinsey & Company, a leading business think tank. These models involved a new type of "deep learning," a "step change revolution" within deep learning that entails expansive artificial neural networks inspired by the billions of neurons connected in the human brain. Unlike earlier models, they can process extremely large and varied sets of unstructured data and perform more than one task.[65]

Back to the Future: The Shift from Absolute to Relative Surplus Value

Digitalization has the potential to exponentially increase the productive power of social labor and therefore holds out the promise to the TCC of a vast increase in the production of relative surplus value. Yet this potential for such an increase in productivity has not been realized. The average growth of output per worker in the United States, for instance, was 2.3 percent a year between 1891 and 1972. It was just 1.4 percent a year between 1972 and 1996, and 1.3 percent between 2004 and 2012, although it recovered historical levels between 1996 and 2004, corresponding roughly to the period in which computerization became generalized in industry and services.[66]

---

[65] Michael Chui et al., The Economic Potential of Generative AI: The Next Productivity Frontier, June 2023, McKinsey & Company, www.mckinsey.com/capabilities/mckinsey-digital/our-insights/the-economic-potential-of-generative-ai-the-next-productivity-frontier.

[66] See Marin Wolf, "Same as It Ever Was: Why the Techno-Optimists are Wrong," in *The Fourth Industrial Revolution: A Davos Reader* (Davos: Foreign Affairs, undated but contents suggest a mid 2010s publication date), pp. 117–118.

Part of the explanation for this so-called productivity paradox may be the time lag between the introduction of new technologies and their adoption. Although the tractor was invented in the late 1880s, just 4 percent of farms in the United States three decades after the invention had one. And it took two decades after personal computers were first introduced into offices for the 50 percent adoption threshold to be crossed.[67] Another may be the need for industrial capitalists to make good on large-scale investments in fixed capital made prior to the new technologies. Moreover, low rates of profit tend to retard investment in new technologies, insofar as an anticipated increase in productivity is not matched by an anticipated increase in profits. However, I suggest that one important factor has been transnational capital's ability to leverage globalization to expand the production of absolute surplus value. The massive increase in the availability of cheap labor opened up by globalization may have until now held back the potential that is latent in the new digital technologies for an explosion in productivity.

But that may change. As Marx noted, "a crisis always forms the starting-point of large new investments."[68] The early years of globalization, to reiterate, allowed the TCC to increase absolute surplus value, that is, by seeking out new pools of cheap and super-exploitable labor around the world, which may have held back the full deployment of digital technologies to advance the forces of production. In seeking these pools of labor, emergent transnational capital was able to take advantage of the uneven development of capitalism around the world, and especially of the relative underdevelopment of the former Third World. It is no surprise, as noted earlier, that the rate of profit increased during the globalization boom from the 1980s into the early twenty-first century before it again declined.[69] Super-exploitation, a concept first introduced in 1973 by the Brazilian dependency theorist Ruy Mauro Marini,[70] involves subjecting workers to low wages, long hours, and intensive work to the point of exhaustion in place of increasing their productivity. As a result, that labor power is

---

[67] *The Economist*, "Artificial Intelligence: Machine Dream," July 22, 2023, p. 55.
[68] Marx, *Capital* Vol. II, p. 189.
[69] See Roberts, *The Long Depression*, chapter one, "The Causes of Depression."
[70] Ruy Mauro Marini, *Dialéctica de la Dependencia* (Buenos Aires: CLCACSO, 1973); first published in English as *The Dialectics of Dependency* (New York: Monthly Review Press, 2022).

remunerated below its value, that is, below the cost of the social reproduction of the worker (see Chapter 2). There have been fierce debates that I cannot revisit here as to whether this super-exploitation constitutes a form of absolute surplus value or a third form of surplus value not identified by Marx.[71]

The key point is that the extreme oppressive conditions of exploitation observed by Marini have been made more widely available to transnational capital through globalization. Yet the more this super-exploitation is extended around the world, the more does it aggravate in the long run the underlying conditions of capitalist crisis and incentivize the TCC to make broad use of the new digital technologies in order to offset the fall in the rate of profit by increasing relative surplus value. Equally if not more important, the TCC has to confront the global revolt. Ongoing social upheavals and escalating class struggle in *both* low-wage and higher-wage zones around the world provide transnational capital with a powerful incentive to undertake a more thoroughgoing automation. Digital restructuring would allow the dominant groups to step up restructuring of time and space in its drive to exercise greater control over the global working class. The new technologies constitute a powerful instrument of social control in two respects. First, they can and are being applied to develop chilling new systems of omnipresent surveillance and repression, as I have explored elsewhere and will return to later on.[72] Second, they allow for the replacement of insubordinate workers with technology. Robots, it has been widely noted, do not go on strike and can work round-the-clock.

The COVID-19 pandemic made clear the fragility of global supply chains and hence of vast global outsourcing networks, as I will discuss in Chapter 3. Reshoring and nearshoring become attractive options for assuring supply in local and national markets. (Note that

---

[71] For some discussion on these debates, see Andy Higginbottom, "Superexploitation and the Imperialist Drive of Capitalism: How Marini's 'Dialects of Dependency' Goes Beyond Marx's Capital," Monthly Review, April 1, 2023, https://monthlyreview.org/2023/04/01/superexploitation-and-the-imperialist-drive-of-capitalism-how-marinis-dialectics-of-dependency-goes-beyond-marxs-capital/. My own view is that Higginbottom is mistaken; the concept of super-exploitation is already contained in Marx's *Capital*. He had already identified a situation in which the worker is paid below the value of her labor power, that is, below her cost of production.

[72] See Robinson, *The Global Police State*.

reshoring or "de-globalization" does not mean that capital ceases to be transnational. It is *transnational capital* that relocates from one place to another as the geography of global capitalism is continuously reconfigured.) But reshoring to high-wage zones means foregoing access to the cheapest pools of labor. Higher wages in the historic core would have to be compensated for by significant increases in productivity. The new technologies, in particular the applications of generative AI, make possible a very significant, even exponential, acceleration in the velocity of accumulation and therefore, *ceteris paribus*, an increase in appropriated surplus value, given that accelerated turnover time in itself does not increase the organic composition of capital. The McKinsey report cited earlier anticipated that generative AI would produce a revolution in productivity in the coming years, predicting that, together with related technologies, work automation could add 0.5 to 3.4 percentage points annually to productivity growth.[73] An increase in relative surplus value is a result of an increase in productivity, whether due to the introduction of new machinery and technology, which is usually the case, and that increases the organic composition of capital, or to superior methods of organizing the production process. In either case, the rate of exploitation is intensified. Despite the hype about the return of industrial policies that bring industry back to the core countries, as I will discuss in detail in Chapter 3, it is highly doubtful that any such reshoring will bring back to rich countries stable, high-skilled, and high-paying industrial and postindustrial jobs, given that the relocation back to the core centers of the global economy will involve high levels of automation.

The flip side of reshoring to rich counties is the automation of plants that were previously offshored. Sweatshops that employ largely young women in cheap labor zones around the world, perhaps the archetypical image of the global economy, may become rarer as the low-skilled and repetitive labor that these sweatshops employ are exactly the type of tasks that are easily automated. The case of Foxconn, the Taiwanese transnational corporation that

---

[73] Michael Chui et al., The Economic Potential of Generative AI: The Next Productivity Frontier, June 2023, McKinsey & Company, www.mckinsey.com/capabilities/mckinsey-digital/our-insights/the-economic-potential-of-generative-ai-the-next-productivity-frontier.

assembles Apple and other electronic devices in China, gives us a sign of a possible shift in capital's strategy from absolute to relative surplus value production in low-wage zones. The company is one of the largest employers in the world, with 1.2 million workers in 2016, more than one million of them in China.[74] It started operations in the late twentieth century through an accumulation strategy based on super-exploitation, but in the 2010s it began a shift to the digital elimination of its workforce. In 2016 the company unveiled plans to automate factories in the face of mounting worker unrest and competitive pressures, leaving them "with only a minimal number of workers assigned for production, logistics, testing, and inspection processes" (in March of that year it announced that it had already automated away 60,000 jobs at one of its giant factories).[75] This strategy of automation appears to be spreading more broadly in China. By the 2020s, China had become the world's largest robotic market, accounting for half of robotic installations worldwide. Robots were used across vast sectors of the economy, including manufacturing, warehousing, logistics, hospitality, health care, and construction.[76] Official Chinese statistics showed a decline of thirty million manufacturing jobs from 1996 to 2014, or 25 percent of the total, even as manufacturing output increased by over 70 percent.[77] Beyond China, there appears to be a substantial shift to automation and robotics in Asia, in both higher-wage countries

[74] Nick Statt, "Iphone Manufacturer Foxconn Plans to Replace Almost Every Human Workers with Robots," *The Verge*, December 30, 2016, www.theverge.com/2016/12/30/14128870/foxconn-robots-automation-apple-iphone-china-manufacturing.

[75] "Apple Manufacturer Foxconn to Fully Replace Humans with Robots," *Futurism*, January 3, 2017, https://futurism.com/apple-manufacturer-foxconn-to-fully-replace-humans-with-robots. By 2017 it had deployed 40,000 of its Foxbot industrial robots.

[76] Su Ng, "Deep Dive: China Shifts to Automation, Industrial Robots to Address Shrinking Workforce and Stay Competitive," *South China Morning Post*, April 7, 2024, www.scmp.com/yp/discover/article/3257925/deep-dive-china-shifts-automation-industrial-robots-address-shrinking-workforce-and-stay-competitive; Robert D. Atkinson, "How Innovative is China in the Robotics Industry?," Information Technology & Innovation Foundation, March 2024, www2.itif.org/2024-chinese-robotics-innovation.pdf.

[77] Erik Brynjolfsson and Andrew McAfee, "New World Order: Labor, Capital, and Ideas in the Power Law Economy," in *The Fourth Industrial Revolution: A Davos Reader*, p. 98, published by *Foreign Affairs*, no specific editor, no indicated place or year of publication.

such as Japan and South Korea and in lower-wage countries such as Vietnam and Thailand, a topic to which I will return in Chapter 2.[78]

Putting aside this automation of *industrial* production, what about the surge in offshoring to low-wage zones in recent years of low- and also high-skilled *service* work, from data entry and call centers to accounting, engineering, financial analysis, and computer programming? Digital offshoring, unlike the overseas relocation of production facilities, is virtually frictionless and does not add transportation and other ancillary costs such as customs charges. When work is carried out remotely, it does not matter where it is performed. Yet even for services, new AI-driven digital technologies such as interactive voice response systems are reducing the requirement for direct person-to-person communication and may lead to the automation of call centers and other digital services around the world. We may see in the coming years a mix of nearshoring and reshoring to rich countries and increased automation in areas that in earlier years became labor-intensive industrial processing zones and service centers, such as China's Guangdong Province. In the long run, it may be that offshoring is a historical way station on the road to automation. Needless to say, I am pointing here to tendencies underway and to the *potential* of the digital revolution, not to the realization in the present of that potential. In analyzing and theorizing the implications of digitalization, we are as much speculating into the future, on how the arc of capitalism's epochal crisis may play out in the coming years and decades, as we are identifying current processes.

We can affirm with some certainty, however, that any new burst of global accumulation based on digital technologies, even if it pulls the global economy momentarily out of stagnation, will in the long run

---

[78] For automation in Southeast Asia, see two reports by Meticulous Research, a market research company: *Asia-Pacific Industrial Automation Market*, September 2023, and *South East Asia Industrial Automation Market by Component, Mode of Automation, End User, and Geography*, August 2023. For Vietnam, see *The Manufacturing Outlook*, "The Rise of Automation and Robotics in Vietnam's Manufacturing," December 15, 2023, www.themanufacturingoutlook.com/news/the-rise-of-automation-and-robotics-in-vietnam-s-manufacturing-nwid-1538.html. For Thailand, see "Thailand's $45 Billion Leap to Industry 4.0," *Asian Robotics Review*, 2024; *Linkedin*, "Industry 4.0 and the Rise of the Smart Factory in Thailand: Challenges and Opportunities," July 21, 2023, www.linkedin.com/pulse/industry-40-rise-smart-factories-thailand-challenges-opportunities.

end up aggravating underlying crisis tendencies. We have seen that digitalization greatly accelerates the process whereby machinery and technology replace human labor, thus expanding the ranks of those who are made surplus and marginalized. As we will see in Chapter 2, generative AI holds up to the TCC the promise of a revolution in value by radically increasing productivity and also doing away with the need for much troublesome human labor. The processes that push capitalism toward laborless production also push marginal cost toward zero, that is, zero cost for each incremental unit of output. "Nothing has super-charged the competitive dynamic quite like the technology sector," observed the McKinsey report cited earlier. "By building powerful digital platforms and networks, the most successful tech companies have created a model that allows them to scale up to unprecedented size, while driving their marginal costs to almost zero."[79]

It is near impossible that we will ever reach the event horizon of laborless production or zero marginal cost, much less in the near future. Theoretically the organic composition of capital can rise indefinitely. Fully automated production would actually be described as an infinite organic composition! This is, of course, an end point in theory only. The more the system does away with labor and pushes toward zero marginal cost, the more it is faced over the long run with a *crisis of value*, since only living labor can generate value. A revolution in value leads inevitably to a crisis of value. As we saw earlier, the rate of profit has declined in recent decades even though the mass of surplus value has continued to grow. But this situation cannot continue indefinitely. Digitalization may offer capital a way to extend the growth in the mass of surplus value and even the possibility for raising the rate of surplus value for a time. But over the long run, *ceteris paribus*, the extension of the digital replacement of human labor must lead to a reduction in the total volume of value produced, to be followed by a reduction in the total volume of surplus value produced, a point when there is no more living labor for dead labor to consume, a crisis in the production and the realization of surplus value so much so that the destruction or devalorization of capital on a world scale would be

---

[79] James Manyika, "Playing to Win: The New Global Competition for Corporate Profits," McKinsey Global Institute, October 20, 2015, www.mckinsey.com/mgi/overview/in-the-news/playing-to-win-the-new-global-competition-for-corporate-profits.

cataclysmic. Note that I am not suggesting such a doomsday scenario is inevitable, certainly not anytime soon, and in any event an ecological collapse, the subject of Chapter 4, may preempt any such structural economic collapse.

Short of these collapse scenarios, digital restructuring, to conclude, may intensify many times over the crisis of overaccumulation to the extent that it radically increases the organic composition of capital and therefore places downward pressure on the rate of profit at the same time that the replacement of workers by technology aggravates overproduction/underconsumption. But if digital transformation were to be coupled with significant redistributive and regulatory reform as countervailing tendencies, it may offer global capitalism a temporary way out of the structural crisis. In theory, digital technologies could raise productivity enough to offset the decline in profit rates and therefore lead to renewed investment in the productive sector. To date, no such reform has occurred. To the contrary, the unbridled predatory expansion of transnational capital has heightened social polarization and mass depravation around the world. Absent radical reform, if not the outright overthrow of global capitalism, an advanced digitalization of the global economy and society will intensify the crisis of social reproduction that is the focus of Chapter 2.

2 | Crisis of Social Reproduction

The Absolute General Law of Capitalist Accumulation in the Age of Globalization

In radical political economy, a theoretical understanding of crisis focuses on capitalism's ability for *reproduction* in its totality. *Social reproduction*, as I use it here, refers to how human beings reproduce their existence from one day to the next, one month to the next, one year to the next, and one generation to the next. Along with all other species, ours must seek to reproduce ourselves, for otherwise life cannot be sustained. If a deer stops grazing, it perishes; if a lion stops hunting deer, it perishes. Whereas other species withdraw directly from nature, our species' unique way of reproducing our existence is to produce – to transform extra-human nature through the collective labor process in order to supply ourselves with the necessities of life. Production of the material means of our existence – food, clothing, shelter, and so forth – is the necessary condition for our reproduction and reproduction is a necessary condition for production, for without social reproduction we perish and are therefore unable to continue to produce. We produce in order to reproduce ourselves. Production and social reproduction are moments in the singular process of our existence. There is a long and complex debate on the definition and meaning of reproduction/social reproduction and its place in Marxist analysis that I cannot revisit here.[1] For the purposes here, we may

---

[1] I use here the concept of social reproduction more broadly than how it applies to the oppression of women and gender relations. I will refer briefly later in this chapter to Marxist feminist approaches under the very broad and debate-filled category of social reproduction theory. For general discussion on social reproduction, see inter-alia: Isabella and Stephen Gill (eds.), *Power, Production and Social Reproduction* (New York: Palgrave, 2003); Tithy Bhattacharya, *Social Reproduction Theory: Remapping Class, Recentering Oppression* (London: Pluto, 2017); Susan Ferguson, *Women and Work: Feminism, Labor and Social Reproduction* (London: Pluto, 2019); Lisa Vogel, *Marxism and*

note that the distinction between production and social reproduction, and between productive and reproductive labor, is entirely methodological. Struggles around social reproduction are not tangential to struggles around production but part of them. Furthermore, they are central to class struggle between capital and labor.

In capitalist society, both production and social reproduction are organized in function of capital accumulation. Once people have been separated from the means of production, the only way they can survive is to work for those who own the means of production in exchange for a wage or salary that allows them to purchase the commodities necessary for survival. The laborer must sell the commodity she has to offer, her labor power, yet even if she is unable to do so, on pain of death she must still be a buyer of commodities, the means of subsistence. Social reproduction becomes dependent on capital (on employment, the wage, and social policies of the capitalist state). At the same time, the capitalist needs exploitable workers in order for production and therefore accumulation (profit-making) to take place. It needs the worker to produce in the factory, the farm, the mine, the warehouse, the office complex, the service industries, and so on. But he also needs the worker to be able to eat, sleep, and procreate so that she can return to work the next day and so that a fresh generation of workers will be available for future exploitation. If the worker is thus dependent on capital to obtain the very means of her existence, that is, to purchase food and other commodities, the capitalist is equally dependent on the worker for his existence. Capital, in fact, is not a "thing" but a *relationship* between capital and labor as a unity of antagonistic opposites. Here is how Marx described this relationship of mutual dependence:

The capital [the wage] given in exchange for labor-power is converted into necessaries, by the consumption of which the muscles, nerves, bones, and brains of existing laborers are reproduced, and new laborers are begotten. Within the limits of what is strictly necessary, the individual consumption of the working class is, therefore, the reconversion of the means of subsistence given by capital in exchange for labor power, into fresh labor-power at the disposal of capital for exploitation. It is the production and reproduction of

the Oppression of Women (Chicago: Haymarket, 2013 [1983]); Martha E. Gimenez, *Marx, Women and Capitalist Social Reproduction* (Chicago: Haymarket, 2019).

that means of production so indispensable to the capitalist: the laborer himself. The individual consumption of the laborer, whether it proceed within the workshop or outside of it, whether it be part of the process of production or not, forms therefore a factor of the production and reproduction of capital; just as cleaning machinery does, whether it be done while the machinery is working or while the machinery is standing. The fact that the laborer consumes his means of subsistence for his own purposes, and not to please the capitalist, has no bearing on the matter. The maintenance and reproduction of the working class is, and must ever be, a necessary condition to the reproduction of capital.[2]

But what happens when capital has no need for regular full-time workers who earn enough to purchase the commodities necessary for their social reproduction? And what happens when capital has no need for workers at all? Marx referred to those who are not employed by capital as the surplus population, more specifically as an industrial reserve army. In the normal course of capitalist development, there is an ongoing increase in constant capital relative to variable capital, or a continuous increase in the organic composition of capital, as I discussed in Chapter 1. This process "constantly produces and produces in direct ratio of its own energy and extent, a relatively redundant population of laborers, i.e., a population of greater extent that suffices for the average needs of the self-expansion of capital, and therefore a surplus-population."[3] Marx continued:

The whole form of the movement of modern industry depends, therefore, upon the constant transformation of a part of the laboring population into unemployed or half-employed hands.... But the greater this reserve army in proportion to the active labor-army, the greater is the mass of a consolidated surplus-population, whose misery is in inverse ratio to its torment of labor. The more extensive, finally, the lazarus-layers of the working-class, and the industrial reserve army, the greater is official pauperism. *This is the absolute general law of capitalist accumulation* (emphasis in original).[4]

In turn, Marx identified three forms of surplus labor: floating, latent, and stagnant. The first two were seen as those who weave in and out

---

[2] Marx, *Capital*, Vol. I, p. 537. Marx goes on: "From a social point of view, therefore, the working class, even when not directly engaged in the labor process, is just as much an appendage of capital as the ordinary instruments of labor. Even its individual consumption is, within certain limits, a mere factor in the process of production" (p. 538).

[3] Marx, *Capital*, Vol. I, p. 590.   [4] Ibid., p. 603.

of the production process in accordance with the cycles of capital accumulation and changes in the division of labor. The third, however, is a group that has been pushed structurally outside of the production process, that is, which is of no *direct* use to capital over entire historical epochs. "The capitalist can now wring from the laborer a certain quantity of surplus-labor without allowing him the labor-time necessary for his own subsistence," observed Marx, capturing this analytical bifurcation of the global working classes into those expelled from the circuits of accumulation and those incorporated under the conditions of super-exploitation. "He can annihilate all regularity of employment, and according to his own convenience, caprice, and the interest of the moment, make the most enormous over-work alternate with relative or absolute cessation of work."[5]

Surplus Humanity

In the epoch of globalization, there has been an ongoing worldwide expansion of the third category to which Marx referred, stagnant surplus labor. What I will call here *surplus humanity*[6] may be a permanent structural phenomenon of global capitalism rather than a transitory dislocation pending absorption into new circuits of accumulation.[7] As the global reserve army of labor becomes ever more saturated and bloated, it may be useful heuristically to establish two analytical categories that overlap, the reserve army of labor and surplus humanity, the latter made up of masses of people who may be locked out of the economy and society for decades, a permanent redundant mass. To Marx's assertion that the accumulation of capital involves the multiplication of the proletariat, we can add that in this age of global capitalism, capital simultaneously produces an historically unprecedented multiplication of surplus humanity, proletarianized to be sure, but too numerous to be useful to capital as a reserve army and too restless and on the move to not be contained through the global police state whose

---

[5] Ibid., p. 511.
[6] As far as I know, the first person to use this term "surplus humanity" was Mike Davis, in *Planet of Slums* (London: Verso, 2006). He did not, however, theorize the concept, as I am attempting to do here by expanding my earlier discussion in William I. Robinson, *The Global Police State* (London: Pluto, 2020).
[7] William I. Robinson, *The Global Police State* (London: Pluto, 2020), chapter two, "Savage Inequalities: The Imperative of Social Control."

contingent end game is extermination. While the absolute number of those excluded is historically unprecedented, we can predict that its ranks will continue to expand, as I will discuss later, unless the current course of capitalist development is altered by government policies, a fundamental change in TCC accumulation strategies forced on it by mass struggle, or otherwise.

The history of capitalist development is a history of the development of a global working class. We are, in the words of the Salvage Collective, living in the *proletarocene*.[8] The global wage labor force, as noted in Chapter 1, doubled from 1.5 billion in 1980 to some three billion in 2006, as workers from China, India, and the former Soviet bloc entered the global labor pool,[9] and then increased by another 500 million by 2018, the largest size of the global labor force in recorded history.[10] In the coming years and decades, hundreds of millions more will swell the ranks of the proletariat, which is now the largest class in world history. Moreover, the global proletariat is truly a *world class*, every member connected to one another through the global circuits of capital, objectively if not subjectively. The concept of surplus humanity amalgamates two categories within the global proletariat, neither of which are stable and that are interpenetrated, insofar as those who are surplus may move into precarious forms of employment, or their participation in the informal sector or underground or illicit economies may be considered labor, if one wants to think of it as such, rather than exclusion and unemployment, whereas those who are in precarious employment arrangements may well become surplus.

This categorical separation of surplus labor from precariously employed labor is therefore slippery since there is movement back and

---

[8] The Salvage Collective, *The Tragedy of the Worker: Towards the Proletarocene* (London: Verso, 2021).

[9] Richard Freeman, "The Great Doubling: The Challenge of the New Global Labor Market," *The Globalist* online magazine, March 5, 2010, www.theglobalist.com/StoryId.aspx?StoryId=4542. The ILO placed the global working class in 2017 at 3.2 billion. International Labor Organization, *World Employment and Social Outlook 2017: Sustainable Enterprises and Jobs: Formal Enterprises and Decent Work* (Geneva: ILO, 2017), https://ilo.org/wcmsp5/groups/public/---dgreports/---dcomm/---publ/documents/publication/wcms_579893.pdf.

[10] International Labor Organization, "World Employment and Social Outlook: Trends 2019" (Geneva, ILO, 2019), p. 5, www.ilo.org/wcmsp5/groups/public/---dgreports/---dcomm/---publ/documents/publication/wcms_670542.pdf.

forth between the porous boundaries of the two contingent categories. For this reason we may consider the concept of surplus humanity as a heuristic device that requires some conceptual stretching. But by the same token, Marx's very concept of stagnant labor as long-term surplus labor outside of the capital circuit faces the same problem. Unless this labor simply lies down to die, it must do something, formal or informal, licit or otherwise, to survive day to day; in one way or another, this activity makes the individual not excluded in the strict sense. In popular parlance, the concept of marginality refers to those who face special forms of oppression, such as ethnic minorities or migrant workers who may be marginalized from full participation in political and civic life. This usage is problematic because it obscures the fact that these groups are not marginalized from capitalist relations of production and exploitation but are exploited under special oppressive conditions, such as migrant workers in agriculture and services who may not have the same legal protections as citizens and can therefore be superexploited. Instead, I use marginality here to denote surplus labor that experiences dispossession and expulsion from the global economy in the sense that Marx meant by the third stagnant category of surplus labor.

Yet as global capitalism continues its relentless drive for expanded accumulation, the global proletariat, both those portions expelled from the formal circuits of capital and those incorporated under conditions of super-exploitation, is in crisis everywhere, under a permanent state of siege. Humanity is becoming exhausted in/by capitalism even as a growing portion of it is chewed up without first being sucked in. Long-term structural un- and underemployment, below-subsistence wages, eking out an existence in the licit and illicit informal street economies of the world's megacities, the displacement of hundreds of millions of people by climate change, economic collapse, wars, natural disasters, and political persecution – all this and more makes it increasingly difficult, and in many instances, impossible, for billions of people to survive, that is to reproduce themselves, their families, and their communities. "Capital cares nothing for the length of life of labor-power," argued Marx in his discussion on the forms of surplus labor.

All that concerns it is simply and solely the maximum of labor-power, that can be rendered fluent in a working-day. It attains this end by shortening the extent of the labor's life, as a greedy farmer snatches increased produce from the soil by robbing it of its fertility. Capital that has such good reasons for denying the sufferings of the legions of workers that surround it, is in practice moved as much and as little by the sight of the coming degradation and final depopulation of the human race, as by the probable fall of the earth into the sun.[11]

The phrase "surplus humanity" does nothing to capture the depths of misery that billions of people go through daily: poverty, disease, unemployment, homelessness, malnutrition, social exclusion, racism, xenophobia, forced migration, incarceration, state violence, and other forms of social violence and humiliation. Those expelled must scramble to find ways to assure the reproduction of their own lives in an environment that is extremely hostile and restrictive, in which they are criminalized de jure or de facto. The march of appropriation continuously closes off more and more spaces for reproduction. Those desperate to survive at all costs will turn in their anguish to dangerous and often deadly treks to find employment in other countries, to surrogate pregnancy, to trafficking themselves sexually (while many are also forcibly trafficked), and to petty crime and social violence as those preyed upon by capital in turn prey upon other victims around them, and even to the sale, usually illicit, of one's organs. It is no surprise that the global trade in organs is booming. One U.S. reporter who broke a story on how a hospital in India was arranging for illicit kidney transplants was inundated with emails from people around the world – from India and Bangladesh, to Germany, Russia, Croatia, Colombia, Peru, Kenya, Nigeria, and even the United States – inquiring if he could help them to arrange an international sale (in Iran, the one country that operates a legal, government-managed market for the sale of kidneys, the organ seller earns less than $4,000).[12] Surplus humanity has been reduced, not to selling its labor to capital, but to literally selling its flesh and blood so that capital may exist.

More than two billion people across the globe work in the informal sector.[13] Labor in the informal sector and the underground economy

---

[11] Marx, *Capital*, Vol. I, pp. 253, 256.
[12] Shashank Bengali, "I Reported on Illicit Kidney Trade, Then Offers Piled Up," *Los Angeles Times*, October 1, 2018, p. A2. Some of those people who contacted the reporter were not the impoverished desperate for survival but opportunists, such as a man from Cameroon who proposed a business deal to sell his countryfolk for a cut.
[13] ILO, *World Employment and Social Outlook 2017: Sustainable Enterprises and Jobs: Formal Enterprises and Decent Work*.

is unwaged labor in the sense that capital does not provide it with a wage. What happens when it becomes impossible to achieve social reproduction in the informal sector? Primary exploitation refers to the exploitation that takes place in the capital–labor relation at the point of production of wealth, where capitalists directly appropriate from labor surplus value that is the source of profits. Surplus humanity cannot be directly exploited, that is, subject to primary exploitation. But unless they are to quietly die of starvation, they must enter into the market in the sphere of circulation to obtain their basic necessities, by hook or crook, by all sorts of survival strategies, including crimes of survival ("street crime" and often petty property crime). Informality encompasses a wide range of licit and illicit activities with no work-based social protection or guaranteed income, ranging from street vending, unregulated homework in global and domestic value chains, agriculture, waste picking, domestic work, and panhandling.

The ILO estimates that 61 percent (63 percent for men and 58 percent for women) of the global employed population, or two billion people, attempt to scratch by in the informal economy. In India, to take one example, out of a working-age population of one billion, only 100 million have formal jobs. The rest are relegated to casual work or to joblessness.[14] This estimate, however, does not include illicit activities in the underground economy, including a range of survival crimes such as the sale of drugs, petty theft, or fraud. While not all informal workers are from poor households, there is a significant overlap between informality and poverty. When the ILO data is broken into "developed" and "developing" countries (these terms are themselves problematic), a full 92 percent of men and 87 percent of women who work in developing countries do so in the informal sector (compared to 19 and 18 percent in developed countries), that is, the vast majority must turn to a wide range of often-ad hoc survival strategies.[15] In a nutshell, the vast majority of workers in the former Third

---

[14] *The Economist*, "How Strong is India's Economy," April 27, 2024, p. 9.
[15] Note that informal employment includes those who are "self-employed," meaning simply that whatever activity they are engaged in, they are not working for someone else, and those who work for others. Florence Bonnet, Joann Vanek and Martha Chen, "Women and Men in the Informal Economy: A Statistical Brief," International Labor Organization, Manchester, UK, January 2019, pp. 4–5, www.ilo.org/wcmsp5/groups/public/---ed_protect/---protrav/---travail/documents/publication/wcms_711798.pdf.

World labor in the informal sector. However, this sector has always been functionally linked to the formal sector in a myriad of ways, including as a bastion of informal and unregulated social reproduction and for the provision of services to the formal sector.[16]

Does the TCC need to achieve the social reproduction of billions of people for its own reproduction? Is this mass of surplus humanity simply expendable for global capitalism? Capital has no immediate use for those thrust out of the economy, although they serve to hold down all wages and as a vast reserve army of labor to be tapped into when needed. But when this army reaches billions of people, as we are discussing here, a certain threshold has been reached. The system can *and does* simply discard them wholesale and turn to strategies of containment. Not part of the formal economic system, they have no acknowledged existence in the capitalist social order except as actual or potential dangers through uncontrollable social violence or rebellion. The global police state becomes an instrument imperative to ruling class strategies of containment, to capitalist reproduction itself.

Mass incarceration, to take one example, is spreading very rapidly from the United States to Latin America, Europe, Asia, and elsewhere as capitalist states expand incarceration as a strategy to contain surplus humanity, a topic I will return to in Chapter 5. In 2023 the Salvadoran government inaugurated its draconian mega-prison, Center for the Confinement of Terrorism, the largest in the world at the time, with a capacity for 40,000 prisoners. Not to be outdone, China, Turkey, the Philippines, Thailand, and India, among other countries, also opened or announced plans to construct such mega-prisons. There were more people worldwide in prison in 2023 than ever before. Those people locked up everywhere faced conditions of extreme overcrowding, were subjects for the application of radical new social control technologies, suffered extraordinarily high death rates, lacked access to legal aid and to adequate medical care, and faced alarming escalation of prison violence.[17] Generally missing from official reports, journalistic headlines, and the prison abolition movement is a class analysis of the

---

[16] See, inter-alia, discussion in Manuel Castells and Alejandro Portes, eds., *The Informal Economy: Studies in Advanced and Less Developed Countries* (Baltimore: Johns Hopkins University Press, 1989).

[17] Penal Reform International and Thailand Institute of Justice, "Global Prison Trends 2023," https://cdn.penalreform.org/wp-content/uploads/2023/06/GPT-2023.pdf.

relationship of the new mass incarceration to global capitalism and its crisis, including the exponential expansion of the surplus population worldwide and the fact that the vast majority of those incarcerated come from the lowest rungs of the global proletariat who have been brutally marginalized in the sense that I defined it earlier.

The more the ranks of surplus humanity expand, the more genocidal pressures build up. Genocide cannot be ruled out, whether by intention or, more likely, simple neglect along with containment strategies by capitalist states. In historical instances where the ruling classes have had no need for the labor of those who have been conquered, the oppressed, often delineated along ethnic or national lines, have been subject to genocidal pressures. The ruling class in the United States, for instance, incorporated Africans as slave labor in earlier centuries. No matter how brutalized and immiserated by their oppressors, the slaves were commodities whose preservation the slavers required. In contrast, the U.S. ruling groups needed the resources of the indigenous – specifically, their land – but had no use at all for their labor, as the labor supply came from enslaved Africans and free European proletarians. Hence the indigenous were subject to a centuries-long genocide that in North America reduced their numbers from some 20 million to barely 300,000 by the turn of the nineteenth century.[18] Palestinians faced a similar situation at the hands of the Israeli state, as witnessed by the genocide in Gaza, as I write these lines in mid 2024.

There may be other instances of genocidal pressures in global capitalism today, but I suggest here instead that the mass of surplus humanity may more often face a different form of genocide, not by intention but by containment, that is, by keeping surplus humanity out by physical or digital walls and simply letting millions die off. A virtually limitless supply of labor means that capital has little material incentive to commit to social reproduction absent organized mass struggle that leaves it no other political option but to respond to mass needs. Excess population whose labor may never be required may as well lay down and die as far as capital is concerned – the better to prevent popular uprisings. We should ponder how it is that the death of some six million Congolese and the displacement

---

[18] The horror story of the genocide of the North American indigenous is told by Roxanne Dunbar-Ortiz in *An Indigenous People's History of the United States* (Boston: Beacon Books, 2015).

of some seven million more in the three decades of conflict in that country, from the 1990s into the 2020s, many in the same regions as diamonds, cobalt, gold, and other minerals are extracted through the crudest form of plunder and exploitation by transnational corporations – and indeed, many of these victims died in conflicts over transnational capitalist access to those minerals – has barely registered a blip on the global capitalist radar.[19] I will return to this discussion in the concluding chapter.

Capitalism's Twofold Character and the Commodification of Social Reproduction

Fundamental to the Marxist political economy approach is recognition of capitalism's twofold character, simultaneously a process of producing the material needs of society and of generating private profit. These two logics, one private and the other social, are in antagonistic contradiction to one another. Without countervailing pressure to the drive toward the endless accumulation of capital, social reproduction becomes impossible. We saw in Chapter 1 that through globalization more and more areas of society are being converted from the logic of use value to that of exchange value. Use values are things that human being need and want and that their labor produces *in order to* satisfy these needs and wants. Exchange values are things (values) that are produced in the capitalist mode of production not in order to satisfy human need but in order to be exchanged in the market for a profit. This is to say that the capitalist system produces the material needs of society only by producing private profit.

Yet meeting the needs of society is not something that the TCC seeks to achieve; it is simply a byproduct of its pursuit of accumulation. The imperative of profitability runs up permanently against

---

[19] Council on Foreign Relations, "Conflict in the Democratic Republic of the Congo," *Global Conflict Tracker*, June 2023 update, www.cfr.org/global-conflict-tracker/conflict/violence-democratic-republic-congo. See also, Anjan Sundaram: "Why the World's Deadliest Wars Go Unreported," *Foreign Policy*, May 29, 2023, https://foreignpolicy.com/2023/05/29/international-news-war-reporting-media-central-african-republic-congo/; International Organization for Migration, "Record High Displacement in DRC at Nearly 7 Million," October 30, 2023, www.iom.int/news/record-high-displacement-drc-nearly-7-million; Siddharth Kara, *Cobalt Red: How the Blood of the Congo Powers Our Lives* (New York: St. Martins Press, 2023).

social need. This contradiction between social reproduction and private accumulation is exploding into an unprecedented worldwide crisis of social reproduction. However – and this is key – *this crisis of survival* is an existential crisis for billions of people, but it is not necessarily a crisis for the system. It becomes a crisis for capitalism itself only under unusual circumstances, when whole populations collapse, when vital infrastructure can no longer be maintained, when so many people are locked out of consumption that markets collapse, and when production and capital accumulation are impeded by this crisis in social reproduction. It also becomes a crisis for the system when the increasingly desperate struggles for survival lead to mass rebellion that undermines the stability and regularity that capitalism needs to function, when it blocks capital's access to resources, or when it even comes to threaten capital's political control.

Crises, let us recall, grow out of working- and popular-class struggles that force capital to discipline and replace workers by increasing the organic composition of capital and by the violent search for the cheapest labor. We saw in Chapter 1 that emerging transnational capital sought to restore profit rates by a campaign to disorganize and dispossess the popular classes, to undermine and reverse their growing class power. This involved *stripping working people of their means of social reproduction.* "Rising unemployment was a very desirable way of reducing the strength of the working class," bluntly explained Alan Budd, the chief economic advisor to former British prime minister Margaret Thatcher, whose government played a major role in launching neoliberalism and capitalist globalization in the 1980s. "What was engineered – in Marxist terms – was a crisis in capitalism which re-created a reserve army of labor and has allowed the capitalist to make high profits ever since."[20]

Capital's twofold strategy was to transfer the cost of reproducing labor from the wage to states – and then to cut back state spending on social reproduction – and at the same time to commodify the means of social reproduction so as to turn them into profit-making activities. Neoliberal policies first introduced in the 1980s by Thatcher and her U.S. counterpart Ronald Reagan and subsequently spread around the world were less an imperative of fiscal stability in the first instance than of capital's class struggle against the working and popular classes. The attack on social

---

[20] As cited in David McNally, Global Slump: The Economics and Politics of Crisis and Resistance (Oakland: PM Press, 2011), p. 115.

reproduction achieved both political and economic objectives – control and profit – for emergent transnationally oriented political and economic elites. As they became increasingly enmeshed in global circuits of accumulation, their sights shifted from national to global markets. They began to abandon programs of local and national development requiring mass consumption and became less dependent on the social reproduction of large swathes of the domestic population as either workers or consumers.

It must be reiterated that as capitalism expands, it commodifies everything. If capital's bloody birth through primitive accumulation involved the original commodification of land and labor, the juggernaut of commodification went on to progressively conquer all that lay outside of its sphere. By the late twentieth and early twenty-first centuries, transnational capital turned to a vicious commodification (privatization) of the means of social reproduction (housing, health care, water, sanitation, etc.). In the 2010s, for instance, transnational private equity firms spent hundreds of billions of dollars buying up hospitals, physicians' practices, nursing homes and hospice centers, and ambulance companies.[21] Neoliberal restructuring has resulted in the ongoing privatization of educational systems in both the historic core and periphery, opening them up to transnational capital as a new space for accumulation. Direct and indirect student fees, for instance, shift the costs of training and prepping future workers for exploitation by capital to the workers themselves. Those who cannot afford these fees do without education – 244 million children had no access to schooling in 2022[22] – predisposed to join the ranks of surplus humanity. The privatization of higher education establishes the university as a brain trust for the TCC, which has invaded the university and the educational system more generally, in every sense,

---

[21] Gretchen Morgenson and Emmanuelle Saliba, "Private Equity Firms Now Control Many Hospitals, ERs and Nursing Homes. Is It Good For Health Care?" *NBC News*, May 13, 2020, www.nbcnews.com/health/health-care/private-equity-firms-now-control-many-hospitals-ers-nursing-homes-n1203161. Marxist class analysis historically categorized physicians as members of the petty-bourgeoisie or of the new middle classes. Yet in the United States by the 2020s, a majority of doctors were proletarians. The percentage of doctors that owned their own medical practices went from 72.1 in 1988 to 45.9 in 2018. Ibid.

[22] "244M Children Won't Start the New School Year," UNESCO press release, September 1, 2022, www.unesco.org/gem-report/en/articles/244m-children-wont-start-new-school-year.

from converting education into a for-profit activity to commissioning and appropriating research (often publicly funded) and generating a major new source of financial speculation through student loans and privatized teacher and university pension systems.[23]

While there is still much room for further commodification (social reproduction can *never* be fully commodified without exterminating human life), the capitalist agents of globalization and neoliberalism radically extended the privatization of social reproduction as a strategy simultaneously for accumulation and for disciplining the working and popular classes. The more the system commodifies spheres of society that are essential for social reproduction, the more the political and social dimensions of the general crisis become aggravated. Ongoing destabilization of socioeconomic conditions and mounting threats to survival are a key underlying cause of rising political conflict, civic strife, social upheavals, and low- and high-intensity wars around the world. These contradictions and antagonisms are played out in the political, cultural, and ideological realms, in the so-called "superstructure," such as in the appeal of fascism, the turn toward authoritarianism and dictatorship, Islamic, Christian, Hindu, and other fundamentalisms, the attacks on gender and sexual nonconformity, and cultures of hyper-masculinity. These should be seen ultimately as often-depraved responses to the crisis in social reproduction.

The Exploitation of Female Reproductive Labor and the Production of Surplus Labor

Thus far I have been referring to social reproduction in a more generic sense as the reproduction of human existence. But as in all social

---

[23] On the privatization of education, see inter-alia: William I. Robinson, "Global Capitalism and the Restructuring of Education: Producing Global Economy Workers and Suppressing Critical Thinking," in Robinson, *Into the Tempest: Essays on the New Global Capitalism* (Chicago: Haymarket Press, 2018); Francesc Pedró, Gabrielle Leroux, and Megumi Watanabe, "The Privatization of Education in Developing Countries. Evidence and Policy Implications," UNESCO, Paris, 2015, https://unesdoc.unesco.org/ark:/48223/pf0000243824; "False Promises: How Delivering Education Through Public-Private Partnerships Risks Fueling Inequality Instead of Achieving Quality Education for All," Oxfam Briefing Paper, April 2019, https://oxfamilibrary.openrepository.com/bitstream/handle/10546/620720/bp-world-bank-education-ppps-090419-en.pdf.

relations, the process of reproduction, however so we define it, is gendered. There is a rich literature on the gendered *labor* of reproducing human beings that divides the totality of the human labor process into productive and reproductive labor. The distinction between the two, it cannot be overemphasized, is entirely methodological, insofar as all labor is reproductive labor, and moreover, insofar as reproductive labor is itself productive labor in the sense that it involves the production of our existence. Marx had divided labor into productive and nonproductive labor, the first referring to labor that is specifically employed by capital and that generates surplus value in the production process. This division, again, is entirely methodological, insofar as productive labor cannot be realized absent nonproductive labor in the circuits of circulation, for example, public transportation transports workers to points of production, and commercial sector workers make possible the realization of surplus value into profits. Such nonproductive labor, "even though it does not create surplus value, does create his [the capitalist's] ability to appropriate surplus value, which, as far as this capital is concerned, gives exactly the same result; i.e., it is its source of profit.... It is labor that *realizes* values but does not create any [my emphasis]."[24] Debate over the nature and utility of such a separation, even if for methodological purposes, has gone on for decades.

Much Marxist feminist theorizing on the nature of capitalism (and more generally class society) and the oppression of women takes a "social reproduction" approach that centers women's role in procreation (specifically, giving birth, lactation, suckling, and child rearing) and domestic or household labor as the foundations of the special oppression of women in a male-dominated gender order. Marxist feminist debates have revolved around whether these activities constitute productive labor in the sense that they generate surplus value, and most have concluded that they do not, although they certainly constitute a subsidy for capital insofar as the capitalist class is absolved of responsibility for assuring the household social reproduction of the worker. Rather, domestic or household labor produces use values yet is indispensable to the reproduction of capitalism by achieving the reproduction of workers. Unpaid workers are not *directly* exploited by capital insofar as they do not produce surplus value, but to the

---

[24] Marx, *Capital*, Vol. III, pp. 407, 411.

extent that unpaid labor reproduces paid labor or simply integrates into market relations, it becomes subsumed under the hegemony of capital. Moreover, while domestic labor was assumed to be female (in fact it historically has been), women have steadily entered the ranks of the proletarian wage-labor force as capitalism has developed, giving rise to an important literature on sex-segmented labor markets, gender inequality in the capitalist production process, the feminization of poverty, and the international division of reproductive labor. The "global assembly line" that employs armies of young, mostly female workers, intensely exploited and tightly controlled by male bosses in corporate sweatshops and export-processing zones around the world, as I mentioned previously, has been one of the quintessential images of capitalist globalization.[25]

The crisis of social reproduction and the pressures toward the disintegration of popular class families and communities, it should be obvious, falls back with devastating impacts onto women and their children. If women workers have experienced the so-called double shift, whereby their first shift is for the capitalist employer in often sex-segmented labor markets and the second is for household-based family reproduction, millions of women thrust into the ranks of informality and surplus humanity face the impossibility of reproducing their families. Historically, capital and the state need to regulate the biological capacity to produce the next generation of workers, which, in the view of Marxist-feminist theory, constitutes an underlying material basis for the oppression of women in capitalism. For capital, the

---

[25] Among the many works that take the "social reproduction" perspective are: Lisa Vogel's classic study, *Marxism and the Oppression of Women* (Chicago: Haymarket, 2013 [1983]), and Martha E. Gimenez, *Marx, Women and Capitalist Social Reproduction* (Chicago: Haymarket, 2019). The publication by June Nash and María Patricia Fernández-Kelly (eds.) of *Women, Men, and the International Division of Labor in the Early Years of Globalization* (Albany: State University of New York Press, 1983) set the stage for a mass of subsequent research on women workers in the global assembly line and in the international division of labor. See also Maria Mies's famous study, *Patriarchy and Accumulation on a World Scale: Women in the International Division of Labor* (London: Zed Press, 1986). Rhacel Salazar Parreñas coined the phrase "international division of reproductive labor" in *Servants of Globalization: Women, Migration, and Domestic Work* (Stanford: Stanford University Press, 2001). See also the very useful collection of essays in Barbara Ehrenreich and Arlie Russell Hochschild, *Global Woman: Nannies, Maids, and Sex Workers in the New Economy* (New York: Henry Holt and Company, 2002).

womb, and hence female sexuality, has always been a site that had to be controlled. Heteronormativity and gender conformity are not simply backward cultural practices that pop up out of nowhere; they are essential for the control over the process of reproducing and controlling exploitable labor. Colonial regimes encouraged women to breed as much as possible to supply labor that had to be pressed into service on plantations, in mines, on railroad construction, and as personal servants. The ruling groups became concerned after decolonization and with the spread of revolutionary movements in the former Third World that women were breeding future rebels. The CIA warned that "demographic pressures" were "important underlying determinants of political instability in Third World countries vital to U.S. interests." Policy shifted to population control, which should not under any circumstances be confused with reproductive rights. Now, women from the popular classes and their reproductive labor experience a further degradation as they move from producing workers for transnational capital to producing expendable surplus humanity and as states withdraw from social reproductive services.[26]

The debate on gendered reproductive labor in the household is part of a larger problematic of the relationship between paid and unpaid work and between exploitation and appropriation. Paid work finds its alter ego in unpaid work; the two are mutually constitutive and form a larger unity. Wage labor cannot be reproduced without "un-waged," that is, unpaid labor outside of commodity production but linked to the circuit of capital and forming part of the totality of the social relations of capitalism. It becomes of secondary importance to resolve the debate as to whether unpaid labor is unproductive labor insofar as unpaid labor does not produce value but makes value production possible. Throughout its history, capitalism has depended on the appropriation of unpaid work together with externalization of other costs, such as environmental degradation. Unpaid or unwaged labor in the household, the community, informal sectors, and reserves that have yet to be formally subsumed into the capital–labor relation do not fit into the Marxist value equation. It is literally *devalued*. In its circuits of accumulation, capital exploits wage workers and appropriates

---

[26] As cited in Information Project for Africa, *Excessive Force: Power, Politics, and Population Control* (Washington, DC: Information Project for Africa, 1995), p. 33.

unwaged work. Appropriation and exploitation are two moments in a singular process of capital accumulation.

Observing that the quantitative estimates for unpaid work range from 70 to 80 percent of world GDP,[27] geographer and political economist Jason Moore has made the bold claim that we must distinguish between the value (commodity) *form* and the value *relation*. In making this distinction, Moore has offered a critical conceptual input into the debate on productive and unproductive labor and into the nature of the crisis of social reproduction:

> Every act of exploitation (commodified labor power) depends on an even greater act of appropriation (of unpaid work/energy). Wage-workers are exploited; everyone else, human and extra-human [nature], is appropriated. These movements of appropriation produce the necessary conditions for the endless accumulation of capital (value in motion). In other words, value does not work unless most work is not valued. The law of value under capitalism is, then, comprised of two moments. One is the endless accumulation of capital as abstract social labor. The other, the ceaseless expansion of the relations of exploitation and appropriation, joined as an organic whole. This perspective stresses the historical and logical *non-identity* between the value-form and its necessarily more expansion value-relations.... The relations of reproduction cut across the paid/unpaid work and human/extra-human boundaries. In this, the historical condition for socially necessary labor-time is socially necessary unpaid work."[28]

Moore, whose work I will discuss further in Chapter 4, insists that we should reconceptualize capitalism as a system whose chief contradictions turn on the antagonism and interdependence of commodity relations and the totality of the conditions of reproduction.[29] He observes, correctly in my view, that world capitalist development has been marked by the uneven globalization of wage work dialectically joined to the expansion of unpaid work as a condition for capitalist reproduction. "The meaningful distinction is between the zone of paid work (the exploitation of commodified labor-power) and the zone of unpaid work (the reproduction of life)."[30] As I have suggested here, however, the reduction in

---

[27] Jason W. Moore, *Capitalism in the Web of Life: Ecology and the Accumulation of Capital* (London: Verso, 2015), p. 64.
[28] Moore, *Capitalism in the Web of Life*, p. 54.
[29] Moore, *Capitalism in the Web of Life*.
[30] Moore, *Capitalism in the Web of Life*, p. 69.

the need for the former (commodified labor power) as capital turns to relative over absolute surplus value production aggravates the crisis of social reproduction. To the extent that capital no longer needs the social reproduction of a great many people, and to that extent, it does away with the need for the reproductive labor of women and others who are not directly exploited inside the circuits of production.

Globalization, let us reiterate, increasingly turns female proletarians from reproducers of labor power required by capital into reproducers of supernumeraries for which capital has no use. Female labor, already devalued when it is unwaged, is further devalued, and women denigrated, as the function of the domestic (household) economy moves from rearing labor for *incorporation* into capitalist production to rearing supernumeraries. This helps explain the movement to dismantle Keynesian welfare benefits in a manner which disproportionately affects women, the relentless attacks on reproductive rights (see later), and the impetuousness with which the neoliberal model calls for the elimination of even minimal social spending and safety nets that often mean, literally, the difference between life and death. It is not surprising that women and their children form the majority of those in poverty, make up two-thirds of the 800 million illiterate adults, and are more likely than their male counterparts to experience acute precarity. Three-quarters of countries in the world have laws that discriminate against women economically. Nearly 800 million women have experienced gender-based violence, while every ten minutes a woman is killed in such gender-specific violence.[31] The ever-greater degradation and devaluation of female proletarians in times of epochal crisis and mass social anxiety form a deep structure that breeds pandemics of degradation, of misogyny, and of aggression and violence against women, generating an escalating worldwide crisis in gender relations.

Planet of Paupers and Billionaires

Seen from the logic of human need and available resources, the crisis of social reproduction is an irrational absurdity. Mass deprivation cannot be accounted for by a lack of resources. As far back as

---

[31] See: Oxfam International, "Gender Justice and Women's Rights," 2023, www.oxfam.org/en/what-we-do/issues/gender-justice-and-womens-rights; United Nations, "International Day for the Elimination of Violence against Women," 2024, www.un.org/en/observances/ending-violence-against-women-day.

1998, the United Nations Development Program observed that a mere $40 billion dollars in annual investment – an amount that would not even register the tiniest financial blip in the global economy! – could eradicate the worst forms of poverty around the world and cover the bill for basic education, health, nutrition, reproductive health, family planning, and safe water and sanitation for all.[32] But capitalism's logic of accumulation is at war with the social logic of human well-being. As Thatcher's economic advisor Alan Budd made clear, capital's strategy of commodifying social reproduction means leaving it to unfettered market forces that, through their own spontaneous workings, produce poverty, destitution, and inequality. Seen from this logic, the more desperately immiserated the working class, the more desperate it is to survive, all the better for disciplining and exploiting the proletariat. Social austerity measures around the world in the age of capitalist globalization have included cutbacks in social welfare, income and value added sales tax, regressive income tax, cuts in public employment, escalating fees for public services, massively defunding and privatizing public health, education, old age pensions, and other public assets, and so on. In 2013, according to one study, some 5.8 billion people, or 80 percent of the global population, were affected by such austerity measures.[33]

Data on the immiseration around the world of the working and popular classes is widely available. The World Bank reported that in 2020 over 700 million people subsisted in extreme poverty, on less than $2.15 a day – that is, teetering every day on the brink of life and death – and that progress in eradicating extreme poverty had "ground to a halt."[34] The Bank also reported that nearly half the world – 3.4 billion people – lives on less than $5.50 a day, well below the Bank's poverty line of $6.85 a day[35] (according to other

---

[32] United Nations Development Agency, *Human Development Report 1998* (New York: Oxford University Press, 1998), p. 37, https://hdr.undp.org/system/files/documents/hdr1998encompletenostatspdf.pdf.

[33] This data from an IMF report was cited in Saskia Sassen, *Explusions*, p. 24.

[34] The World Bank, "Global Progress in Reducing Extreme Poverty Grinds to a Halt," press release, October 5, 2022, www.worldbank.org/en/news/press-release/2022/10/05/global-progress-in-reducing-extreme-poverty-grinds-to-a-halt.

[35] The World Bank, "Nearly Half the World Lives on Less than $5.50 a Day," press release, October 17, 2018, www.worldbank.org/en/news/press-release/2018/10/17/nearly-half-the-world-lives-on-less-than-550-a-day.

data, half the world lives on less than $3.00 a day[36]), while upward to 80 percent of the world lives on less than $10 per day. In the United States, food insecurity increased by 40 percent between 2021 and 2024, while poverty increased 67 percent during this period and 80 percent of families reported living paycheck to paycheck in 2024.[37] World Bank data on poverty tends to be conservative and tells us nothing about access to sanitation, safe drinking water, health care, education, adequate housing, and other resources upon which survival depends. According to UN data, 2.2 billion people lacked access to potable water in 2024 and 3.5 billion lacked adequate sanitation.[38] The number of those facing these conditions may increase in the coming years as underemployment, unemployment, and precarious employment rise. Already in 2023, of the world's 1.2 billion youth fifteen to twenty-four years old, 25 percent were unemployed and unable to access education or training programs, and another 30 percent were underemployed or employed in the informal economy, according to the World Bank.[39]

On the other extreme of the spectrum, in 2022 the world's ultra-wealthy included 62 million millionaires and billionaires whose combined wealth exceeded $190 trillion, or more than double the entire global gross domestic product that year of $85 trillion.[40] According to the development agency Oxfam, just one percent of humanity owned over half of the world's wealth in 2018 and the top 20 percent own 94.5 of that wealth, while the remaining 80 percent had to make do with just 5.5 percent

---

[36] Phillips, *Titans*, p. 116.

[37] Emily Batdorf, "Living Paycheck to Paycheck Statistics 2024," *Forbes*, April 2, 2024, www.forbes.com/advisor/banking/living-paycheck-to-paycheck-statistics-2024/; Stephen Semler, "A Couple of Charts to Explain a Harris Loss," Polygraph, Newsletter 275, November 5, 2024, www.stephensemler.com/p/a-couple-charts-to-explain-a-harris?utm_campaign=post&utm_medium=web.

[38] United Nations, "Press Release: Water Crises Threaten World Peace," March 22, 2024, www.un.org/sustainabledevelopment/blog/2024/03/un-world-water-development-report/.

[39] Diego Angel-Urdinola, Gemma Rodon, and Nicolas Torres, "Youth Economic Disengagement: A Harsh Global Reality to Remember on World Youth Skill Day," *World Bank Blogs*, July 13, 2023, https://blogs.worldbank.org/en/education/youth-economic-disengagement-harsh-global-reality-remember-world-youth-skills-day.

[40] Credit Suisse, "Global Wealth Report 2022," Credit Suisse Research Institute, 2022, file:///Users/user./Downloads/global-wealth-report-2022-en.pdf.

Table 2.1 *Shares of World Income 1965–2014*

	Percent of total world income				
Population	1965	1970	1980	1990	2014
Poorest 20%	2.3	2.2	1.7	1.4	Combined
Second 20%	2.9	2.8	2.2	1.8	80% =
Third 20%	4.2	3.9	3.5	2.1	5.4
Fourth 20%	21.2	21.3	18.3	11.3	
Richest 20%	69.5	70.0	75.4	83.4	94.5

Compiled from various sources indicated in endnotes.

(Table 2.1).[41] This data, however, is misleading since within the wealthiest one percent of humanity, it is the top one-twentieth of one percent (0.06 percent), some 40 million people, including more than 36 million millionaires and 2,600 billionaires, that actually controls the world and its wealth.[42] Its 2023 Oxfam report, "Survival of the Richest," warned that billionaire fortunes were increasing by $2.7 billion a day even as 1.7 billion or more workers lived in countries where inflation was outpacing wages and that the richest one percent of humanity grabbed for itself nearly two-thirds of all new wealth created since 2020. In 2022, in the midst of a global food and energy crisis, the top ninety-five food and energy corporations more than doubled their profits, according to the report, making $306 billion in windfall profits and paying out $257 billion of that to rich shareholders, at the same time as some one billion people went hungry and another two billion suffered from food insecurity.

Despite this poverty amidst plenty, three-quarters of the world's governments, warned the 2023 Oxfam report, were planning austerity-driven public sector spending cuts, including health care and education, by a whopping $7.8 trillion over the next five years.[43] Such

---

[41] Oxfam (London), *Wealth: Having it all and Wanting More*, March 4, 2018 at the Oxfam website, http://policy-practice.oxfam.org.uk/publications/wealth-having-it-all-and-wanting-more-338125. Here is a longitudinal Table 2.1 compiled.

[42] Peter Phillips, *Titans of Capital: How Concentrated Wealth Threatens Humanity* (New York: Seven Stories Press, 2024), pp. 18, 49.

[43] Oxfam, "Survival of the Richest: How We Must Tax the Super-Rich Now to Fight Inequality," January 2023, www.oxfam.org/en/press-releases/richest-1-bag-nearly-twice-much-wealth-rest-world-put-together-over-past-two-years.

obscene wealth polarization skews global production more and more toward luxury goods for the consumption of the affluent. In 2022, for instance, the total number of cars sold worldwide decreased by 1.3 percent, but the sale of Rolls Royce vehicles increased by 8 percent.[44] Kering corporation, which owns fashion labels such as Gucci and Balenciaga, reported a 14 percent rise in profits in 2022, while profits increased by nearly 25 percent for LVMH, owner of Tiffany and Louis Vuitton, and by some 33 percent for Hermes and Richemont, owner of Cartier and other luxury brands.[45] Transnational capital has little incentive to organize production around the consumption needs of the great majority. Already by 2005, a team of stock market analysts at Citigroup warned that the global economy was becoming a "plutonomy" in which growth was driven by small high-income clusters. They advised wealthy investors to avoid purchasing stock in industries producing for mass consumption and to instead invest in companies producing luxury goods and services for the super-rich concentrated in "globalized enclaves" around the world.[46]

A New Round of Global Enclosures

Capitalist expansion in the latter decades of the twentieth into the twenty-first century involved ongoing waves of primitive accumulation in the Third World countryside, subjecting hundreds of millions around the world to depeasantization and proletarianization.[47] Displacement has generated a vast army of internal and transnational migrants who

---

[44] *The Economist*, "High-Performance Motoring," January 14, 2023, p. 59.
[45] *The Economist*, "Keeping Their Shine," June 3, 2023, pp. 52–53.
[46] See Citigroup, "Equity Strategy: Plutonomy: Buying Luxury, Explaining Global Imbalance," October 16, 2005, pp. 1–2, www.lust-for-life.org/Lust-For-Life/CitigroupImbalances_October2009/CitigroupImbalances_October2009.pdf. For discussion, see Robert Cox and Eliza Rosenbuam, "The Beneficiaries of the Downturn," *New York Times*, December 28, 2008, accessed on April 9, 2019 at www.nytimes.com/2008/12/29/business/29views.html.
[47] See, inter-alia: Farshad A. Araghi, "Global Depeasantization, 1945–1990," *The Sociological Quarterly*, 36(2), 1995; Deborah Bryceson, Cristobal Kay and Jos Mooij, *Disappearing Peasantries: Rural Labor in Africa, Asia, and Latin America* (Rugby: Intermediate Technologies Publications, 2000); Mohd Anzar, "Depeasantization as a Social Process," *Indian Journal of Jurisprudential Studies*, 1(1), 2020, file:///Users/user./Downloads/DepeasantizationasaSocialProcess.pdf.

have swelled the ranks of those super-exploited and those structurally marginalized. The International Organization on Migration, a United Nations agency, reported in 2015 that there were 232 million international migrants and 740 million internal migrants.[48] The United Nations High Commission for Refugees (UNHCR) reported that 2023 set a record of 110 million people forcibly displaced by conflicts.[49] The International Labor Organization (ILO), another United Nations agency, reported that 1.53 billion workers around the world were in "vulnerable" (precarious) employment arrangements in 2009, representing more than 50 percent of the global workforce,[50] and that in 2018 a majority of the 3.5 billion workers in the world "experienced a lack of material well-being, economic security, equality opportunities or scope for human development."[51]

While the data varies from one reporting agency to another and on the categories of analysis, there can be little doubt that in the coming years there will be more hundreds of millions of people uprooted, fleeing the collapse of whole regions. Some of those uprooted may be super-exploited through incorporation into the global factories, farms, mines, and service complexes as precarious labor. But there will be great masses of those displaced who cannot ever be absorbed into a global labor market that has become ever more saturated. They will face being relegated to marginal existence and converted into surplus humanity. The ILO reported as early as the turn of the century that some one-third of the global labor force had been made superfluous.[52] Even the CIA felt compelled to warn in 2002 that "by the late 1990s a staggering one billion workers representing one-third of the world's labor force, most of them in the South, were either unemployed or underemployed."[53]

---

[48] *World Migration Report 2015* (IOM: Geneva, 2015), p. 2.
[49] Emma Farge, "Global Level of Forced Displacement Climbs to Record 110 Million, UN says," *Reuters*, June 13, 2023, www.reuters.com/world/global-level-forced-displacement-climbs-record-110-mln-un-2023-06-14/.
[50] International Labor Organization, *Global Employment Trends 2011: The Challenge of Job Recovery* (Geneva: ILO, 2011).
[51] International Labor Organization, "World Employment and Social Outlook: Trends 2019" (Geneva, ILO, 2019), p. 2, www.ilo.org/wcmsp5/groups/public/---dgreports/---dcomm/---publ/documents/publication/wcms_670542.pdf.
[52] International Labor Organization, *World Employment Report 1996–97* (Geneva: ILO/United Nations, 1997).
[53] As cited in Mike Davis, *Planet of Slums*, p. 199.

As disturbing as this data may be, all signs suggest that the ranks of surplus humanity will continue to expand sharply. The UNHCR warned in 2021 that more than twenty million people are forced each year to leave their homes due to extreme weather events.[54] A 2020 study by the U.S. National Academy of Sciences predicted that for every additional one-degree centigrade rise in the average global climate, a billion people will be forced to abandon their locations and to endure insufferable heat.[55] Drawing on UN data, a widely cited 2021 report by the Institute for Economics and Peace estimates that people living in 151 countries face exposure to destabilizing ecological threats, and that 1.2 billion people living in thirty-one high-risk countries, largely in South Asia, Sub-Saharan Africa, and the Middle East, and North Africa, could become climate refugees by 2050 as the climate crisis generates water and food shortages, greater exposure to natural disasters, and temperatures too hot for human existence (see Chapter 4 for further discussion on the climate crisis).[56]

A global land rush appears to be a leading edge of primitive accumulation in the new century, a vast new round of global enclosures and commodification of nature not seen since the colonial era that displace and proletarianize local populations. Land grabs are defined as the purchase, leasing, or concessional use for commercial purposes by companies from abroad of land that had previously been used communally, by small-scale landholders, or as public lands and nature reserves, and therefore outside of the value relation. Transnational investors have acquired vast tracts of land around the world since the early 2000s for agribusiness, tourism, and extractive activity such as mining, logging, and fossil fuels; the establishment of special economic zones; control over water resources; or in many cases, simply as speculative investment outlets for overaccumulated capital (sometimes in the form of carbon offsets). The intensity of this global land rush has

---

[54] See UNHCR, "Climate Change and Disaster Displacement," www.unhcr.org/en-us/climate-change-and-disasters.html.
[55] Chi Xu, Timothy A. Kohler, Timothy M. Lenton, Jens-Christian Svenning, and Marten Scheffer, "Future of the Human Climate Niche," Proceedings of the National Academy of Sciences, May 26, 2020, accessed on December 6, 2021 at www.pnas.org/content/117/21/11350.
[56] Institute for Economics and Peace, "Ecological Threat Report 2021: Understanding Ecological Threats, Resilience and Peace," Sydney, October 2021, www.visionofhumanity.org/wp-content/uploads/2021/10/ETR-2021-web.pdf.

Crisis of Social Reproduction 79

been unprecedented, with upwards to 225 million hectares (one hectare is 2.47 acres) seized by transnational investors from around the world in the first decade of the twenty-first century alone (to put this in perspective, this represents nearly 2 percent of the entire land surface of the earth[57]). Investors in this leading new round of global capitalist expansion have come from corporations as well as financial conglomerates from around the world, including from North America, the EU countries, China, Saudi Arabia and the Gulf states, South Africa, Brazil, and many other countries, although land grabbers also include local capitalists and land barons in the affected countries.[58]

This new round of expansion shifts resources from food production to commercial export crops, and especially so-called flexicrops, such as soy and palm oil that have multiple uses (food, feed, fuel, and industrial material) and therefore can quickly and profitably be marketed worldwide. Transnational agribusiness deepens the enmeshment of the local in global markets and heightens the dependence of the global working class on the TCC. The risks of such investment are shifted onto local populations who must face the diversion of water supplies to agribusiness and tourism, deforestation, and other devastating environmental consequences, while investors operating through the circuits of global finance can pick up and leave at any moment.

---

[57] See United Nations Food and Agricultural Organization (FAO), "Land Statistics and Indicators, 2000–2021," Rome, 2023, https://openknowledge.fao.org/server/api/core/bitstreams/5c8b2707-1bcf-4c29-90e2-3487e583f71e/content.

[58] Note that data on the total amount of land grabbed is inconsistent, depending on the definition (see my definition above). For the 225 million hectares figure, I rely on Oxfam Briefing Paper, "Land and Power: The Growing Scandal Surrounding the New Wave of Investments in Land," September 22, 2011, https://oxfamilibrary.openrepository.com/bitstream/handle/10546/142858/bp151-land-power-rights-acquisitions-220911-en.pdf?sequence=32. See also: Saska Sassen, *Expulsions: Brutality and Complexity in the Global Economy* (Cambridge: Harvard University Press, 2014), chapter two, "The New Global Market for Land"; "The Global Land Grab," The Transnational Institute (Amsterdam), February 2013, file:///Users/user./Downloads/landgrabbingprimer-feb2013-1.pdf; Kyle Frankel Davis, et al., "Transnational Agricultural Land Acquisitions Threaten Biodiversity in the Global South," *Environmental Research*, February 2, 2023, https://iopscience.iop.org/article/10.1088/1748-9326/acb2de/pdf. According to the Land Matrix database, a total of 31 million hectares have been affected in Africa, 16 million in Asia, 11 million in Latin America, and 38 million in Eastern Europe. https://landmatrix.org/.

African countries have been the most affected by land grabs, although this global market for land has also expanded rapidly in Asia and Latin America as well as in the former Soviet Eurasia. Peru has been the most heavily affected country in the world, with sixteen million hectares seized in the first two decades of the twenty-first century, much of it for mining operations. In Africa, the Democratic Republic of the Congo (DRC) has been the most heavily affected, with more than nine million hectares seized during this period, largely for mining and agribusiness.[59]

The financialization of transnational capital discussed in Chapter 1 makes the new round of capitalist expansion throughout the former Third World, and increasingly in the former First World as well, exceptionally volatile and risky. Total global liquidity, a measure of cash and credit in the world economy, rose to an all-time high of some $170 trillion in 2023,[60] a vast pool of cash and credit that transnational capitalists can draw on to snatch up assets around the world wherever and whenever the opportunity arises. The securitization of all sorts of assets and commodities makes them tradables that can be leveraged. Agricultural and extractive commodities are traded in speculative futures markets. As Michael Gordy notes in his study on risk, the impermanent, footloose nature of securitized global financial flows means that transnational finance capital can take huge risks in affected communities beyond what would be acceptable, for example, with more long-term greenfield or fixed investment. Transnational finance capital makes money not by permanence but, all to the contrary, by constantly moving money. The shareholders and investors of global corporations come from everywhere and, as Gordy observes, "whose sense of connection to local environments is extremely tenuous where it exists at all." Real estate, speculation, agribusiness, tourism, "all these and more are seen only as 'profit centers' through the prism of transnational capital accumulation."[61] Risk is offset to local

---

[59] On the DRC and Peru, see "The Countries Most Affected by Landgrabs," Statista, November 11, 2022, www.statista.com/chart/19044/countries-most-affected-by-land-grabs/.

[60] Naomi Rovnick and Harry Robertson, "Tranquility Reigns Over Markets Still Awash with Cash, For Now," *Reuters*, June 13, 2023, www.reuters.com/markets/global-markets-liquidity-2023-06-14/.

[61] Michael Gordy, *Disaster Risk Reduction and the Global System: Ruminations on a Way Forward* (New York: Springer, 2016).

populations who are more and more vulnerable to natural disasters, political instability, and military conflict.

A 2020 report by the Land Inequality Coalition notes that land inequality worldwide is significantly higher than generally reported and that the land grab trend directly threatens the livelihoods of some 2.5 billion people involved in smallholder agriculture – that is, the world's remaining peasants and small farmers. The report observed that from the early twentieth century through to the 1970s, agrarian policies focused on small-scale producers and family farms that, together with agrarian reform, had actually reduced somewhat land inequality. But this changed from the 1980s and on, the period that here we have identified as globalization. Widespread poverty, unemployment, hunger, disease, exclusion, violent conflict, social disintegration, migration, urban inequality, and spatial segregation all follow in the wake of this ongoing transnational corporate agroindustry takeover of the global food system and the seizure of land that holds valuable mineral, forestry, and energy resources. In 2020 just one percent of farms in the world operated 70 percent of farmland supplying corporate food systems. Even at that, transnational capital does not necessarily need to own or operate farmland in order to exercise its domination and exploit agricultural labor. In the remaining 30 percent of farmland it does not operate, it exercises indirect control through such mechanisms as controlling the supply of seeds, fertilizers, and other inputs; control over prices and marketing; and contract farming.[62]

Global agribusiness mediates food production and distribution around the world. As populations uprooted into the countryside stream into urban areas, the land is freed up for agribusiness, mining, and tourism. The more the teeming masses in megacities become dependent on the global food system controlled by agribusiness and the financial interests invested in it, the more they are vulnerable to price fluctuations and food shortages. By 2030, forty-one cities will have more than ten million inhabitants, up from thirty-one in 2016, and two-thirds of the world's population will live in an urban

---

[62] Ward Anseeuw, Giulia Maria Baldinelli, et al., "Uneven Ground: Land Inequality at the Heart of Unequal Societies," International Land Coalition/Oxfam, https://d3o3cb4w253x5q.cloudfront.net/media/documents/2020_11_land_inequality_synthesis_report_uneven_ground_final_en_spread_low_res_2.pdf.

area by 2050.[63] A third of the world's population lives in a slum.[64] Amin estimated in the early 2000s that the popular classes (by which he means the working classes, whether employed or unemployed, laboring in the formal or the informal economy) accounted for some three-quarters of the world's urban population, and that the precarious subcategory represented two-thirds of the popular classes on a world scale. "The main social transformation that characterizes the second half of the twentieth century can be summarized in a single statistic: the proportion of the precarious popular classes rose from less than one-quarter to more than one-half of the global urban population, and this phenomenon of pauperization has reappeared on a significant scale in the developed centers themselves," he observed. "This destabilized urban population has increased in a half-century from less than a quarter of a billion to more than a billion-and-a-half individuals, registering a growth rate which surpasses those that characterize economic expansion, population growth, or the process of urbanization itself."[65]

Ongoing enclosures, at the same time as they expel whole communities and open new spaces for capital accumulation, have given rise to a new system of transnational labor mobility and recruitment, making it possible for dominant groups around the world to reorganize labor markets in an effort to weaken labor and maximize the extraction of surplus value. Masses of transnational migrant workers are made vulnerable and susceptible to super-exploitation by national borders and the division of the global working classes into citizen and immigrant labor. Transnational migrant workers are disenfranchised. They generally exist in a state of liminal legality or

[63] United Nations Department of Economic and Social Affairs, "Around 2.5 Billion More People Will Be Living in Cities Projects New UN Report," press release, undated, www.un.org/en/desa/around-25-billion-more-people-will-be-living-cities-2050-projects-new-un-report.
[64] Calculated on the basis of World Bank country data, "Population Living in Slums (% of Urban Population)," https://data.worldbank.org/indicator/EN.POP.SLUM.UR.ZS?view=chart.
[65] Samir Amin, "World Poverty, Pauperization and Capital Accumulation," *Monthly Review* (online), October 1, 2003, https://monthlyreview.org/2003/10/01/world-poverty-pauperization-capital-accumulation/?utm_source=Tricontinental+English&utm_campaign=8c9cb1b47e-EMAIL_CAMPAIGN_2019_02_01_02_25&utm_medium=email&utm_term=0_9fbe436b65-8c9cb1b47e-190488593.

illegality, or of temporary residency within national borders. Lacking in civil and political rights and forced to enter labor markets under the permanent threat of deportation or worse, they are subjected to work under conditions more degraded than citizen labor, and as a result, the conditions of their labor place a general downward pressure on wages.

There are two points to be made here with regard to social reproduction and its crisis. First, although the migrant labor population expands around the world, this takes place at the same time as the conditions for social reproduction collapse in the migrants' home country, imperiling the whole system of migrant labor supply. Closely related, as whole regions and countries collapse in the face of the escalating global crisis, the system of transnational labor supply will become – already is becoming – overwhelmed by hordes of migrants who cannot be absorbed into the labor markets of the zones of more advanced accumulation. In this case, ruling class strategies of containment become paramount, and borders between national jurisdictions become war zones and zones of death. Countless thousands have died in recent years along the U.S.-Mexico border and North Africa-Middle East-Europe corridors and in other borderlands between surplus humanity and zones of intense accumulation in the global economy, as I will discuss in Chapter 5.

Second, what we have in this system of global migrant labor mobility and recruitment is the transnational separation of the sites of labor power and the sites of its reproduction. Migrant worker remittances back to their countries of origin approached $900 billion in 2024. To the extent that the possibility for social reproduction in the migrants' home region collapses, the extended family network of these workers becomes dependent on remittances from migrant workers, which shot up to almost $900 billion worldwide in 2024 from a mere $25 billion in 1990, although the true value may be up to 50 percent higher than official figures since many prefer to use informal methods to send money. This is a 3,500 percent increase in a very short time. It underscores just how rapid displacement has taken place during the period of globalization and the extent to which the mechanism of global nomadic movement has escalated in the desperate search for survival. If China is excluded, remittances are the largest source of external finance for countries in the historic periphery taken as a whole, exceeding foreign direct investment and official "development" aid combined.⁶⁶ The crisis of social reproduction would be considerably more acute than it already is in the absence of this transnational movement of migrant labor and the reverse flow of its wages.

Digitalization: Super-Exploitation and Automation Revisited

While the center-peripheral structure of transnational class relations forged through the centuries of colonialism and imperialism has been experiencing substantial transformations, it remains true that the global division of labor involves significant distinctions in national and regional participation in the global economy, that labor is more intensely exploited in the former Third World, and that the absolute savagery of capital is more fully on display. It would be tempting to frame increasing immiseration in terms of inequality between the traditional core and periphery because immiseration is more widespread and severe in the latter, but this would be a mistake, analytically and also politically, for three reasons. First, exclusion and immiseration are taking place in both. Second, work is becoming ever-more precarious in both. Third, the language of core and periphery as geographic location is a territorial fetish that reifies what are *social categories*.⁶⁷

---

⁶⁶ Douglas Broom, "Migrant Workers Sent Home Almost $800 Billion in 2022. Which Countries are the Biggest Recipients?", *Forum Agenda*, World Economic Forum, February 2, 2023, www.weforum.org/agenda/2023/02/remittances-money-world-bank/.

⁶⁷ See, inter-alia, William I. Robinson, "Remapping Development in Light of Globalization: From a Territorial to a Social Cartography," *Third World Quarterly*. 23, 6, 2002; *Global Capitalism and the Crisis of Humanity*. While scholars and activists analyze the world in terms of rich and poor countries or center and periphery, the TCC does not look at the world in this way. One Citgroup report from 2005 recommended that its investors see the world as a plutonomy made up "globalized enclaves" and look for a "plutonomy basket of stocks" for investment.

In a plutonomy there is no such animal as "the U.S. consumer" or a "the U.K. consumer," or indeed the "Russian consumer." There are rich consumers, few in number, but disproportionate in the gigantic slice of income and consumption they take. There are the rest, the "non-rich", the multitudinous many, but only accounting for surprisingly small bites of the national pie.

See Citigroup, "Equity Strategy: Plutonomy: Buying Luxury, Explaining Global Imbalance," October 16, 2005, pp. 1–2, www.lust-for-life.org/Lust-For-Life/CitigroupImbalances_October2009/CitigroupImbalances_October2009.pdf.

Globalization has brought about a sweeping expansion of the capital–labor relation at the same time as it has brought about the destruction of the social contract that regulated this relation. The counteroffensive launched by the TCC against the working and popular classes involved an attack on regulated, full-time, stable, tenured employment with job security and social benefits that these classes had struggled for in preceding decades. Capital pushed for a new capital–labor regime characterized by deregulated labor markets and unstable employment, involving casual, contract, part-time, temporary, outsourced, informal, nonunionized, "on-demand," and other forms of precarious work, what in the first generation of literature on this labor regime was referred to as a shift from Fordist to post-Fordist or flexible accumulation.[68] Precarious work involves the ongoing withdrawal of the state from the protection of labor and the erosion of reciprocal obligations on the part of the state and capital to labor, or even any notion of social reproduction of the worker as a part of the labor or the social contract. These reciprocal obligations are replaced by a one-sided domination by capital and a capitalist state that, for the most part, is no longer disposed to provide a buffer to this domination.

The epoch of globalization, as we saw in Chapter 1, has involved a two-fold process. Transnationally mobile capital has sought out cheap labor, or super-exploitation, in low-wage zones around the world rather than digitalize the full sequence of production and circulation. At the same time, it has used digital technologies in higher-wage zones to restructure local forces into a mass of increasingly deskilled, routinized, and fragmented "on-demand" labor that is pushed into precarious work arrangements and wage stagnation or even real decline along with an inner core of high-paid, high-skilled workers who constitute aristocratic layers of the working class, often mistakenly referred to as the "middle class." The concept of the *precariat* captures the notion of proletarians who labor under these unstable, precarious work arrangements.[69] As we shall see later, new digital technologies extend the condition of precariousness worldwide for all sorts of work,

---

[68] See, inter-alia: David Harvey's now-class study, *The Condition of Postmodernity* (Hoboken: Wiley-Blackwell, 1991); Ash Amin (ed.), *Post-Fordism: A Reader* (Hoboken: Wiley-Blackwell, 1995).

[69] The term was first introduced by Guy Standing in *The Precariat: The New Dangerous Class* (New York: Bloomsbury, 2011). For my discussion, see William I. Robinson, *The Global Police State* (London: Pluto Press, 2020).

including white- and blue-collar work, service work, and increasingly professional and managerial work. This latter category of workers has alternatively been referred to as immaterial labor, cognitive labor, and knowledge work, among other terms. The notion of a "professional managerial class" has become increasingly popular in recent years. This stratum, however, does not constitute a class separate from the proletariat, and as we will see later, it is facing a very rapid destabilization. Precariatization will sweep through all areas in the labor process absent a change of course in the patterns of global capital accumulation.

Living standards and work conditions rose in the twentieth century, and especially in the brief period of post-WWII prosperity, for major sectors of the working classes in the core, following mass struggles for unionization and state regulation of the labor market, along with the expansion of middle and professional strata as capitalism further developed. Following Marx, who observed that colonialism "converts one part of the globe into a chiefly agricultural field of production for supplying the other part, which remains a chiefly industrial field,"[70] theories of imperialism and of the capitalist world-system pointed to the history of colonialism and the international division of labor between core and periphery it imposed to explain extreme global inequality. They argued that a portion of the core working classes had become a labor aristocracy as a result of the transfer of wealth from the periphery and its redistribution in the core, although the steady rise in core worker productivity also played an important role. In the formerly colonized world, much smaller groups of urban workers and middle and professional classes experienced stable employment in the Fordist sector of urban industry and services. We want to remember, however, that the historical condition for broad swaths of the working classes in both the traditional periphery and core prior to the mid twentieth-century Fordist-Keynesian social contract was in fact the most extreme exploitation and immiseration. The prosperity they experienced in the twentieth century was *not* the norm for the long sweep of world capitalist history. Here is Marx in *Capital* quoting an English magistrate's report in 1860:

Children of nine or ten years are dragged from their squalid beds at two, three, or four o'clock in the morning and compelled to work for a bare subsistence until ten, eleven, or twelve at night, their limbs wearing away, their

[70] Marx, *Capital*, Vol. II, p. 425.

frames dwindling, their faces whitening, and their humanity absolutely sinking into a stone-like torpor, utterly horrible to contemplate.... The system is one of unmitigated slavery, socially, physically, morally and spiritually. What can be thought of a town which holds a public meeting to petition that the period of labor for men shall be diminished to eighteen hours a day? We declaim against the Virginian and Carolinian cotton-planters. Is their black-market, their lash, and their barter of human flesh more detestable than this slow sacrifice of humanity which takes place in order that veils and collars may be fabricated for the benefit of the capitalists?[71]

In the twenty-first century, living standards and life chances remain far superior in the traditional core than in the periphery for most workers, but the "Thirdworldization" of the First World and downward leveling have progressed in the era of capitalist globalization. As far back as 1998, the United Nations Development Program reported that mass deprivation is not just the lot of poor people in the former Third World. More than 100 million people in rich countries suffered in that year a similar fate as the poor in poor countries. According to the report: "Nearly 200 million people are not expected to survive to age 60. More than 100 million are homeless. At least 37 million are without jobs, often experiencing a state of social exclusion. Many conclusions about deprivation apply to them with equal force."[72] One University of Glasgow study found that government austerity policies in the United Kingdom had caused 300,000 excess deaths.[73] In the United States, nearly four in ten households, or 38 percent, lacked enough money to cover a $400 emergency expense, according to the federal government, up from 32 percent in 2021.[74] More than half of U.S. households do not receive a steady income, relying on contingent work opportunities as they become available, while 80 percent report living paycheck to paycheck.

---

[71] Marx, *Capital*, Vol. 1, pp. 233–234.
[72] United Nations Development Agency, *Human Development Report 1998* (New York: Oxford University Press, 1998), p. 2, https://hdr.undp.org/system/files/documents/hdr1998encompletenostats.pdf.
[73] University News, "Over 300,000 'Excess' Deaths in Great Britain Attributed to UK Government Austerity Policies," October 5, 2022, www.gla.ac.uk/news/archiveofnews/2022/october/headline_885099_en.html.
[74] Will Daniel, "Turbulence Ahead': Nearly 4 in 10 Americans Lack Enough Money to Cover a $400 Emergency Expense, Fed Survey Shows," *Fortune*, May 23, 2023, https://fortune.com/2023/05/23/inflation-economy-consumer-finances-americans-cant-cover-emergency-expense-federal-reserve/.

To Super-Exploit or to Automate?

The TCC's globalization strategy, we have seen, rested heavily on leveraging the newfound transnational mobility of capital to increase the production of absolute surplus value in the former Third World. Now a second generation of digital technologies may open the way for changes in its worldwide accumulation strategies. If labor is cheaper than the adoption of digital technologies, then corporations are more likely to seek out the production of absolute over relative surplus value, *ceteris paribus*, especially if wages sink below the actual value of labor power. Marx described such a situation for an earlier era of industrial capitalism in Europe:

> In the older countries, machinery, when employed in some branches of industry, creates such a redundancy of labor in other branches that in these latter the fall of wages below the value of labor-power impedes the use of machinery, and, from the standpoint of the capitalist, whose profit comes, not from a diminution of the labor employed, but of the labor paid for, renders that use superfluous and often impossible.

He went on to observe that English capitalists chose not to adopt a rock-breaking machine invented in the United States for the mining industry "because the 'wretch' who does this work gets paid for such a small portion of his labor, that machinery would increase the cost of production to the capitalist."[75] Similarly, he observed, "In England, women are still used instead of horses for hauling canal boats because the labor required to produce horses and machines is an accurately known quantity, while that required to maintain the women of the surplus-population is below all calculation."[76]

A change in capital's accumulation strategies depends on a cold calculation: Is it more profitable to employ super-exploited labor or to employ digital technology in place of living labor? But the capitalist does not necessarily freely exercise this choice. Under the compulsion of competition and class struggle from below, capitalists must employ the latest technologies and production methods lest they are run out of business. Free competition, in the words of Marx, "brings out the inherent coercive laws having power over every individual

---

[75] Marx, *Capital*, Vol. I, pp. 371–372.
[76] Karl Marx, *Capital*, Vol. I (New York: International Publishers, 1967 [1867]), p. 372.

capitalist."[77] Super-exploitation has become a less attractive option to transnational capital to the extent that the laboring masses push back against the downward pressure on wages, that extreme exploitation generates social unrest and political crises that undermine the conditions for stable capital accumulation, and that competition in the face of prolonged stagnation forces capitalists to raise productivity. Again Marx: "The automation, as capital, and because it is capital, is endowed in the person of the capitalist, with intelligence and will; it is therefore animated by the longing to reduce to a minimum the resistance offered by that repellent, yet elastic barrier, man."[78] Ironically, the more workers struggle against capitalist exploitation, the more capital has an incentive to replace them with digital technology, to throw them into the ranks of surplus humanity. It matters not if capital continues to pursue a strategy of intensified exploitation by seeking out the cheapest labor or by automating; either strategy – or any combination of the two – aggravates the crisis of social reproduction.

Mainstream economists claimed that workers worldwide would gain from globalization because wages would rise as employers ran out of new pools of cheap workers to tap into. This claim ignored capital's option to switch from extracting absolute to relative surplus value through new technologies. The super-exploitation strategy has followed a pattern of continuously shifting production sequences from one low-wage zone once worker struggles start to raise the wage bill or political risks to a new zone where workers are less organized and more exploitable. Hence Nike, which began operations in Oregon in the 1960s, shifted production first to Japan in the 1970s, then to South Korea and Taiwan in the 1980s, and from there to China, Vietnam, and Indonesia in the 1990s, each move chasing cheaper labor. Then in 2013, Nike announced in the face of rising wages in Indonesia that to reduce labor costs throughout Asia, it would turn toward increasing automation, in the notorious words of Nike chief financial officer Don Blair, to "engineer the labor out of the product" through "technology and innovation," including robotization and 3-D printing.[79]

---

[77] Marx, *Capital*, Vol. I, p. 257.   [78] Marx, *Capital*, Vol. I, p. 380.
[79] Barney Jopson, June 27, 2013, *Financial Times*, www.ft.com/content/277197a6-df6a-11e2-881f-00144feab7de; Jennifer Bissell-Linsk, "Nike's Focus on Robotics Threatens Asia's Low-Cost Workforce," *Financial Times*, October 22, 2017, www.ft.com/content/585866fc-a841-11e7-ab55-27219df83c97.

It is possible, I suggest probable, that we are reaching a point in the pressures placed on capital by the mounting global crisis, by working- and popular-class struggles, competition over shares of oversaturated markets and shrinking shares of total surplus value, and political crisis, that the TCC will choose to undertake a more general shift toward digitalization throughout global value chains. Already by the 2020s, the plummeting real cost of robots made them cheaper than living labor even in low-wage zones around the world. In fact, according to one business report, robotization is spreading more rapidly to manufacturing in these low-wage zones than in higher-wage zones.[80] In India, five times fewer workers were required to operate a factory in 2007 than in 1980.[81] (As I already noted earlier, in India out of a working-age population of one billion, only 100 million have formal jobs at a time when the country is actually experiencing a boom in industrialization.) This process is already underway even in those economic activities long associated with large, highly exploited labor forces, the extractive industries. Across the board, the global extractive industries, from mining to oil and gas and agribusiness, are turning toward automation. In construction, smart robots are now being manufactured to lay bricks and install sheetrock. Robotization has already taken off in agriculture, from automatic harvesters and milking machines to autonomously driven farm vehicles.

The mining sector is emblematic. Robotic hardware and software technologies convert vehicles and equipment such as excavators, drills, and bulldozers into autonomous mining units, spanning remote control, teleoperation, driver assist, and full automation. The China National Coal Group Corporation has employed advanced automatic control equipment to operate the first-ever completed automated mine, a harbinger of widespread automation of the Chinese mining industry.[82]

---

[80] Oxford Economics, "How Robots Change the World: What Automation Really Means for Jobs and Productivity," June 2019, pp. 22–23. https://resources.oxfordeconomics.com/hubfs/How%20Robots%20Change%20the%20World%20(PDF).pdf.

[81] *The Economist*, "How to Get Rich in the 21st Century," January 6, 2024, p. 52.

[82] See, inter-alia, Andrew Hayley, "China Automating Mines to Improve Safety as Coal Output Grows," *Reuters*, April 28, 2023, www.reuters.com/markets/commodities/china-automating-mines-improve-safety-coal-output-grows-2023-04-28/; "The Importance of Automation in the Oil & Gas Industry," *Industlabs*, January 12, 2023,

"The nature of [mining] work itself is evolving, with an increasing focus on automation, algorithms, and a growing need to be digital savvy," observed a 2023 report by *McKinsey & Company*, warning that tens of millions could lose their livelihood in mining in the coming years due to automation.[83] In 2022 the Australian-based Resolute Mining corporation opened up its own fully automated mine in Mali.[84] This tendency toward automation is long term. Nonetheless, the global contraction in employment in extractive industries is already well underway.

We get a glimpse in the mining sector of the simultaneous increase of both relative and absolute surplus value, each intensifying the rate of exploitation, in distinct branches of the industry. In 2023 there were more than 3.7 million formal mining sector workers worldwide, 1.5 million of them in the rich countries, alongside some thirteen million people, many of them women and children, who attempted to scratch by on informal, small-scale mining – often simply scavenging, even digging for minerals by hand – with a fatality rate of ninety times higher than formal sector mining in the rich countries, according to an ILO report. The report added that upward of 100 million people depend on this informal mining.[85] As formal sector extractive work automates, many of these mine workers are thrown into the ranks of the surplus population, whereas many informal miners – whom according to the ILO are low-paid, seasonal, and highly precarious – already exist in a permanent crisis of social reproduction, facing a day-to-day struggle for survival. This world of mining is a microcosm of the violent class relations of global capitalism. Nowhere is more revealed than in the Congo, where, as elsewhere, the two sectors are integrated,

https://industlabs.com/news/oil-and-gas-automation; Linly Ku and Isabel Serna, "The Impact of Automated Farming on the Agriculture Industry," *PlugandPlay*, April 25, 2023, www.plugandplaytechcenter.com/resources/how-automation-transforming-farming-industry/.

[83] "Has Mining Lost Its Luster? Why Talent is Moving Elsewhere and How to Bring Them Back," McKinsey & Company, February 14, 2023, www.mckinsey.com/industries/metals-and-mining/our-insights/has-mining-lost-its-luster-why-talent-is-moving-elsewhere-and-how-to-bring-them-back.

[84] Molly (no surename given), "Sizing Up Syama: The World's First Fully Automated Mine," Mining Technology, January 19, 2022, www.mining-technology.com/features/sizing-syama-worlds-first-fully-automated-mine/?cf-view.

[85] "Small-Scale Mining on the Increase in Developing Countries," ILO, press release, May 17, 1999, www.ilo.org/global/about-the-ilo/newsroom/news/WCMS_007929/lang--en/index.htm.

as the informal mining scavengers whose land has often been usurped by local governments in the service of transnational mining capital, typically sell what they manage to dig up to the mining conglomerates or to agents who in turn deliver to the corporations in exchange for a cut. Even as these informal mine workers generate enormous profits for the mining transnationals, the repressive forces of the state and the corporations keep them dependent, downcast, and destitute. Glencore, a commodities giant with two mines in the Congo, "reckons that some 2,000 people sneak into its pits every day," reports *The Economist*. It is worth citing the report at length:

> Other companies have even more robbers to contend with. Last year Congolese soldiers chased thieves out of a mine owned by China Molybdenum where it was reckoned, 10,000-odd people were then illegally digging. While big firms take in millions, many of the little guys [in the Congo] languish in jail. The prison in Kolwezi, the largest city in the mining region, is crammed with men caught stealing copper and cobalt. More than a hundred inmates occupy one stinking room, sitting in rows on the ground, each wedged between another's legs. Prisoners are allowed to use the toilet only once a day, so they often urinate in their cloths.... In Kolwezi, shiny jeeps slide past beggars on roadsides. Dusty makeshift settlements, similar to Kawama, abut the city, while Chinese casinos and swanky hotels occupy the center. A cynic might see here a microcosm of Congo itself, where mineral wealth is hogged by a powerful few, while the many scramble to get by, and pray to stay out of jail.[86]

The work in such sites as the Congolese mines is so absolutely and totally degraded, so totally below the cost of its labor power, so emblematic of what Marini meant by super-exploitation, that in the ledgers of global capital it could hardly be considered as an expenditure on variable capital. Mining in the Congo represents the outer bounds of precarious work in the global economy, akin to modern-day slavery made possible by the ever-more prevalent conditions of extreme vulnerability. This "new slavery" is defined by Bales as violence to compel labor and the laborer's complete loss of control. He identified three basic forms of slavery: chattel slavery, debt bondage, and contract slavery. At the time Bale published his widely cited study at the turn of the twenty-first century, *Disposable People*, he estimated the number of people enslaved in these ways at 27 million

---

[86] *The Economist*, "Congo's Cobalt: The Ugly Rush," October 17, 2020, pp. 40–41.

worldwide.[87] In 2022, the ILO estimated that some 50 million people were held in modern-day slavery.[88]

Putting aside these extreme forms of exploitation, the coupling of generative artificial intelligence (henceforth, AI) with the Internet of Things (IoT) and the power of quantum computing signals a seismic shift that could bring about a revolution in the forces of production bound to generate new relations of production around the world characterized by more intense forms of exploitation as well as heightened exclusion. AI makes it possible to replace much living with digitalized dead labor in jobs hitherto more resistant to automation and, at the same time, to achieve the deskilling and degradation of work for those who remain in employment. Digital deskilling reduces the costs of equipping labor power with advanced skills and knowledge and therefore lowers the cost of labor power. The more degraded the workers' conditions, the less is the outlay the capitalist must spend on variable capital, and therefore the less is the value of the total capital employed (constant + variable) and the more, *ceteris paribus*, surplus value is extracted. This degradation and the automation of work in any combination achieve an increase in surplus value production but only at the cost of aggravating the crises of overaccumulation and social reproduction.

It must be stressed that I am not proposing a much-hyped "end of work" scenario. There will still be billions of workers. Rather, I wish to highlight in this section a clear tendency for workers to be replaced by digital technologies in many previously labor-intensive areas and, perhaps more important, the application of digital technologies to downgrade existing occupations, including the professions, along with a more widespread precariatization of work that aggravates the overall crisis of social reproduction (and of legitimacy, as I will discuss in Chapter 5). There has been substantial automation of industry in core countries over the past half a century alongside the relocation of labor-intensive industry to the traditional periphery that may now be automated, as discussed earlier. What we may now witness is a twin process – a significant automation of services along with the ongoing precariatization of service sector work that is not automated.

---

[87] Kevin Bales, *Disposable People: New Slavery in the Global Economy* (Berkeley: University of California Press, 1999).
[88] ILO, "Global Estimates of Modern Slavery: Forced Labor and Forced Marriage," September 12, 2022, www.ilo.org/publications/major-publications/global-estimates-modern-slavery-forced-labour-and-forced-marriage.

The Automation of Services and Professional Proletarians

Historically, workers displaced from one branch of the economy by the introduction of new technologies were absorbed into new branches of industry and services opened up by those technologies. Much of the work of producing and maintaining the stock of horses, carriages, and so forth, disappeared with the advent of the age of the combustion engine, that in turn employed tens if not hundreds of millions in producing cars, roadways, gasoline, and so on. But now digitalization threatens to do away with the need to absorb and chew up masses of workers in new branches of the economy. The trope on robots taking over and making living labor redundant has been circulating for decades. Why may things be different now? What sets apart advanced forms of AI and the accompanying IoT from earlier digital technologies is that it involves machine learning (specifically, "deep learning"), complex communication and pattern recognition driven by algorithms that AI can itself now create, and as a result, perform tasks that had previously been the exclusive domain of human intelligence.

We should not, therefore, expect the service sector to serve as a buffer to the automation of industry by absorbing those displaced from more traditional industrial activity, as happened from the mid twentieth century until recently, because services themselves are subject to both digital automation and to high levels of precarity. A major portion of service sector work takes place in the sphere of circulation, that is, the work involved in moving goods and services through global production, distribution, and delivery chains, ranging from shipping to warehousing, retail, transport, advertising, hospitality, entertainment, and payments. Many of these areas can and are being digitalized. The number of robots in use worldwide multiplied threefold in the first two decades of the twenty-first century, to 2.25 million (China accounts for some one-fifth of these robots), and is expected to surpass twenty million by 2030. By that year, up to twenty million manufacturing jobs could be replaced by robots, according to one 2019 report by the business consulting firm Oxford Economics. However, it cautioned that those displaced from industry by automation are likely to find that comparable roles in the service sector, such as in transport, construction, maintenance, and office and administrative work, are themselves highly vulnerable to automation. Already, noted in the report, robots were steadily gaining traction in significant sectors of the service economy – in industry jargon, they are now referred to as service robots – from baggage handling in airports to loading inventory in warehouses. As their real costs plummet, robots are becoming cheaper than living labor in both industry and many services.[89]

Digital automation of the global service sector may take many years to become operative, but the transition has already begun. Leading the way are logistics systems. In 2022 one major U.S. freight company, Embark Trucks, announced that in 2024 it would begin employing autonomous long-haul trucks.[90] UPS, FEDEX, and other delivery services announced in 2023 that they would deploy pilotless cargo planes.[91] Autonomous and remotely operated ships, including large cargo ships, are not far behind, and nor are retail and wholesale helicopter and drone delivery, tractors and harvesters, cargo loading, and so on.[92] By the 2020s, a number of Chinese port terminals were moving toward almost complete automation.[93] One McKinsey report found that two-thirds of the 800 senior executives surveyed planned

---

[89] Oxford Economics, "How Robots Change the World: What Automation Really Means for Jobs and Productivity," June 2019, various pages, https://resources.oxfordeconomics.com/hubfs/How%20Robots%20Change%20the%20World%20(PDF).pdf.

[90] "Embark Partners with Real Estate Group to Advance Autonomous Fleet Nationwide," *HDT Trukinginfo*, February 28, 2022, www.truckinginfo.com/10162387/embark-partners-with-real-estate-group-to-advance-autonomous-fleet-nationwide.

[91] Eric Kulisch, "UPS Feeder Airline Intends to Buy 20 Pilotless Cargo Planes," *Freighwaves*, January 30, 2023, www.freightwaves.com/news/ups-feeder-airline-intends-to-buy-20-pilotless-cargo-jets; Jonathan Small, "FedEx and UPS Will Soon be Flying Pilotless Planes. How Safe are They?," *Entrepreneur*, February 1, 2023, www.entrepreneur.com/green-entrepreneur/fedex-and-ups-will-soon-be-flying-pilotless-planes/444111.

[92] Bjorn Hohan Vartdal, Rolf Skjong, and Asun Lera St. Clair, "Remote-Controlled and Autonomous Shipping in the Maritime Industry," Position Paper 2018, *DNV*, 2018; "Pilotless Helicopters Deliver Large Payloads with Precision," *MathWorks*, undated, www.mathworks.com/company/mathworks-stories/pilotless-helicopter-drone-prototype-delivers-large-payloads.html; "Autonomous Electric Tractor Brings Artificial Intelligence to the Field," *MathWorks*, undated.

[93] See: "China's Smart Port Construction Gains Global Attention Despite Headwinds," *Xinjua*, December 16, 2022, www.globaltimes.cn/page/202212/1282015.shtml; Port Technology Team, "Watch China's Biggest Automated Terminal in Action," December 15, 2017, www.porttechnology.org/news/watch_chinas_biggest_automated_terminal_in_action/.

to significantly step-up investment in AI-driven automation in warehouses, grocery stores, call centers, and manufacturing plants.[94] In 2022 in the United States, the twenty fastest growing occupations were all in the service sector and seventeen of them paid below the national median income, some of them below the official poverty line.[95]

Work in personal services that are resistant to automation, such as caregiving, waitressing, and hairstyling, is typically characterized by immobility, low wages, precarity, and often by informality. Moreover, some service sector jobs involve a level of individualized attention and autonomy that make them difficult to automate yet are low skilled and low paid. The work done by an army of "cast members," costume designers, hair stylists, candy makers, custodians, hotel workers, and food service workers at Disneyland and Disney World parks in the United States, for instance, is not easily automated. A damning 2018 report, "Working for the Mouse," gives us a glimpse into the nature of that general service sector work not subject, or less subject, to digital automation. Almost three-quarters of workers reported that they did not earn enough money to cover basic expenses every month and many experienced homelessness – sleeping in their cars or in shelters – food insecurity, and an inability to pay for dental care or prescription drugs. While the job at Disney was the primary source of income for 91 percent of workers, the company only provided full-time employment to 54 percent of their employees.[96]

One report by Goldman Sachs that analyzed the databases detailing the content of over 900 occupations, estimated that up to two-thirds of occupations worldwide could be partially automated by AI in the coming years. Generative artificial intelligence alone could expose 300 million full-time jobs around the world to automation. Generative AI is a type of AI that is capable of generating text or other content in response to user prompts and gained great attention in 2020 when ChatGPT

---

[94] McKinsey Global Institute, "The Future of Work after COVID-19," February 18, 2021, www.mckinsey.com/featured-insights/future-of-work/the-future-of-work-after-covid-19.

[95] Walter Benn Michaels and Adolph Reed Jr., edited by Anton Jager and Daniel Zamora, *No Politics but Class Politics* (London: Eris, 2023), Figure 5, pp. 110–111.

[96] Peter Dreier and Daniel Flaming, "Working for the Mouse: A Survey of Disneyland Resort Employees," Economic Roundtable and Urban & Environmental Police Institute, February 2018, https://economicrt.org/publication/disneyland/.

was publicly launched. This is not to say that the automation of 300 million jobs would result in an equivalent job loss. For one, jobs may be partially automated so that the work itself is degraded and more precarious. And second, many may shift into other service sector jobs that are themselves subject to partial automation and to precariatization. AI replaces living labor with dead labor, and when it does not eliminate jobs, it degrades and precariatizes them.[97] Either way, substantial increases in productivity through partial or complete digital automation will have the effect of raising the organic composition of capital (digital constant capital would be equivalent to physical constant capital in terms of the effect), exacerbating the crisis of overaccumulation at the same time as it aggravates the crisis of social reproduction.[98]

But what about highly skilled and highly paid knowledge work and professional fields? On the one hand, highly skilled labor that is difficult to automate is simply precariatized. For instance, university courses are taught in their majority by adjunct faculty that have doctoral degrees yet live in perpetual poverty, paid a stipend for each course taught with no benefits and no job security. In the United States, about 25 percent of these professors can only get by on public assistance, and nearly a third make less than $25,000 a year, well below the poverty line.[99] On the other hand, if AI is able to replace much manual labor even in the extractive industries, it also revolutionizes the digital world in such a way that it has the potential to degrade and to replace cognitive labor and knowledge work. AI essentially constitutes digital means of production, digital constant capital that can reproduce itself. Marx argued in *The Grundrisse* that at a certain point in the development of production, science and technology become qualitative forces of production that can increasingly generate value independent of "living" human labor (e.g., through automation).[100]

[97] Emily Stewart, "Robots Were Supposed to Take Our Jobs. Instead, They're Making Them Worse," *Vox*, July 2, 2021, www.vox.com/the-goods/22557895/automation-robots-work-amazon-uber-lyft.
[98] Goldman Sachs, "Generative AI Could Raise Global GDP by 7%," April 5, 2023, www.goldmansachs.com/intelligence/pages/generative-ai-could-raise-global-gdp-by-7-percent.html.
[99] Colleen Flaherty, "Barely Getting By," *Inside Higher Ed*, April 19, 2020, www.insidehighered.com/news/2020/04/20/new-report-says-many-adjuncts-make-less-3500-course-and-25000-year.
[100] See discussion in "The Chapter on Capital" (this is the title of the chapter), in Karl Marx, *Grundrisse* (London: Penguin, 1973).

Earlier waves of the computer and information revolution produced highly skilled and highly remunerated workers, especially in the traditional core, while they simultaneously produced mass under- and unemployment, marginality, and exclusion. Low-skilled service work, such as call center customer service, data entry, and accounting, we saw in Chapter 1, is easily automated. But what about more complex tasks such as computer engineering, software design, pharmacology, biotechnology, and medicine? A McKinsey & Company report on the potential of generative AI estimates that AI and related technologies could automate activities across the spectrum of occupations, that the pace of workforce transformation would accelerate, and that half of all work activities would become automated between 2030 and 2060. However, the report singled out the automation of some 60 to 70 percent of knowledge work associated with higher pay and educational requirements, given its increasing ability to understand natural language, and will thus have the greatest impact on knowledge work, including software engineering, computer coding, research and development, the creative content of marketing and sales work, and customer operations, among other tasks.[101]

In core countries, "on-call" work arrangements have been spreading throughout the professions. They generally involved severe underemployment, often on zero-contract hours (meaning that there is no guarantee of any hours at all) and "just-in-time" scheduling, so that workers must show up to work at a moment's notice. Although no aggregate global data was available for on-call labor, it appeared that these arrangements, and especially zero-contract hours, were rising steeply in the traditional core countries.[102] The return to piecework through digitalized remote work, whether through a computer screen or driving an Uber, means that capital offsets to labor the cost of the means of production and also that capital need not concern itself with the direct discipline of labor since these computerized and digitalized

---

[101] Michael Chui et al., The Economic Potential of Generative AI: The Next Productivity Frontier, June 2023, McKinsey & Company, file:///Users/user./Downloads/the-economic-potential-of-generative-ai-the-next-productivity-frontier.pdf.

[102] International Labor Organization, "Working Time and Work-Like Balance Around the World" (Geneva: ILO, 2022), pp. 13–14, 42, www.ilo.org/wcmsp5/groups/public/---ed_protect/---protrav/---travail/documents/publication/wcms_864222.pdf.

piecemeal forms of work instill discipline of their own account. Among the millions that are either made superfluous or pushed into unstable and precarious work arrangements is a growing army of so-called "gigs" working digitally for the TCC. Much of this work is already controlled by algorithms and is automated, including hiring, reviewing, and paying workers, and so on. The paradox is that as automation advances, it also generates new tasks that can be performed by "on-demand" workers hired for piecemeal microtasks at below-subsistence wages, so that there is an endless cycle of automation and the degradation of work. In their study, *Ghost Work*, Gray and Suri observe:

> Billions of people consume website content, search engines, queries, tweets, post, and mobile app-enabled services every day. They assume that their purchases are made possible by the magic of technology alone. But, in reality, they are being served by an international staff, quietly laboring in the background. These jobs, dominated by freelance and contingent work arrangements rather than full-time or even hourly wage positions, have no established, legal status. Sometimes these jobs are given heft as harbingers of the 'Second Machine Age' or 'Fourth Industrial Revolution' or part of a larger digital or platform economy. Other times they are simply glibly called gigs.[103]

This on-demand work can be farmed out online to workers anywhere around the world. These workers represent a new level of commodification of labor and alienation of the worker. As Gray and Suri show, workers must acquire their own computer equipment and internet hookup and then constantly monitor the web for individual tasks that are dished out on a piecemeal basis. Workers are given their own unique identifying number so that companies who hire them do not even know their names or their physical location, which can be anywhere in the world where there is a computer terminal and internet service. These workers are not considered employees of the companies that represent a new generation of temp agencies – epitomized by Amazon's Mechanical Turk platform – registering individual workers with a numerical ID and then posting piecemeal tasks to the sites that these companies set up. In turn, any company that needs piecemeal

---

[103] Mary L. Gray and Siddharth Suri, *Ghost Work: How to Stop Silicon Valley from Building a New Global Underclass* (New York: Houghton Mifflin Harcourt, 2019), p. xvii.

digital work is connected with anonymous workers, the recruitment company taking a cut in the pittance paid to the worker for performing the task. They become the epitome of abstract social labor. "From the programmer's perspective, it makes humans seem interchangeable, as each worker is represented by a worker ID, and everything that makes a human a person, such as their beliefs, attributes, and experiences, is stripped away from this identifier."[104] Ironically, many of the tasks assigned to workers involve teaching machines to advance AI. These workers thus create their own redundancy to AI!

The ILO found that the majority of these superexploited on-demand workers are well educated: 37 percent held a bachelor's degree, 20 percent held a postgraduate degree, and one-fourth held a technical certificate or had some amount of university education. The median earnings of these workers across all countries were just $2.16 per hour. Workers in the United States earned less than the federal minimum wage of $7.25 an hour. Only 7 percent of those in Germany earned above the German minimum wage. Thirty-six percent regularly worked seven days a week, while 43 percent reported working during the night, and women workers combined crowdwork with care responsibilities. Moreover, contractors were free to reject without pay a task completed and delivered by any worker. "Despite performing work for many highly successful companies, compensation from crowdwork is often lower than minimum wages, workers must manage unpredictable income streams, and they work without the standard labor protections of an employment relationship," concluded the ILO.[105] Such crowdwork, in sum, aggravates the crisis of social reproduction, involving a more extensive precariatization of labor and a more intensified exploitation by transnational capital operating through several levels of mediation.

---

[104] Gray and Suri, *Ghost Work*, p. 5. On automation and laborless production, also see, inter-alia, George Borg, "Whose Labor? Appropriation and the Very Idea of Full Automation," *Science & Society*, 87(3), 2023, pp. 359–384; Aaron Benanav, "Automation and the Future of Work," New Left Review, No. 119, 2019, pp. 5–38; Nick Dyer-Witherford, Atle M. Kjosen, and James J. Steinhoff, *Inhuman Power* (London: Pluto, 2019); Phil Jones, *Work Without the Worker: Labor in the Age of Platform Capitalism* (London: Verso, 2021).

[105] Janine Berg et al., "Digital Labor Platforms and the Future of Work," International Labor Organization, Geneva, 2018, pp. XVII–XVIII, www.ilo.org/wcmsp5/groups/public/---dgreports/---dcomm/---publ/documents/publication/wcms_645337.pdfpp.

This "ghost work" may be the face of the future. As digitalization advances, more and more occupations may move toward on-demand remote labor. Already by 2016, some 12 percent of U.S. working-age adults did some form of on-demand ghost work. If the rate of growth in such crowdwork continues, 60 percent of global employment will be converted into some form of on-demand work by 2055.[106] Gray and Suri observe that cameras, sensors, internet connectivity, and real-time support make it possible for even such tasks as surgery to become on-demand, in which remote surgeons perform surgery. If this seems like an exaggeration, an open-heart surgery was performed in 2002 on a woman in Strasbourg, France. The surgeon, however, was 3,600 miles away, in New York, sitting at a console with controls for robot arms that manipulated the scalpel and other operating equipment. Such robotic arms dated back decades, but it was only the more advanced CIT, including fiber optics networks, that so reduced the time between the surgeon's movement on a touch screen and the operating equipment that the operation could take place remotely. In fact, the electronic signal produced by manipulation of the controls took only 80 milliseconds to transmit, while the image from the camera to the patient's abdomen was returned to the surgeon in New York in 160 milliseconds after the motion.[107] In effect, the digital technology applied to surgery had, for all practical purposes, obliterated space-time.

We may ask, in conclusion, can state intervention in the economy mitigate the crisis of social reproduction explored in this chapter? In theory, governments could undertake radical redistributive and regulatory reform in order to assure the well-being of billions of people who currently teeter between life and death. But even if governments were intent on doing so, states, even the most powerful among them, run up against the structural power of transnationally mobile capital, a topic to which I will return in Chapter 3. In this regard, capitalist states are not just politically but *structurally beholden* to transnational capital, by which I mean that the reproduction of these states – and of the state managers and political

---

[106] Gray and Suri, *Ghost Work*, p. 169, and see p. 243, endnote 5, for how they derive this figure for 2055.
[107] Thomas H. Maugh II, "Surgery Spans Miles of Ocean, Wires," *Los Angeles Times*, September 20, 2002, p. A30.

elites tied to these states – is dependent on the reproduction of transnationally mobile capital. As conditions for capitalist renewal dry up, as crisis in value intensifies, as obstacles mount to accumulation, as states lose legitimacy, compete with one another, and go to war – all this undermines conditions for new social contracts that "buy" class peace.

3 | *Legitimacy Crisis, Geopolitical Conflict, and Global Police State*

Thus far we have discussed the problems of overaccumulation and social reproduction. But the crisis is politically explosive. States everywhere, unable to cope with economic turbulence and social disintegration, face spiraling crises of legitimacy in the face of mass discontent with the status quo. Popular insurgencies have spread since 2008 as capital attempts to shift the burden of the crisis onto the working classes and as national states turn toward more repressive, authoritarian, and even fascist forms of rule to contain restive populations. Fissures within the ruling groups over how to manage the crisis and stabilize global capitalism are reaching a breaking point as the global capitalist historic bloc constructed in the heyday of neoliberalism from the 1990s until 2008 has all but crumbled and as the post-WWII international order cracks up. The system is moving very quickly toward a general crisis of capitalist rule.

The breakdown of hegemonic order in earlier epochs of world capitalist crisis was marked by political instability, intense class and social struggles, wars, and ruptures of the established international system. We have entered anew a period of worldwide political instability. Key turning points were the 2022 Russian invasion of Ukraine and the West's radical political, military, and economic response to it, along with Israeli's genocidal assault on Gaza that began in 2023 and the West's complicity in it. There is a radical reconfiguration of global geopolitical alignments underway as we move toward political multipolarity, itself an outcome of the transnationalization of capital, which has helped disperse state power in the international system. This takes place, however, within a single integrated global economy. Volatility will be the order of the day. Political decay will be drawn out, unfolding to the drumbeat of continuous, often violent conflicts and the collapse of state authority.

At the heart of these political dimensions of the crisis lies a fundamental contradiction in the organization of global capitalism that we will explore in this chapter: The disjuncture between a globally integrated economy and a nation-state-based system of political domination and capitalist reproduction. World capitalism as a whole requires an authority structure. Yet national governments do not exercise the required transnational political authority to address the crisis. Global elites sought in earlier years of globalization to develop such transnational political authority structures. As far back as the 1970s, with the formation of the Trilateral Commission and the World Economic Forum, emerging transnational elites sought to develop international networks to coordinate policy and impose worldwide the conditions necessary for capitalist globalization. I have discussed these efforts at length, referring to these networks as transnational state (TNS) apparatuses, and cannot reiterate them here.[1]

TNS apparatuses refer not to a "world government" but as an analytical abstraction to the loose yet dense networks of inter- and transnational institutions *together with* national states that have been captured by transnational forces, sometimes directly, as when local representatives of the TCC and their technocrats and political agents win state power, and otherwise when the national state internalizes the logic of transnational accumulation as a consequence of the structural pressure exercised over it by transnational capital. Along with national states, the institutional power network that constitutes the TNS spans established international agencies such as the United Nations and the Bretton Woods institutions, the creation of new ones such as the European Union in 1993, the World Trade Organization in 1995, the G20 in 1999, and a number of national and transnational regulatory and oversight bodies developed in the wake of the 2008 Great Depression intended to assist the global ruling class to take collective action to stabilize the system.

The TNS expresses a class relation between global capital and global labor. It is through TNS apparatuses that the TCC has sought to exercise its class power over the global working classes. These apparatuses served the TCC well during half a century of globalization in cracking open the world to its plunder and exploitation, and in bringing

---

[1] See Robinson: *A Theory of Global Capitalism* (Baltimore: Johns Hopkins University Press, 2004); *Latin America and Global Capitalism* (Baltimore: Johns Hopkins University Press, 2008); and especially Chapter 2 of *Global Capitalism and the Crisis of Humanity* (New York: Cambridge University Press, 2014).

down barriers to its access to resources, markets, and labor around the world. They played a critical role in converting the structural power of the global economy into supranational political domination, in particular by imposing the structural adjustment and free trade policies that opened the world up to transnational capital. However, they have proved ineffective in addressing the crisis. Facilitating plunder and exploitation is one matter and stabilizing global capitalism is quite another. To the contrary, the more freedom that capital has had to appropriate, exploit, and repress, the more it has fanned the political flames of the crisis.

Even in the heyday of neoliberal consensus, the fragmentary nature of TNS apparatuses made the effort problematic given the dispersal of formal political authority across many national states. The inadequacy of these efforts became more apparent as the crisis has escalated and as the political management of global capitalism has slipped from U.S. state managers without it being picked up effectively by TNS apparatuses. Any effort at transnational capitalist unity is undermined by the crisis. While the point should not be overstated, TNS apparatuses are breaking down. The World Trade Organization trade rules, for instance, are being disregarded by the very U.S. national state that so forcefully pushed for them at the height of neoliberal globalization. The disjuncture between a globally integrated economy and a nation-state-based system of political authority makes it difficult, if not impossible, for national states and transnational elites to resolve the crisis of state legitimacy, social control, and international conflict. However, the breakdown of the political organization of world capitalism is not the cause but the consequence of contradictions internal to a globally integrated system of capital accumulation.

A Contradictory Mandate

Capitalist states have a contradictory mandate: They must reproduce capitalist relations of production within their nation-states, but they must also achieve a measure of consent among the working and popular classes in their efforts to stabilize and reproduce the social formations over which they govern. This task is not easily accomplished given the class dynamics of capitalist exploitation. As we saw in earlier chapters, the drive to maximize the extraction of surplus value from labor results in social polarization. The capitalist system, by its very internal dynamics, generates destitution and inequality, which in turn undermines the state's legitimacy. If the source of this destitution and inequality is to be found in the relations of exploitation in the capitalist economy, the state becomes the lightning rod – or as Poulantzas put it, the "point of condensation" – for grievances that originate in the economy.[2] How are states to manage these grievances? On the one hand, the state has to meet the needs of capitalists, for otherwise they will withdraw their capital from circulation and throw the economy into crisis. On the other hand, the more the state caters to the needs of capital, the less it can satisfy the needs of the working and popular classes.

It is only under very special and infrequent historical conjunctures that this is not a zero-sum game; that the state can address enough of the demands of each to achieve broad legitimacy and stabilize the national social order. The "class compromise" of Fordist-Keynesian or social democratic capitalism conjoined with high growth rates, as I discussed earlier, to bring about the "golden age" of nation-state capitalism in the core capitalist countries in the post-WWII period. In Latin America, to take another historic conjuncture, populist projects in the mid twentieth century, such as Peronism in Argentina and, more generally, postcolonial developmentalist projects in the former Third World, held together coalitions for a time being that included both capital and labor in support of nationally oriented industrial and social welfare policies. But these were historic conjunctures that attenuated the sharpest class contradictions by momentarily displacing them into the future. Regulatory and redistributive reform in the twentieth century acted as countervailing tendencies to the tendency toward polarization. But capital went global in the final decades of that century, as we have seen, to escape the constraints on its freedom. By undercutting the national state's ability to capture and redistribute surpluses, globalization brought to an end redistributive nation-state capitalism, leading to the progressive loss of state legitimacy and the

---

[2] See, inter-alia, Nicos Poulantzs, *Political Power and Social Classes* (London: Verso, 1975). For Poulantzas, the capitalist state is a "condensation" of a relation of power between classes in struggle. The dual mandate of national states that I suggest here draws on Poulantzas' insight that the capitalist state contains within its own apparatuses the contradictory interests of both dominant and dominated classes. See Poulantzas, *State, Power, Socialism* (London: Verso, 2014 [1978]).

destabilization of national political systems – the so-called crisis of the nation-state much referred to in the globalization literature.

What comes into sharp focus now is the contradiction between the accumulation function and the legitimacy function of national states. This contradiction has historically reached a breaking point during each major crisis of world capitalism, resolving itself into new rounds of capitalist expansion, new state forms, and new dispensations between the exploiter and the exploited classes. It is again reaching the breaking point, but this time it is inscribed into the epochal crisis of global capitalism. Social scientists such as Jurgens Habermas, Claude Offe, and Alan Wolfe have made theoretical contributions to the legitimation crisis that arises from this contradiction.[3] But their approaches are of limited utility as they tend to address the matter from a methodological nationalism that takes the nation-state as the unit of analysis and appear to be more concerned with the implications of legitimacy crises for the future of democracy and the welfare state than with global political crisis and the reproduction of the world capitalist system.

My concern is to focus on the contradiction between the need that the national state has to promote transnational capital accumulation in its territory in competition with other states and its need to achieve political legitimacy and stabilize the domestic social order. Attracting transnational corporate and financial investment requires providing capital with investment incentives such as low wages and labor discipline, a lax regulatory environment, tax concessions, investment subsidies, privatization and deregulation, and so on – the policies that have been pursued worldwide since the onset of globalization. The result is rising inequality, impoverishment, and insecurity for working and popular classes, precisely the conditions that throw states into crises of legitimacy, destabilize national political systems, and jeopardize elite control.

Any attempt by the state to address the political crisis of legitimacy runs up against the accumulation strategies pursued by the TCC and capitalists' efforts in each country of the world to shift the burden of the crisis onto working and popular classes. The Chinese state, for

---

[3] Jurgen Habermas, *Legitimation Crisis* (Boston: Beacon Press, 1975); Alan Wolfe, *The Limits of Legitimacy* (New York: The Free Press, 1977); Claus Offe, *Contradictions of the Welfare State* (Boston: MIT Press, 1984).

instance, intent on keeping a lid on rising discontent, established in the early 2020s as its goal a reduction in inequality.[4] This inequality escalated as China opened up and integrated into global capitalism starting in the late twentieth century. But the Chinese state must also reproduce transnational capital inside China, which has complicated its effort to reduce inequality.[5] As states try to manage escalating political turmoil, they may pursue policies and a politics of crisis management that come to appear as contradictory and even bewildering. The astute political sociologist must know how to make sense out of what may appear bewildering, to think dialectically, and to see how contradictions play themselves out in unpredictable ways and through multiple levels of mediation.

There are three dimensions of the contradiction between a globalizing economy and a nation-state/interstate-based system of political authority that we want to explore here. First, unable to manage the escalation of political conflict and class struggle produced by the crisis of social reproduction, governments and capitalists increasingly rely on an omnipresent global police state to surveil and repress the popular classes. The balance between consensual and coercive modes of domination has been shifting in many countries around the world toward the latter as states turn toward authoritarian, dictatorial, and even fascist forms of control over these classes. Capitalism has always forced working people to compete with one another, for which it employed a whole host of strategies and forms of oppression, including racism, nationalism, and selective cooptation to fan this

---

[4] See, inter-alia, David Bulman, "Xi Jinping Says He Wants to Spread China's Wealth More Equitably. How Likely is That to Actually Happen?" *ChinaFile*, March 3, 2023, www.chinafile.com/conversation/common-prosperity-China-wealth-redistribution. The article provides a vast wealth of links to other literature discussing the Chinese leadership's plan to reduce inequality.

[5] In the early 2020s, foreign direct investment into China began a sharp decline. If resentment over Chinese state controls and fear of U.S. reprisals were factors in this decline, perhaps the principal one was emerging stagnation and overproduction in China. In response, Chinese president Xi Jinping issued a series of public pleas for transnational corporate investment, including directly to dozens of transnational corporate CEOs at the 2024 China Development Forum and the Boao Forum (Asia-specific versions of the World Economic Forum conclaves), promising that the Chinese state would lift restrictions on capital movements, push forward reforms, and further open up the Chinese market. See, for example, *The Economist*, "Business in China: A New Opening?", April 6, 2024, pp. 49–50.

competition. Capitalist and state efforts to undermine the class unity and consciousness of the exploited is, of course, a very old game. It should come as no surprise that the more the crisis deepens, the more the ruling groups have turned to nationalism, in some cases to a hypernationalism characteristic of fascism.

Second, if nationally based working classes are pitted against one another by transnational capitalists and their agents in states – this is merely an aggregate expression of the competition among all individual workers under capitalism – states must also compete with one another to attract transnationally mobile capital *and* to secure the inflow of resources and raw materials that this capital needs to undertake accumulation as they strive to stabilize their own respective national social orders. This competition provides a part of the explanation for mounting international tensions and geopolitical rivalry. The crisis of overaccumulation and the limits to capitalist expansion amplify these tensions. The chasm is rapidly widening between the economic unity of global capital and political competition among ruling groups who must achieve legitimacy and keep the internal social order of their respective nations from fracturing in the face of the escalating crisis. Economic globalization and the transnational integration of capitals provide a centripetal impulse to global capitalism, whereas political fragmentation gives a powerful centrifugal counterimpulse that is resulting in an escalation of geopolitical conflict and the crackup of the post-WWII international order. The class/capital-theoretic approach I take here requires, to paraphrase Marx, that we exit the noisy abode of international relations that captures news headlines, which centers on state-level analysis, and instead seek the causal original of inter-state conflict in the contradictions of global capital accumulation.

And third, there is growing tension and complexity in the relationship between national states and transnational capital as well as between distinct fractions of capital. We want to avoid the twin traps of falling into a dualism of the economic and the political or of collapsing the economic and the political into one and instead focus on the dialectical unity of the two and the tension between them. Unlike earlier modes of production where the politically ruling class was also the economically dominant class, under capitalism the group extracting surplus labor from the laboring classes is not necessarily the group that has *direct* control over the state. Yet the political sphere is not extraneous to capitalist relations of production. To the contrary, it orders and organizes those relations, providing coercive power and the ideological reproduction it requires. The mechanisms by which the capitalist state reproduces capitalism, and the theoretical explanation for why it does so, remain areas of intense debate. The key point here is that transnational capital is reproduced globally, but legitimacy is reproduced nationally. This contradiction between the political and the economic constitution of global capitalism becomes more acute as the global crisis intensifies. The contradictory mandate of states places them not only in conflict with one another but may also place them in conflict with transnational capital. If capital has always been dependent on the state to provide the conditions for accumulation, the state has in turn been dependent on capital for its own reproduction and that of the social order over which it governs.

Globalization tipped the balance in recent decades in the relationship between capital and the state. It gave the TCC, and especially transnational finance capital, newfound structural power over national states, and with it the ability to manipulate crises of state legitimacy and the international tensions generated by these crises. As we shall see, the relationship between transnational capital and the national state becomes more complicated as the contradiction between accumulation and legitimation is transferred to the global field. There is underway a very significant spatial reconstruction of the worldwide patterns of accumulation and a geopolitical reconfiguration of global capitalism driven by this now globalized contradiction. But we must move beyond the realist nation-state/interstate framework of analysis to make sense of these three interwoven dimensions and to grasp the changes underway.

The Breakdown of Consensual Domination

The global police state is a response to both the political and the economic dimensions of the crisis. Rather than a theory of the state, the global police state is a heuristic instrument of analysis that helps us see how the coercive domination of capital is becoming deeply embedded in new strategies of accumulation, or to say this another way, how expanding systems of mass surveillance, repression, and warfare constitute in themselves a strategy of accumulation. In Chapter 1 I referred to militarized accumulation and accumulation by repression as mechanisms for sustaining accumulation in the face of chronic stagnation.

The global police state facilitates accumulation in a dual sense. First, it serves as a sledgehammer to violently crack open new spaces for profit-making worldwide and to repress those who resist. Second, in and of themselves, military conflict and control, surveillance, and repression of the popular classes are enormously lucrative outlets for overaccumulated capital. But in addition to helping capital to expand and to profiteer from war and repression, global police state also refers to the ever-more ubiquitous systems of mass social control, surveillance, and repression to contain the global working classes and criminalize surplus humanity at a time when worldwide inequalities and mass deprivation have never been so acute and when popular rebellion is breaking out everywhere. As I will discuss further below and in Chapter 5, the more the global economy is driven by militarized accumulation and accumulation by repression, the more the effort to sustain these forms of accumulation fuels interstate conflict.

In two earlier books, *The Global Police State* and *Global Civil War*, I expounded on the concept of global police state and its relationship to the spread of popular insurgencies around the world in the wake of the 2008 Great Recession.[6] A 2020 survey found that a majority of people around the world (56 percent) believed in that year that capitalism was doing more harm than good. Majorities rejected capitalism in many Asian, European, Gulf, African, and Latin American countries.[7] From 2017 to 2024, more than 400 major anti-government protests swept the world, in rich and poor countries alike, 132 countries in all, toppling some thirty governments or leaders and sparking an escalation of state violence against protesters.[8] Some of these mass struggles appeared to be acquiring a radical anti-capitalist character.[9]

---

[6] William I. Robinson, *The Global Police State* (London: Pluto Press, 2020); *Global Civil War: Capitalism Post-Pandemic* (Oakland: PM Press, 2022).
[7] Mark John, "Capitalism Seen Doing 'More Harm than Good' in Global Survey," *Reuters*, January 19, 2020, www.reuters.com/article/us-davos-meeting-trust/capitalism-seen-doing-more-harm-than-good-in-global-survey-idUSKBN1ZJ0CW. In fact, only in Australia, Canada, the United States, South Korea, Hong Kong, and Japan did majorities disagree with the assertion that capitalism currently does more harm than good.
[8] Carnegie Endowment for International Piece, "Global Protest Tracker," at https://carnegieendowment.org/publications/interactive/protest-tracker. The tracker is interactive and regularly updated.
[9] For a survey and discussion of the global revolt and the challenges that it faces, see Robinson, *Global Civil War*.

Socialist ideology and politics have made a comeback among young people untainted by the virulent anti-communism of the Cold War. In all of their diversity, these mass struggles have a common underlying denominator: An aggressive global capitalism in crisis that is pushing to expand on the backs of masses who can tolerate no more hardship and deprivation.

The ruling classes must figure out how to keep accumulating capital in the face of stagnation and at the same time maintain control by keeping a lid on rebellion. The savage inequalities I discussed in earlier chapters are politically explosive and to the extent that the system is simply unable to reverse them or to incorporate surplus humanity, it turns to ever more violent forms of containment to manage immiserated populations.[10] The dominant groups have ramped up transnational systems of social control, repression, and warfare – from mass incarceration and militarized border walls to deadly new modalities of policing, paramilitarism, and omnipresent systems of state and private surveillance. The global order as a unity is becoming increasingly repressive and authoritarian as the apparatuses of the global police state become embedded in every country. States and transnational capitalists may face one another in fierce competition over expanding the frontiers of global accumulation and dividing up shares of surplus value, yet every capitalist on the planet needs a global police state to repress and control the working and popular classes, while every capitalist state serves this mandate. As I shall discuss later, each national state deploys the global police state in its own territory to crush resistance, while the U.S. and other interventionist powers deploy it extraterritorially around the world.

The Italian communist Antonio Gramsci developed the concept of hegemony to refer to a particular relation of social domination in which subordinate groups lend their "active consent" to the system of domination. Projects of hegemony involve not merely rule but political and ideological leadership of the dominant groups based on a set of class alliances and political blocs they have constructed. However, the possibility of hegemonic or consensual domination rests not just on the dominant groups achieving their political and ideological leadership

---

[10] Robinson, *The Global Police State*; Transnational Institute (TNI), "State of Power 2021," (Amsterdam: TNI, May 16, 2021), www.tni.org/en/publication/state-of-power-2021.

but also on material foundations. No would-be ruling class can exercise hegemony without developing diverse mechanisms of legitimation and securing a social base – a combination of the consensual integration through material reward for some and the coercive exclusion of others that the system is unwilling or unable to co-opt. The ruling groups must provide some sort of material (economic) "payoff" to significant enough sectors among the subordinate groups to allow for these sectors' social reproduction and stability, that is, for their well-being. The exclusion of billions and the socioeconomic destabilization of many of those who had achieved some level of stability in the earlier eras, especially in the rich core countries of world capitalism, are now making it increasingly difficult for the ruling groups to reproduce hegemonic control.

The breakdown of hegemony has helped fuel the militarization of the global economy and society. The various wars, conflicts, and campaigns of social control and repression around the world involve the fusion of private accumulation with state militarization. In this relationship, the state facilitates the expansion of opportunities for private capital to accumulate through militarization, such as by facilitating global weapons sales by military-industrial-security firms, the amounts of which have reached unprecedented levels. The twin dimensions of global police state – first as an outlet for overaccumulated capital and second as an instrument of mass repression as hegemonic control breaks down – make it increasingly difficult to maintain "democratic" systems. These two dimensions feed off of one another and lend themselves to fascist political tendencies. The ruling groups cannot stabilize their domination, and therefore the system of worldwide capitalist exploitation, on coercion alone, yet they are compelled by the loss of legitimacy to turn toward coercive domination. New political dispensations are more willing to deploy the global police state without concern for legitimacy. This is a political contradiction internal to global capitalism. The crisis of legitimacy may be a necessary condition for any working-class movement to overthrow capitalism because the masses must come to see the system that rules them as illegitimate. However, dictatorship, authoritarianism, and fascism are the least propitious political conditions for mass struggle from below.

Whether in its early twentieth- or early twenty-first-century iterations, fascism is always a particular *response* to capitalist crisis involving militaristic and chauvinistic nationalism and externalizing tensions onto communities that serve as scapegoats, whether Jews in Nazi Germany, Palestinians in Palestine/Israel, Muslims in India, immigrants around the world, amorphous "terrorists" and "criminals," or onto other countries that must be portrayed as enemies. The downward mobility and destabilization of working classes, the destruction of the old labor aristocracies, the demise of the middle classes, the ravages of neoliberalism, and the political backlash against globalization generate the recruiting grounds for twenty-first-century fascism. Far-right forces draw on well-known nationalist, populist, xenophobic, racist, and masculinist repertoires to channel rising social anxiety, uncertainty over the future, and mass anti-systemic sentiment into support for neo-fascist programs. The discourse of "law and order" manipulates legitimate fear over insecurity, rising crime, and social violence, themselves inevitable consequences of inequality and deprivation. New forms of cultural hegemony achieved through digital technologies and spectacles seek to manipulate cognition and depoliticize those experiencing fragmented lives by sublimating frustrated desires, pent-up libido, and primal fears toward titillating dreams of consumption and flights into fantasy worlds.

The core of twenty-first-century fascism is the triangulation of transnational capital with reactionary and repressive political power in the state and a neo-fascist mobilization in civil society. It is this mobilization of the disaffected among the working and popular classes that distinguishes fascism from other forms of authoritarianism or from mere dictatorship. The crisis of global capitalism makes it increasingly difficult for the capitalist state to represent itself as some universal interest; it is revealed to represent nothing more than the naked self-interest of (transnational) capital and corrupt politicians that serve its interests. If the loss of legitimacy allows hyper-nationalist, right-wing populist, and fascistic discourses to claim themselves of saviors from an imagined enemy, there is no actual praxis behind the discourse that could reconstitute an historic bloc involving enough of the subordinate and allied classes to reconstruct hegemony. Nationalist, populist, and anti-globalist rhetoric notwithstanding, most instances of twenty-first-century fascism involve not a departure from global capitalism but a more despotic management of it. These projects seek to violently unblock accumulation through new political and ideological scaffolding that may forsake traditional mechanisms of democratic legitimation for other forms of legitimation achieved through hypernationalism and the sublimation of mass anxiety onto internal and external scapegoats.

The fight against fascism is necessarily a fight against the TCC. Global capitalists may seek alliances with fascist movements in order to do away with democratic constraints or popular challenges to the extractive accumulation of capital. The election of the fascist Jair Bolsonaro as president of Brazil in 2019 was indicative. The TCC had banked (literally) on Bolsonaro in 2018 and was delighted with his victory. As in the United States under Trump, Bolsonaro proposed the wholesale privatization and deregulation of the economy, opening up the amazon to lumber, mining, and transnational agribusiness interests, regressive taxation and general austerity, alongside mass repression and criminalization of social movements and vulnerable communities that opposed this program. As one journalist noted at the time of Bolsonaro's electoral victory, the "world's capitalists are salivating over the new investment opportunities" that he promised.[11] Capital markets and Brazilian funds spiked on the world's stock exchanges the day after his electoral victory. Here we see the "wages of fascism" for a global capitalism in crisis.

On the other hand, however – *and this is crucial* – the TCC, embedded as it is in global, not national, markets and circuits of accumulation, does not support national state restrictions on these markets and circuits. Fascist movements, with their populist discourse and hypernationalism, are prone to policies that may restrict capital's freedom, which helps us understand why much of the TCC has been wary of casting its lot with the fascist option. This appears to be especially so, for example, in the European Union (EU), where far-right and neofascist parties have gained a significant following in civil society and a presence in political institutions across the EU, from where they have championed protectionist and populist policies that are a threat to the transnational capital. The TCC, recall, lobbied heavily against BREXIT in 2016, and in Germany, corporate managers have campaigned against the far-right Alternative for Germany (AfD) due to

---

[11] Jake Johnson, "After Win by Brazilian Fascist Jair Bolsonaro, World's Capitalists Salivate Over 'New Investment Opportunities'," *Common Dreams*, October 29, 2018, www.commondreams.org/news/2018/10/29/after-win-brazilian-fascist-jair-bolsonaro-worlds-capitalists-salivate-over-new.

the threat it posed of a German withdrawal from the EU.[12] The TCC wants the coercion and control over the oppressed that fascism offers, but it does not want the national restrictions on the freedom of transnational capital that many far-right and neofascist projects propose.

The Political and the Economic: The State and (Transnational) Capital

The problem of the relationship between capital and the state is rooted in a more expansive theoretical matter, that of the relationship of the political to the economic, that has been debated for many years by social scientists. The Greek social theorist Nicos Poulantzas developed the concept of the relative autonomy of the state based on the formal separation of the political from the economic sphere and the function of the state in securing social cohesion.[13] However, this relationship between economics and politics, between capital and political elites, is mediated in complex ways that are often tension-ridden. The capitalist state forms a unity with capital, but we cannot collapse the two into one, just as the political and the economic are a unity that cannot be collapsed into one. While capital has the sole objective of maximizing accumulation, capitalist states have the contradictory mandate that I discussed earlier and must manage the political fallout of the crisis. In its attempt to secure legitimacy and assure the reproduction of the social order, the capitalist state can and often does impose restraint on capital, pursue policies that contravene capitalist interests, or push the process of capital accumulation

---

[12] Thomas Klikauer, "German Industry & the Far-Right in 2024," *Z Magazine*, June 13, 2024, https://znetwork.org/znetarticle/german-industry-the-far-right-in-2024/.

[13] Poulantzas, *Political Power and Social Classes*. Poulantzas refers to the autonomy of the political realm from simplistic class influence; autonomy does *not* mean *independence* from capital. If it is the relative autonomy of the capitalist state that allows it to reproduce capitalism, I am arguing here that the crisis undermines that ability. Poulantzas can be considered the principal Marxist theorist of the capitalist state in the late twentieth century, yet there was an impressive barrage of such theorizing starting with the 1970s crisis. For discussion, see: Clyde W Barrow, *Critical Theories of the State: Marxist, Neo-Marxist, Post-Marxist* (Madison: University of Wisconsin Press, 1993); Bob Jessop, *The Capitalist State: Marxist Theories and Methods* (Oxford: Martin Robertson, 1982); Jessop, *The Future of the Capitalist State* (Cambridge: Polity, 2002). In my view, this late twentieth century theorizing petered out because it was unable to address the transformations involved in capitalist globalization.

in certain directions. The leading states in the international system are at this time pushing transnational capital to undertake spatial restructuring and effecting a geopolitical reconfiguration of world politics.

Yet impositions on capital run up against the self-same capitalist state's drive to promote (transnational) capital accumulation. As discussed by the French philosopher Louis Althusser, overdetermination refers to how multiple forces within a larger unity that are often contradictory or opposed to one another are active in any given political situation.[14] Most observers, fixed as they are in a state-centrism and a nation-state/interstate framework of analysis that attributes global political dynamics to capitalist competition among nation-states, fail to see how the political contradictions generated by the legitimacy crisis can overdetermine the economic impulse toward transnational integration. The extent of control that capitalists are able to exercise over the state varies in accordance with the tenor of class struggle and capitalist crisis. In the late twentieth and early twenty-first centuries, the emergent TCC managed to exercise a more direct, instrumental control over the state in pursuit of its globalization agenda. But this level of instrumental control now appears to give way to greater state autonomy in response to the crisis. Politics, including geopolitics, may come to *overdetermine* economics. This is not the sole explanation for the escalation of geopolitical conflict – far from it – but it is a crucial part of the story that is obscured by approaches that box transnational phenomena into a realist nation-state/interstate straightjacket.

The spatial reconfiguration of the global economy is driven as much by the crisis of state legitimacy as by the economic considerations of transnational capital. The breakdown of global trade networks during the 2020 economic meltdown triggered by the COVID-19 pandemic and the chaotic economic reopening from 2021 to 2023 revealed the vulnerability of far-flung global supply chains as international transportation and logistical infrastructure broke down. A logjam of container ships waiting to dock and unload could be seen in major ports around the world during the reopening. At one point in 2021, a massive container ship beached in the Suez Canal, clogging up global

---

[14] See "Contradiction and Overdetermination" in Louis Althusser, *For Marx* (London: Verso, 2006). There is also the larger theoretical discussion on the relative autonomy of the state that I cannot take up here. But it is important to remember that official state discourse is not to be taken at face value.

merchant sea traffic. As we saw previously, globalization has involved the fragmentation and decentralization of industrial production and distribution processes into numerous intermediate phases that are geographically scattered around the world and functionally linked to one another. More than 50,000 merchant ships operate in the oceans, the largest of which are loaded with up to 24,000 containers.[15] Intermodal transportation, introduced in the late twentieth century, standardized the size and design of these containers and the ships, trains, planes, and trucks that transport them around the globe.

The interruption from 2020 to 2023 of these global trade and supply networks so emblematic of globalization underscored just how dependent every country has become on this globally integrated system and, from the viewpoint of both states and capitalists, highlighted key fragilities in the global economy. In the early twenty-first century, trade in intermediate goods, such as semiconductors and other industrial inputs, accounted for a full 56 percent of all trade in goods and 73 percent of services trade among the rich countries of the Organization of Economic Cooperation and Development that dominate the global trade system.[16] In the mid 2010s, transnational corporations (TNCs) accounted for 80 percent of global trade and cross-border supply chains accounted for 60 percent of that trade.[17] If global shipping is disrupted, so too are industrial production and distribution networks in each country. The breakdown during the height of the pandemic of these networks led academics and pundits to declare that the world was moving to a period of "deglobalization" as corporations turned to the nearshoring or reshoring of production and supply chains that had previously been offshored.

In fact, however, an analysis of the data and of the underlying structural transformations underway suggests a more complex picture. The TCC is

---

[15] Zahra Ahmed, "Top 22 World's Largest Container Ships in 2024," *Marine Insight*, April 11, 2023 [updated for 2024], www.marineinsight.com/know-more/top-10-worlds-largest-container-ships-in-2019/.

[16] OECD, "Trade in Intermediate Goods and International Supply Chains in CEFTA," CEFTA Issues Paper 6, 2013, p. 3, www.oecd.org/south-east-europe/programme/CEFTA%20IP6_Trade%20in%20Intermediate_Web%20and%20Print.pdf.

[17] Richard Dobbs, Tim Koller, Sree Ramaswamy, Jonathan Woetzel, James Manyika, Rohit Krishnan, and Nicoló Andreula, "Playing to Win: The New Global Competition for Corporate Profits," McKinsey Global Institute, September 2015, Executive Summary, file:///Users/user./Downloads/mgi%20global%20competition_executive%20summary_sep%202015.pdf, p. 3.

too dependent on an open and integrated global economy for ongoing accumulation of capital on a world scale to withdraw back into the confines of "national" economies, even if its members wanted to disentangle themselves into national capitalist groups. Globalization scholars Steger and James show how the leveling off of cross-border trade in goods and a dip in cross-border financial flows after the 2008 crisis was more than compensated for by a massive increase in global digital connections, so that instead of deglobalization, there is a shift from "embodied globalization," by which they mean the physical mobility of human beings, and "object-related globalization," which refers to the mobility of physical objects, to what they term "disembodied globalization," which pertains to intangible global transactions such as those I discussed in Chapter 1.[18] Even at that, however, the volume of trade in goods rebounded from the 2008 collapse, the 2015 recession, and the 2020 pandemic meltdown, reaching an all-time high in 2021.[19] It was expected to rise by more than 5 percent for the 2024–25 two-year period.[20]

In the 2020s, the TCC and governments began to set up new nodes in worldwide trade networks in order to reduce dependence on a few key nodes and reduce supply chain volatility, creating in the process denser webs and new geographic patterns of cross-border integration. In Chapter 1 I discussed how transnational capitalists are in a constant process of relocating their global production and supply chains in their search for optimal accumulation conditions. In the early 2020s, a full 90 percent of global shippers set about to diversify their supplies.[21]

---

[18] Manfred Steger and Paul James, "Disjunctive Globalization in the Era of the Great Unsettling," *Theory, Culture, and Society*, 37(7–8), 2020.

[19] United Nations Conference on Trade and Development (UNCTAD), "Global Trade Update," May 2021, https://unctad.org/system/files/official-document/ditcinf2021d2_en.pdf.

[20] Sam Fleming, Valentina Romei, and Martin Arnold, "Global Trade Growth Set to More Than Double This Year," *Financial Times*, May 7, 2024, G www.ft.com/content/3451ba03-28fc-4300-8813-af66bb743bf4. In 2017, of the 126 policies issued in 65 countries, 74 percent favored greater globalization, while only 14 percent established restrictions. Center for China and Globalization, "Report on Chinese Enterprise Globalization 2018," June 24, 2018, http://en.ccg.org.cn/archives/58337.

[21] FreightWaves (a freighter trade association annual report), "The State of Freight 2023," November 2023, www.freightwaves.com/wp-content/uploads/2023/11/21/FW-SONAR-State-of-Freight-November-2023.pdf. The trade association website Lloyd's List offers vast information on all-things global freight, https://lloydslist.com/markets/containers#.YX3NxKBlBTY.

We see a mix of nearshoring and reshoring to rich countries and increased automation in labor-intensive industrial processing zones and service centers. Putting aside the economic motives of the TCC to nearshore, what interests us here are the political motives for this spatial reorganization. The corporate managers of the global economy are engaged in geographic restructuring in accordance with how the political winds are shaping the opportunities for and constraints on accumulation around the world. Transnational capitalists (including Chinese transnational capitalists themselves) are relocating from China to Vietnam, for instance, because of Chinese state constraints on their freedom, U.S. state pressure, or cheaper labor, while some Chinese-based transnational capitalists are investing directly in the so-called industrial renaissance in the United States.

Mexico illustrates the link between crises of state legitimacy and changing spatial patterns of global accumulation. The country experienced in the 2020s a new wave of industrialization driven by transnational corporate relocation of their operations into its territory for economic and political reasons that cannot be separated from one another. The North American Free Trade Area (NAFTA), which was initially negotiated in the early 1990s in the heyday of the late twentieth century globalization boom, was renegotiated in 2018 at the insistence of U.S. president Donald Trump, with his proclaimed nationalist and protectionism agenda. The renegotiated trade treaty erected new tariff walls and restrictions that reconfigured the relationship of the North American regional economy to the larger global economy into which it is inextricably integrated. Getting inside the regional tariff wall proved to be a powerful incentive for transnational corporations to relocate industrial production of intermediate and finished goods from elsewhere, especially from Asia, to Mexico, whose government provides tariff- and duty-free programs to attract transnational investment for reexport to U.S. and Canadian markets. In the early 2020s, tens of billions of dollars in Asian- and especially Chinese-based investment poured into Mexico, with billions more coming from the EU countries, Latin America, and elsewhere. In 2023 alone, some fifty industrial parks were under construction in Mexico, almost half by Chinese investors and another 20 percent by Koreans. Trade between the United States and Mexico approached $800 billion.[22]

---

[22] Natalie Alcoba, "Politics and Convenience Drive Mexico to Be US's Top Trading Partner," *Aljazeera*, February 13, 2024, www.aljazeera.com/

What appeared as the export of "Mexican" goods and services to the United States and as U.S.–Mexico "bilateral" trade was actually the movement of transnational capital through shifting global networks. Far from resulting in a regional deglobalization, the trade agreement deepened the transnationalization of capital, converting what were international trade flows between Asia and the Americas to transnational investment flows, pushed in that specific direction by U.S. state policy. These are global economic spaces that touch down in national political spaces. Regional booms may appear as "deglobalization," but these booming regional circuits are integrated into a singular global economy. As has already been well-studied, the thunderous boom of the Chinese economy in the late twentieth and early twenty-first centuries drew other regions even more deeply into the globalized circuits, whether through the massive increase in Latin American and African raw materials exports to Asia, the integrative economic tapestries weaved by the Belts and Roads Initiative, or the surge of Chinese-based transnational investment into North America and Europe and the reverse flow of Western investment into China.

Global capitalism is a heterogeneous political space. Market (economic) compulsion is mediated by state (political) coercion, without which the production and circulation of capital could not function. The nation-state serves transnational capital as a core site for organizing power, a space for the TCC to plunder and extract, and a reserve of resources, exploitable labor, and markets. For the TCC, national state apparatuses exist to open, and keep open, access to this plunder and extraction and for the repression of popular resistance to its predation. As the hegemonic fraction of capital on a world scale, the TCC seeks to reduce, if not abolish, encumbrances that limit its space for production and accumulation, to convert the world into a single integrated field for accumulation. National spaces present for the TCC a constantly evolving kaleidoscope of opportunities and constraints for accumulation as capital fluidly shifts from one space to another around the world and as national states try to influence this pulsating

economy/2024/2/13/politics-and-convenience-drive-mexico-to-be-uss-top-trading-partner; Enrique Hernández, "Nearshoring: Mexico Ya Es el Centro Manufacturero de las Empresas Chinas," *Forbes*, November 10, 2022, www.forbes.com.mx/nearshoring-mexico-ya-es-el-centro-manufacturero-de-las-empresas-chinas/?fbclid=IwAR3Tx3EC-mswoT0Fa2r3VyD7QOS2k09P6mYiIehyahilfkLgohQ5jH8y_qc.

movement to their advantage. The TCC is not tethered to territory and does not identify with any one nation-state or operate in a place-bound logic (space and territory are distinct concepts and categories of analysis, yet they are typically conflated). But it must nonetheless rely on and contend with states whose contradictory mandate may impede the freedom of capital to dictate the terms of its own reproduction.

The uneven and combined development of capitalism is a structural condition for world capitalist reproduction. Uneven development, especially the relative underdevelopment of the former Third World, has historically given capital important advantages in its worldwide accumulation strategies. Political heterogeneity, however, is a double-edged sword for the TCC. It allows transnational capital to pit national states and nationally bound working classes against one another. But it may also curtail the absolute freedom of transnational capital to accumulate. The globally integrated system of production, finance, and services controlled by the TCC operates as a unit synchronized in real time, but its sequences traverse nationally differentiated spaces. Each state operating within its national spaces has to deal with the problems of legitimacy and reproduction of the internal social order. The crises of legitimacy and interstate conflict give rise, as we have been discussing, to nationalist, populist, and protectionist tendencies that reflect contradictory attempts to refound state legitimacy under the destabilizing conditions of capitalist globalization. States push nationalist and xenophobic discourses in an attempt to sublimate and externalize social and political tensions onto vulnerable groups, political rivals, or more peripheral regions.

Every U.S. administration in the twenty-first century has imposed tariffs and other protectionist measures of one sort or another. Yet this protectionism has decidedly *not* been directed at keeping out "foreign capital" but at attracting transnational corporate and financial investors. "America is open for business," U.S. president Donald Trump declared to these investors at the 2018 meeting of the global elite gathered for the annual conclave of the World Economic Forum in Davos, Switzerland, shortly before imposing tariffs on China, the EU, and other countries. "Now is the perfect time to bring your business, your jobs and your investments to the United States."[23] Transnational

---

[23] Joah Bierman, "A Sales Pitch for Davos Globalists," *Los Angeles Times*, January 26, 2018, p. A3.

capitalists will invest wherever they find the best conditions to make a profit. Protectionism offers the TCC incentives to invest inside rather than outside the borders of a particular country. State subsidies, tariffs, dirigisme, and other nationalist economic policies have been on the rise around the world to attract transnational capital in search of investment opportunities. Governments around the world adopted over 1,500 policies in the early 2020s to promote specific industries in their territories compared to almost none in the 2010s.[24] Each state seeks to reduce risks to its internal economy in the face of global financial turmoil and political instability by doubling down on these policies in order to force, or incentivize, TNCs to spatially restructure their accumulation strategies. Successive U.S. administrations in the twenty-first century pursued subsidies, tax credits, and tariffs to entice transnational investors, triggering subsidy and protectionist wars among the United States, the EU, and China.[25] This is a radically different protectionist regime than in the nineteenth and twentieth centuries, when it sought to *keep out* foreign capital in order to boost domestic capital. As the crisis deepens now, politics may come to overdetermine economics, or, to say this another way, the political interests of states may trump the economic interests of transnational capitalists.

The TCC has opposed protectionism and state interference in accumulation strategies. Capital's rationale for going global was to escape national economic, techno-industrial, and social constraints on the rate of profit and it has no intention of returning to the confines of the nation-state. The US Chamber of Commerce, the National Association of Manufacturers, the National Retail Federation, and other corporate bodies opposed US tariffs and other measures against China.[26]

---

[24] The Economist, "The Great Regression: Globalization in Reverse," May 11, 2024, pp. 13–15.

[25] See: Patricia Cohen, "The Global Turn Away from Free-Market Policies Worry Economists," *New York Times*, April 17, 2024, www.nytimes.com/2024/04/17/business/economy/industrial-policies-global-economy.html; Simon Evenett, Adam Jakubik, Fernando Martín and Michele Ruta, "The Return of Industrial Policy in Data," IMF Working Papers, WP/24/1, International Monetary Fund, January 2024, file:///Users/user./Downloads/IMF%20-%20Return%20of%20Industrial%20Policy%202024.pdf. *The Economist*, "The Great Regression: Globalization in Reverse," May 11, 2024, pp. 13–15.

[26] See, inter-alia, Ana Swanson, "U.S. Weighs Tariff Relief but Some Fear China Will Take Advantage," *The New York Times*, March 15, 2020, www.nytimes.com/2020/03/15/business/economy/us-china-tariffs-coronavirus.html.

Chinese- and U.S.-based transnational capitalists want access to the markets of both nations. They want to freely exploit U.S. and Chinese workers and to circulate their capital unimpeded by states. The U.S. and the Chinese states began to take measures in the mid 2020s, against the wishes of the TCC, to undercut transnational capital integration among U.S.- and Chinese-based transnational corporate and financial conglomerates. These conglomerates are inextricably cross-invested among themselves and around the world, a process that, far from reversing, actually *deepened* in the first half of the 2020s even in the midst of the New Cold War.[27] U.S.–China financial integration accelerated during the second and into the third decade of the century.[28]

In 2022, the Biden administration restricted investments in Chinese entities involved in semiconductors, microelectronics, and artificial intelligence systems. But it did so in the face of opposition from Nvidia, Intel, and Qualcomm, three of the world's largest U.S.-based chipmakers.[29] "Industry is united: we don't want this," declared one corporate consultant.[30] Most observers attribute global political dynamics to capitalist competition among nation-states but fail to see how the political contradictions generated by the legitimacy crisis feed back into economics. As U.S.–China tensions heated up in the late 2010s, for instance, U.S.-based

---

[27] The Rhodium Group publishes ongoing reports on the inextricable entanglement of U.S. and China-based transnational corporate capital and finance. See https://rhg.com/research-topic/china/. See also Jerry Harris, "China's Threat to Global Capitalism: Nationalist Nonsense," *Socialism and Democracy*, 3(1), 2021, pp. 92–115.

[28] Ronald W. Cox, "The Crisis of Capitalism Through Global Value Chains," *Class, Race and Corporate Power*, 7(1), 2019, https://digitalcommons.fiu.edu/cgi/viewcontent.cgi?article=1134&context=classracecorporatepower.

[29] Tripp Mickle, David McCabe, and Ana Swanson. "How the Big Chip Makers Are Pushing Back on Biden's China Agenda." *The New York Times*, October 5, 2023, www.nytimes.com/2023/10/05/technology/chip-makers-china-lobbying.html?searchResultPosition=1. China consumed in 2022 more than 70 percent of the world's semiconductor products, but it only produced 15 percent of them, and at that, the least technologically sophisticated ones. Marco D'eramo described the Biden move as a declaration of world war, given the pivotal role of semiconductors in China's economic rise and its extreme dependence on a global microchip industry over which the U.S. state is able to exercise a significant degree of control. See Marco D'eramo, "Circuits of War," *Sidecar* (*New Left Review*), November 14, 2022, https://newleftreview.org/sidecar/posts/circuits-of-war.

[30] As cited in Ana Swanson and Lauren Hirsch, "U.S. Aims to Curtail Technology Investment in China," *The New York Times*, February 9, 2023, www.nytimes.com/2023/02/09/business/us-china-investing-tech-biden.html.

transnational corporations were hesitant to swap board seats with Chinese-based firms with which they were cross-invested. Their hesitancy was not due to intercorporate competition but because they feared that Trump's political rhetoric over China would bring them political difficulties.[31] "Companies find themselves pushed in all directions" as governments try to manipulate corporate behavior, observed *The Economist*. "Businesses cannot hide from politics and geopolitics."[32]

This is a similar story for U.S.–Russia relations. Russian natural resources are highly coveted by global investment capital, and in the aftermath of the breakup of the Soviet Union in 1992, several trillion dollars in foreign investment poured into the country. The 2022 Russian invasion of Ukraine was a boon to military-industrial corporations (see Chapter 5). However, Western sanctions imposed on Russia forced a withdrawal of Western-based financial investment firms and other transnational corporate investors from Russian markets. The sanctions imposed a suspension of trading of Russian securities in Western stock markets. Hence, both Russian and Western state policies forcibly disentangled transnational capital from Russia and forced a reordering of transnational accumulation patterns in the Eurasian region. Yet many Western-based corporations continued to do business as usual in Russia, finding ways to get around war and sanctions.[33] "The war in Ukraine has exposed how multinational corporations have become less willing to fully comply with the directives of any single government, including the U.S., when it conflicts with their financial interests," observes Ruehl in *Eurasia Review*, noting that many Western-based companies, even in the midst of war, have continued to operate in both Russia and Ukraine. Similarly, the largest Chinese-based commercial drone company, DJI, became the largest provider of drones to *both* Russia *and* Ukraine. "Instead of marching in lockstep with Washington," he concludes, "companies appear more willing to try to maintain ties to the U.S. while simultaneously maintaining and building ties with countries hostile to it."[34]

---

[31] *The Economist*. "Snowbalization," January 26, 2019, www.economist.com/leaders/2019/01/24/the-steam-has-gone-out-of-globalisation.
[32] *The Economist*, "The Overstretched CEO," August 12, 2023, p. 9.
[33] Phillips, *Titans*, pp. 203–210.
[34] John P. Ruehl, "How Corporations are Fueling Geopolitical Tensions and Global Conflicts in the 21st Century," *Eurasia Review*, June 19, 2024, www.eurasiareview.com/19062024-how-corporations-are-fueling-geopolitical-tensions-and-global-conflicts-in-the-21st-century-oped/.

Nonetheless, the Russian invasion of Ukraine and its aftermath have contributed to an ongoing spatial reorganization of the global economy in such a way, to reiterate, that *politics becomes overdetermined*. Rather than seeing growing interstate rivalry and geopolitical conflict as a clash among national capitalists – the evidence does not support such an interpretation – we want to focus on how the nationalist and protectionist measures taken by states lead transnational capitalists to adjust their own global accumulation strategies in ways that may end up generating new patterns of transnational capitalist competition. There may come a point where state strategies for reconstituting domestic legitimacy fan such interstate conflict and geopolitical rivalry that they make impossible further transnational capitalist integration across the national borders of competing states. Silicon Valley venture capital firms, for instance, had to shelve plans in 2023 for expanding their investments in China, while at the same time their Chinese counterparts faced rapidly escalating political difficulties in the United States. The political will of states facing crises of legitimacy is bending and restricting the circuits of transnational capital accumulation. Deals for Chinese start-ups that included U.S. investors declined 88 percent between 2021 and 2023, from $47 billion to $5.6 billion.[35]

The structure of global capital and the relationship within that structure between transnational capital and local, national, and regional fractions is a matter of empirical research, as is the possibility that state capital, in which state managers and capitalists overlap, may be pulled into conflicting directions. Even at that, however, we generally find that what appear as national capitals are quite transnational. The global financial system, including the murky world of shadow banking, acts as a mechanism for the transnational integration of capitals in ways that require us to move beyond surface appearance. There are some 100 offshore financial centers, for instance, that operate beyond the control of individual states and often outside of official ledgers. In order to avoid sanctions following the 2022 Russian invasion of Ukraine, the Russian-based oil giant, Rosneft, raised some $15 billion in these financial centers through a joint venture with the Qatari Investment Authority and the Swiss-based trading and mining

---

[35] For these details, see Erin Griffith, "Silicon Valley Venture Capitalists Are Breaking Up With China," *The New York Times*, February 21, 2024, www.nytimes.com/2024/02/21/technology/silicon-valley-vc-china.html.

conglomerate Glencore, a deal managed by a Singapore company owned in turn by a London-based firm, interlocking these capitals to one another. The deal, according to researchers Hendrikse and Fernandez, "shows how the rich and powerful hide and transfer their assets, including large transactions of geopolitical significance, in complete anonymity." Uncovering the tangle of global financial capital "allows us to counter the idea that the many nationalists currently rising across the world are 'challengers' to the global order."[36]

Harris observes with regard to U.S.–Chinese economic integration that state-owned enterprises (SOEs) dominate significant sections of the Chinese economy, but transnational capital from the United States (and around the world) has invested heavily in SOEs. Blackrock, the largest investment management firm in the world, has multi-billion-dollar investments in the Bank of China, ICSB, China Construction Bank, China Life Insurance, China Pacific Insurance, CITIC, SINOPEC, PetroChina, China Rail Construction Corporation, China Engineering General Corporation, China Telecommunications, and China Communications Construction Corporate, among others. This same pattern holds for other leading global financial conglomerates, including HSBC, JP Morgan, State Street, Vanguard, UBS, Invesco, Barclays, Deutsch Bank, BNP Paribas, and many others.[37] When any of these SOEs, or, for that matter, private Chinese-based corporations, invest around the world, their transnational coinvestors also profit. Both state and private Chinese-based corporations have also invested extensively in U.S.-based TNCs, among them AIG, Apple, Bank of America, Blackstone, Citigroup, Coca-Cola, Johnson & Johnson, Morgan Stanley, Motorola, News Corp, and Visa, among others. As I noted in the Introduction, and as has now been widely researched and documented, the leading global corporate and financial conglomerates are so transnationally entangled among themselves that separating them out into national boxes or into clearly delineated companies, much less countries, is simply impossible – they constitute

---

[36] Reijer Hendrikse and Rodrigo Fernandez, "Offshore Finance: How Capital Rules the World," Amsterdam, Transnational Institute, January 16, 2019, https://longreads.tni.org/stateofpower/offshore-finance.

[37] Jerry R. Harris, "Who Leads Global Capitalism? The Unlikely Rise of China," *Class, Race and Corporate Power*, 6(1), 2018, pp. 8–10, https://digitalcommons.fiu.edu/cgi/viewcontent.cgi?article=1119&context=classracecorporatepower.

a self-invested network of interlocking capital that spans the globe. As one UNCTAD report noted in 2016, "corporate nationality, and with it the nationality of investors in and owners of foreign affiliates, is becoming increasingly blurred."[38]

The economic and the political are two moments in a larger totality that form a tension-ridden and contradictory unity. To say that transnational capital is not tethered to *territory*, as I insist, is not to say that it is not tethered to *national states*, not as geographic spaces but as centers of power. The state is an institutionalized relationship of power. The extent to which clusters of transnational capital may retain special relationships with the nation-states from whose cocoon they sprung is as well a matter of empirical research. But we do not want to confuse national capital that operates outside of national borders with transnational capital.[39] No historic process is static; all processes are subject to reversals that do not return us to the status quo ante but to a new set of circumstances.

A more expansive analysis, especially with regard to complex levels of mediation, will have to await another study. However, it is clear that the state and the TCC can have conflicting objectives. Unlike global capitalists, state managers and political elites reproduce their status within the nation-state and in relation to the international system. Yet states and state elites, in order to reproduce themselves, must reproduce *not national* but *transnational* capital. By explaining the escalation of geopolitical conflict as national economic rivalry, we not only simplify this relationship; we end up committing the error of economism. The capitalist state, by definition, must reproduce capital. To say this does not mean that the capitalist state is a mere instrument of capital. Its policies may contradict those of specific capitalist groups or, under certain historical circumstances, of capital as a whole.

---

[38] Ibid.
[39] Some capitals are able to do so across multiple borders and in the global system at large, while others are more limited in their scope, yet they enter global circuits through the financial system and other mechanisms of integration. There are local and national capitalist groups that do not have the same capacity as transnational capitalists and compete over local and regional control. The temptation here is to make some inappropriate distinction between "national capital" and "imperialist capital," which is an utter analytical and ideological confusion. It is a matter of empirical investigation as to whether more local and nationally grounded fractions of capital are able to influence states in their interests or in their competition with transnational capital.

The Escalation of International Tension and Geopolitical Conflict

We have established that *inter*-national tensions derive from the very dynamics of global capitalism. Key to understanding the escalation of these tensions as the epochal crisis deepens is the relationship of the TCC to states and the relationship of states to different class groups within the totality of global capital. In production, capital and labor confront one another. In the market, capital confronts capital in competition. Oligopolist clusters of transnational capital compete over world market shares and shares of world surplus value. They do so against a background grid of multiple political jurisdictions that constitute both obstacles and opportunities. The challenge we face is how to explain the escalation of geopolitical tensions and interstate conflict so epitomized by the Ukraine conflict and the New Cold War between the United States and China, *despite* transnational capitalist integration. If this conflict cannot be attributed to competition among national capitalist groups, how do we explain it? The class/capital-theoretic attempts to explain the state form, interstate conflict, and geopolitics as derivations, in the first instance, of social and class forces as these forces develop historically, globally, and in struggle. The focus is on the relationship of state forms and state cadres to transnational capital accumulation. There are looming theoretical issues that I cannot address here. Suffice it to note that this relationship becomes more complicated in times of crisis and transformation, especially when the national state that serves as a hegemonic anchor for world capitalism, in this case the United States, enters into decline.

Robert Cox, the leading figure in the Gramscian school of international relations, suggested in his 1987 landmark study, *Production, Power, and World Order*, that international relations develop out of the interaction among "state-civil society complexes."[40] Dutch political economist Kees van der Pijl identifies what he calls a Lockean heartland at the center of the global political economy, comprised of the core Anglophone states of the world capitalist system that originally fostered the development of capitalist social relations. This liberal state-society complex of the Lockean heartland has faced distinct historical

---

[40] Robert W. Cox, *Production, Power, and World Order: Social Forces in the Making of History* (New York: Columbia University Press, 1987).

challenges from rival Hobbesian "contender states," first from France, Germany, and Italy from the eighteenth to the mid twentieth centuries, then from the Soviet Union, and now from China. Van der Pijl argues that state managers – in his terms, a "managerial cadre" – play a greater role in the structure of the global political economy and the international system in major crises such as the 1930s, the 1970s, and, I argue, since 2008. If not checked by popular mobilization, the intervention of this cadre may assume authoritarian forms.[41]

Van der Pijl's approach helps us understand how escalating international tension and geopolitical conflict derive from the relationship of state elites in different countries to global capital accumulation. World capitalist crises open up room for state elites to mold the transnational environment in such a way that gives their national social formations advantages in the organization of world capital accumulation. Following Van der Pijl, I suggest as a proposition requiring further study that state managers as status groups from weaker or "Hobbesian states" would tend to have a more contentious relationship to transnational capital in the age of globalization, *especially at moments of crisis and transformation such as the present*, since they must do more to "refract" global accumulation into their territories and exercise greater control over it than in the "Lockean states" in order to secure their own reproduction and the reproduction of the national social formations over which they govern.

I differ with van der Pijl, however, on the notion of state cadre as a "state class." Classes in the Marxist approach are defined by their relationship to the process of production. State managers or cadre, in my view, constitute a bureaucratic or administrative caste. Distinct bureaucratic states and political elites may be interwoven with capitalist groups, but they are not necessarily capitalists. They form a distinct stratum whose interests do not necessarily coincide with those of various capitalist groups in competition. However – and this is the crux of the matter – a state cadre can only reproduce itself by reproducing capital, specifically in the age of globalization, *transnational* capital. The state form in the Marxist approach is ultimately derived from the political economy of civil society. Global capital is now embedded

---

[41] Kees van der Pijl, *Transnational Classes and International Relations* (New York: Routledge, 1998).

in every nation-state, in the political economy of every national civil society. Following Van der Pijl, Senalp, Kucucker, and Sengor-Senalp argue, and I concur, that contending approaches to the organization of transnational space have acquired at this time world-historic significance, in which "neoliberal capitalism embedded in the West is locked in battle with a state-directed capitalism" centered especially in China.[42]

Van der Pijl claims that in the Hobbesian contender states, "the social-economic power of a ruling class is not differentiated from the political role of a governing class."[43] I do not believe, however, that we can collapse the distinction. There may be gradations of differentiation between the economically dominant classes and the politically ruling classes, insofar as this relationship is *less* differentiated in the Hobbesian than in the Lockean states. We are more likely to see statist versions of capitalism when, for one or another historical reason, capitalist hegemony in civil society is weak and tenuous, and as a result, political and economic elites must rely more directly on state power in civil society and over capital for their own development – and for the development of capitalism within national borders. In China, Russia, and other "Hobbesian" state capitalist systems, the bourgeoisie has to share surplus value with state elites and bureaucracies. Such "strong states" in earlier moments in the world capitalist system carried out "revolutions from above," or what Gramsci called passive revolutions, in which states imposed themselves on civil society, undertaking transformations from above to hasten bourgeois class formation and to bring about a more effective and hegemonic capitalist development.[44] In the age of capitalist

---

[42] M. Gursan Senalp, M. Can Kucucker, and Esra Sengor-Senalp, "Transnational Rivalries and Left Politics: An Amsterdam School Perspective on Turkey's 'Ergenekon' Trials," *Science & Society*, 86(3), 2022, p. 255.

[43] Kees van der Pijl, "Arab Spring, Turkish Summer? The Trajectory of a Pro-Western 'Moderate Islam.'" *NOREF Report*, 2012b, as cited and discussed by Senalp, Kucucker, and Sengor-Senalp, p. 255 and on.

[44] See, inter-alia, the classical works by Ellen Kay Trimberger, *Revolution from Above: Military Bureaucrats and Development in Japan, Turkey, Egypt, and Peru* (Piscataway: Transaction Books, 1978), and by Theda Skocpol, *States and Social Revolutions: A Comparative Analysis of France, Russia and China* (Cambridge: Cambridge University Press, 1979). For Gramsci on passive revolution, see various sections in Antonio Gramsci, *Selections from Prison Notebooks* (New York: International Publishers, 1971, esp. pp. 104–114. Gramsci writes (p. 105):

globalization, these states may be more likely to contest the unrestricted freedom of transnational capital or to intervene in the circuits of global accumulation.

This is certainly the case for China, a country that experienced a transition to capitalism starting in the late twentieth century after several decades of socialist transformation in such a way that transnational capital has achieved its dominance in the economy but not its hegemony in Chinese society or the more direct forms of control over the Chinese state typical of the so-called Lockian states. The Chinese state capitalist model rests on a complex of state-private companies. More than 130,000 state-private joint ventures represented a third of all registered capital in the country in 2019.[45] Capitalism with Chinese characteristics has involved the rise of a powerful Chinese TCC contingent, fused with a state-party elite dependent on the reproduction of capital, and superrich and high-consumption middle classes, fueled by a devastating wave of primitive accumulation in the countryside and escalating exploitation of hundreds of millions of Chinese workers. Chinese state capitalism has not followed the neoliberal route to transnational capitalist integration. The state plays a key role in the financial system, in regulating private capital (which accounts for three-fifths of output and four-fifths of urban employment[46]), in massive public expenditure, especially in infrastructure, and in planning. This has allowed it to develop twenty-first-century infrastructure, to undertake cutting-edge Research & Development, and to guide capital accumulation into aims broader than that of immediate profit-making, something that the Western capitalist states have not been able to accomplish in recent decades due to the more thorough subordination of the state to private capital and the rollback of public sectors, privatization, and deregulation it has entailed.

> This fact is of the greatest importance for the concept of "passive revolution" – the fact, that is, that what was involved was not a social group which "led" other groups, but a State which, even though it had limitations as a power, "led" the group which should have been "leading" and was able to put at the latter's disposition an army and a politico-diplomatic strength.

[45] *The Economist*, "The Party Capitalists," November 20, 2021, pp. 59–60.
[46] Keith Bradsher, "China's Economy is Slowing, A Worrying Sign for the World," *New York Times*, January 17, 2022, www.nytimes.com/2022/01/16/business/economy/china-economy.html.

As the crisis deepens, competition between the Western model of neoliberal capitalism, to which the state cadre in the traditional core countries are beholden for their advantage in interstate competition, and the Chinese model of state capitalism explains at least a part of the rising U.S.–China geopolitical conflict. U.S. policy toward China in the first two decades of the twenty-first century sought to open China up to transnational capital – to break with continued state control over the financial system, to allow foreign investors more than a 49 percent share in corporate ownership, to remove trade restrictions, and so on. Chronic stagnation in the global economy is resulting in intensified transnational corporate competition for shares of total global surplus value.[47] However, far from a decoupling, U.S.–China financial integration actually accelerated during the second and into the third decade of the century.[48] In 2024, U.S.-based investors held $1.1 trillion in equity issued by Chinese-based companies.[49] Ronald Cox observes, and I concur, that the Chinese state acts to mediate the political and economic conditions necessary to expand global capitalism into a vast global value chain network, and that the key battle within transnational conglomerates is over the extraction of surplus value from the China market. The fight over the distribution of surplus value does not pit "Chinese" and "U.S." capital against each other but transnational clusters against one another and in relation to a Chinese state that mediates this competition in such a way as to advance the interests of those clusters closest to it.

Scholars and pundits alike have framed escalating interstate conflict in terms of a declining U.S. hegemony and the rise of a Chinese competitor. Li argues that the U.S.-centric capitalist world system will be replaced in the next few decades by an Asia-centered world order.[50] Wallerstein has predicted that the U.S.-centered system will not survive

---

[47] James Manyika, "Playing to Win: The New Global Competition for Corporate Profits," McKinsey Global Institute, October 20, 2015, www.mckinsey.com/mgi/overview/in-the-news/playing-to-win-the-new-global-competition-for-corporate-profits.
[48] Ronald W. Cox, "The Crisis of Capitalism Through Global Value Chains," *Class, Race and Corporate Power*, 7(1), 2019, https://digitalcommons.fiu.edu/cgi/viewcontent.cgi?article=1134&context=classracecorporatepower.
[49] Rhodium (a corporate research firm), "China" section, continually updated, accessed here on March 29, 2024, https://rhg.com/research-topic/china/.
[50] Minqi Li, *The Rise of China and the Demise of the Capitalist World Economy* (London: Pluto, 2008).

into the second half of the twenty-first century.[51] In Arrighi's analysis, world capitalism experiences long waves in its development that he calls systemic cycles of accumulation. These cycles have played out in four "long centuries" since 1400, each associated with a hegemonic center – from the Italian city-states to the Netherlands, followed by Britain and then the United States, and now shifting toward China. Each hegemon goes through a period of ascent involving material expansion followed by a decline characterized by financialization in the center.[52] Hegemonic stability theory developed by international relations scholars last century argued similarly that the international system remains stable when there is a single dominant world power, or hegemon, but then becomes destabilized in the transition from one hegemon to another.[53]

These comparative historical approaches are of great historical importance but of limited utility in understanding the trajectory of the current crisis. This is because no new nation-state power can supply the political authority necessary to stabilize the now-inextricably integrated global economy (much less to reverse the ecological meltdown that is the topic of Chapter 4). The crisis of hegemony in the international system takes place within this single, integrated global economy even if a model of Chinese state capitalism were to become generalized. No national or regional economy can survive outside of its integration into the larger global economy. Neither can any single state, no matter how powerful, control the process of global accumulation. The United States progressively lost this ability as capitalist globalization advanced. The U.S. position as a hegemonic anchor of world capitalism is crumbling, and with it, the ability of the U.S. state to determine outcomes. The new wave of U.S. interventionism worldwide in recent decades that some referred to, confusingly, as "the new imperialism,"[54] has been, at least in part, a desperate and futile

---

[51] P. Schouten, "Theory Talk #13: Immanuel Wallerstein on World-Systems, The Imminent End of Capitalism and Unifying Social Science," *Theory Talks*, 2008, accessed on December 10, 2021 at https://iwallerstein.com/wp-content/uploads/docs/THYTLK13.PDF.

[52] Giovanni Arrighi, *The Long Twentieth Century; Money, Power, and the Origins of Our Times* (London: Verso, 1994).

[53] For a review of the literature from this approach, see Robert Gilpin, *The Political Economy of International Relations* (Princeton: Princeton University Press, 1987).

[54] See most notably David Harvey, *The New Imperialism* (New York: Oxford University Press, 2005).

attempt by U.S. policymakers to recover the ability to regulate global capitalism and to determine outcomes.

What about Imperialism?

Escalating interstate competition and geopolitical conflict has been framed by many as a new stage of inter-imperialist rivalry, an approach that remains highly problematic for reasons that I have expounded on elsewhere.[55] I am not convinced that we should retain the term, if not the concept, of imperialism in place of coming up with new ways to conceive and speak of transnational exploitation and political and military interventions of states in relation to that exploitation.[56] Most Marxists and non-Marxists alike fixate on the extra-economic processes alone, such as military intervention or political domination, and moreover tend to separate the critique of imperialism from that of capitalism. If we start the analysis of imperialism with the economic, we are forced to focus on the transnationalization of capital and the rise of a globally integrated production, financial, and service system through which global capital controls resources and exploits global labor. The questions we must then ask are: Who is doing the exploitation and who is being exploited in the global capitalist system? How can we understand the political and military processes that facilitate these worldwide relations of exploitation? What is the relationship between U.S. interventionism and transnational capital accumulation? What are the *class interests* behind what the U.S. state does around the world?

---

[55] See, inter-alia, the following publications by William I. Robinson: "The Travesty of 'Anti-Imperialism'," *Journal of World-Systems Research*, 29(2), 2023, https://jwsr.pitt.edu/ojs/jwsr/article/view/1221/1628; *Global Capitalism and the Crisis of Humanity*, Chapter 3, "Beyond the Theory of Imperialism," "Imperialism, Anti-Imperialism, and Transnational Class Exploitation," and "On Imperialism: Reply to the S&S Symposium," both in "Symposium on Imperialism and Anti-Imperialism," *Science & Society*, 88(3), 2024.
[56] The problem lies, in part, in making transhistoric categories of analysis that are historical. In each historic epoch of capitalism, "categories of analysis have a distinct character that breaths through them," notes researcher Tarang Saluja. "Understanding the Logic of Settler-Colonialism, Repression, and Necropolitics from the Perspective of Transnational Penetration: Changes in the Function of Land from National to Transnational Accumulation," 2024, p. 33. Unpublished manuscript provided to the author.

If imperialism refers to the appropriation of resources and the exploitation of labor by capital across national borders and the flow of the surplus value therein extracted back across borders, then there is no doubt that such imperialism now occurs all over the world, in multiple directions, and there are numerous imperialist states, including in the former Third World. This proposition is problematic – not, however, because it implicates so-called "oppressed nations" in the former Third World in the global webs of capitalist exploitation, but because, to begin with, it frames imperialism in terms of oppressed and oppressor (or imperialist) nations. A nation cannot exploit another nation. This is an utter reification. Classes exploit and are exploited. Imperialism has always been a *violent class relation* not between countries but between global capital and global labor, a *class project* mediated, however, through a world economy politically divided into national jurisdictions and by the uneven accumulation of capital on a world scale. How do we understand this relationship in the contemporary era of globalized capitalism, that is, the relationship of transnational capital and class to the state, and specifically to the nation-state?

As we have already discussed, capitalism is by its very nature expansionary. In this sense, imperialism refers to an economic (class) relationship facilitated by extra-economic political, military, and ideological processes. As capital expanded out violently from its original Western heartland, it plundered and exploited the colonial regions and extracted out of them surplus value that was accumulated in metropolitical centers. But these relations of appropriation and exploitation, and the subsequent flows of surplus value, now take place all over the world and do not resemble the earlier structure in which Western colonial capital simply syphoned out surplus value from the colonies and deposited it back in colonial coffers. These transnational class relations come into focus once we replace the notion of imperialism as a relationship among countries with an analysis that focuses on the webs of transnational class exploitation mediated through states.

My detractors will raise at least two objections: the center-periphery structure of world capitalism and the massively outsized role of U.S. control and interventionism around the world. On the first, there remains an international division of labor and a center-peripheral structure of transnational class relations forged through the centuries of colonialism and imperialism. While this structure has been experiencing substantial transformations,⁵⁷ it remains true that labor is more intensely exploited in the former Third World and the absolute savagery of capital is more fully on display. The North-South divide does not explain but is explained by transnational class dynamics. The uneven development of global capitalism benefits the TCC of all countries insofar as its members can access the cheapest labor and other accumulation considerations around the world. The relationship of the core-periphery structure of the world economy to global capitalism cannot be understood in terms that correspond to earlier centuries, and especially not in terms of some bourgeoisie in peripheral regions oppressed by metropolitan capital and prepared to join class alliances with workers and peasants of the countries where they (but not necessarily their capital) reside, and as if there is some fundamental difference if exploitation is between people born in the same country or those born in different countries. The toiling masses of the former Third World are superexploited by transnational capital. But who is doing this exploitation is not an "oppressor nation" and not necessarily Western-based capital but transnational capitalists from around the world.

When Lenin published in 1917 his famous essay *Imperialism: The Highest Stage of Capitalism*,⁵⁸ much of the former Third World consisted of colonies, had not fully transitioned into capitalism, and did not have powerful bourgeoisies that operated across the globe. Now, powerful transnational corporate and financial conglomerates from the former Third World – from so-called "oppressed nations" – export their capital, appropriate resources, and exploit labor around the world in the same way as European imperial powers did in Lenin's time. Already in 2015, the fifty largest companies from "emerging markets" increased from 19 to 40 percent the portion of their revenue from overseas activity, while more than half of all corporate revenue growth from 2015 to 2025 was expected to come from these

---

⁵⁷ A global, rather than international, division of labor is a more useful conception. Moreover, as I have discussed elsewhere, center and periphery cannot be conceived as territory. See, inter-alia, Robinson, 2002, 2014. William I. Robinson, "Remapping Development in Light of Globalization: From a Territorial to a Social Cartography," *Third World Quarterly*, 23, 2002, p. 6.
⁵⁸ The essay is available here: www.marxists.org/archive/lenin/works/1916/imp-hsc/imperialism.pdf.

companies.⁵⁹ The Brazilian-based transnational conglomerate, Vale, one of the world's largest integrated mining companies, ceased being a "Brazilian" company in the twenty-first century.⁶⁰ It has operations on every continent and exploits tens of thousands of workers in the traditional North American and European core.

But there are countless other examples. The Indian-based Tata conglomerate is the single largest manufacturing employer (and therefore capitalist exploiter of labor) in the United Kingdom.⁶¹ Chinese-based corporations operate in every continent, including throughout North America and Europe, where they exploit U.S. and European workers. Mexican-based transnationals invest throughout the Americas and beyond, exploiting workers of all nationalities, as do Gulf-based capitalists. Moreover, as we have already seen, when we set about to analyze the structure of global capital, we find an expanding complex of interlocked networks that crisscross the world and a very high degree of transnational integration, especially through the circuits of global finance. Private and state corporations based in China control most of the production of cobalt in the Congo, in the process brutally exploiting Congolese miners and plundering the country.⁶² Yet global corporate and financial conglomerates from around the world are invested in these Chinese-based corporations. In turn, that cobalt goes back to industrial circuits in Asia where iPhones and other electronic equipment are manufactured by transnational capital and marketed worldwide. When we study the actual structure of ownership of Apple, to take the case of iPhones, we find that transnational capitalists and financial holding companies from around the world are invested in the company.⁶³

---

⁵⁹ Richard Dobbs, Tim Koller, Sree Ramaswamy, Jonathan Woetzel, James Manyika, Rohit Krishnan, and Nicoló Andreula, "Playing to Win: The New Global Competition for Corporate Profits," McKinsey Global Institute, September 2015, Executive Summary, file:///Users/user./Downloads/mgi%20global%20competition_executive%20summary_sep%202015.pdf, pp. 10, 13.

⁶⁰ Thiago Aguiar, *The Shifting Ground of Globalization: Labor and Mineral Extraction at Vale S.A.* (New York: Boston: Brill, 2023).

⁶¹ *The Economist.* "Tata for Now." September 10, 2011, www.economist.com/britain/2011/09/10/tata-for-now.

⁶² For discussion, see Siddharth Kara, *Cobalt Red: How the Blood of the Congo Powers Our Lives* (New York: St. Martins Press, 2023).

⁶³ On the Apple value chain and the structure of ownership, see William I. Robinson, *Can Global Capitalism Endure?* (Atlanta: Clarity, 2022).

The US state has played the preponderant role for much of the past half century in making the world available to and safe for transnational capital, as a battering ram to force open space for capital to accumulate and as a wrecking ball to smash apart any resistance to it. It has wielded a battery of political, military, and economic instruments in this endeavor, from military interventions and the orchestration of coup d'états, to the application of economic sanctions, structural adjustment programs, free trade agreements, and financial leverage.[64] Rather than sealing off intervened regions to capitalists from other countries, this U.S. interventionism has *opened them up* to transnational capital regardless of national origin.[65] Globalization has opened up new spaces for capital exports from China and other countries traditionally in the periphery, among them the Gulf states, Turkey, Mexico, Brazil, and India. Capitalists from these countries are able to invest in the former Third World without first sending in their own military forces or organizing coup d'états because five centuries of colonialism and imperialism already opened up the world to transnational capital and, until recently, the U.S. interventionist machine has kept it open.

The United States props up repressive governments in Latin America, as does France in Africa, whereas in these same countries Chinese or other transnational investors exploit labor but do not intervene politically or militarily to prop up repressive states. What is the relationship here between Western intervention and Chinese capitalist exploitation? We return again to the relationship between the economic and the political, in this case the relationship of capital to the state, and specifically, the relationship between U.S. interventionism and

---

[64] Once we clear away the smoke and mirrors of political rhetoric, even NATO interventions have served the purpose in the first instance of opening up space for the TCC. One 2016 report on the ongoing wars in the Middle East issued by the Atlantic Council, which was founded in 1961 by NATO members and whose board of directors reads like a veritable who's who of the top global corporations, was unambiguous in calling for U.S. led NATO intervention for the purpose of promoting neoliberal economic policies that open up the region to transnational corporate investment. The objective, it stated, "is to support and facilitate 'Big Bang' Regulatory Reforms to foster greater trade, investment, and economic integration, with a special focus on empowering entrepreneurs." See Madeline K. Albright and Stephen J. Hadley, "Middle East Strategy Task Force: Final Report of the Co-Chairs" (New York: Atlantic Council, 2016), p. 5.
[65] See, inter-alia, my discussion in Chapter 3, "Beyond the Theory of Imperialism," in Robinson, *Global Capitalism and the Crisis of Humanity*.

transnational capital accumulation. At the *political* level, it is U.S.-led Western states that are principally, if not exclusively, carrying out international coercive control and aggression against the working and popular classes and against targeted states, whereas at the *economic* level, there is nothing specifically U.S. or Western about intensifying capitalist exploitation and plunder around the world.

Vietnam, to take one example, was bombed back into the Stone Age by the United States, left destroyed and in ruins in the nineteenth and twentieth centuries by French and U.S. imperialists, and then subjected to devastating sanctions, forcing the country open for transnational capital. Now Chinese-based, Western-based, Indian-based, Saudi-based, and Mexican- and Brazilian-based capitalists, along with Vietnamese capitalists themselves, can trade and invest in Vietnam and exploit Vietnamese labor thanks to the historic role of imperialism. The traditional Western core already did the dirty work. There is nothing intrinsically – as distinct from historically – Western about imperialism. It historically had a Western identity because capitalism was born in the West and expanded out from there. This is a very tough analysis for some on the international left to swallow, but that does not make it less true. In this age of globalized capitalism, there is no fundamental difference in exploitation between people born in the same country or those born in different countries, no self-determination of the working classes within capitalism, and no anti-imperialist struggle that is not anti-capitalist. Capital has no nationality. If this was so in the past, it is more than ever true today.

The relationship between Western intervention and exploitation by capitalists from the former Third World, between political and military intervention and the class exploitation that it makes possible, is brought home by the case of the Las Bambas copper mine in Peru. The indigenous communities of the highland province of Apurímac waged bloody struggles in the early 2020s against the open-pit copper mine, one of the largest in the world, that left scores dead and injured. The mine has been owned and operated since 2014 by the Chinese state-private transnational mining conglomerate MMG (the 25 percent that is private includes global investor groups from other countries). In 2022 the government approved the mine's expansion, violently evicting indigenous communities that had blocked roads and camped on mine property. The Peruvian state legally sells policing services to mining companies, enabling MMG to purchase physical force from the police to advance copper extraction by violent means.[66] The global police state entered in the form of the Peruvian military and police forces. In the wake of the 2022 U.S.-backed coup d'état against a left-oriented president, Pedro Castillo, the United States stepped up its training and supplying of the police that were then used by the Chinese corporation to protect their investments.[67] The global police state propped up by the United States made Peruvian copper and labor available to Chinese-originated transnational capital. The "U.S. imperialism" and "inter-imperialist rivalry" perspective utterly misunderstands the nature of such transnational capitalist exploitation and oppression.

The Peruvian case draws out the often-bewildering contradictions between interstate competition and transnational capitalist exploitation – contradictions between the economic *trans*-national and the political *inter*-national. The disjuncture between a globalized economy and a nation-state-based system of political authority that I have placed at the very center of analysis in this chapter generates enormous geopolitical tensions that destabilize the international order and, as we have seen, may overdetermine the process of transnational capitalist integration. The globally integrated economy cannot for much longer continue to operate within a post-WWII international political order that is anachronistic and utterly incapable of stabilizing the system. The political and economic architecture of this post-World War order was already crumbling prior to the 2022 Russian invasion of Ukraine. That invasion and the West's radical political, military, and economic response to it were but its *coup de grâce*.

The end of Western domination of world capitalism is upon us as the center of gravity of the global economy shifts to China. But China will not become a new hegemon. We are moving into a multipolar or polycentric world polity within a single integrated global economy exhibiting several overlapping centers of intense transnational accumulation, such as the North American free trade bloc, the EU,

---

[66] Fabricio Rodríguez "Authoritarian Practices Between 'Para-Coloniality' and "Cheap Security: When Chinese State Capital Meets Neoliberal Copper Mining (and Protests) in Las Bambas, Peru." *Globalizations*, April 19, 2022, www.tandfonline.com/doi/full/10.1080/14747731.2023.2179813.

[67] Prensa Latina, "Concern Over U.S. Arms Supply for Repression in Peru," August 2, 2023, www.plenglish.com/news/2023/08/02/concern-over-u-s-arms-supply-for-repression-in-peru/.

and a Sino-centric Asian economic region, each interlocked with one another. No national or regional economy can survive outside of its integration into the larger global economy. Zones of intense accumulation are not national or regional but global spaces that are magnets for transnational capital. Here we find spaces of intense extractive, industrial, and commercial activity along with labor and raw material supply corridors from within or often outside these zones. This is not a nation-state but a global class geography. The nation-state/interstate system is a political grid superimposed over an integrated economic structure ridden by explosive contradictions.

The political control afforded to the U.S. state by a dollar-denominated global economy is at odds with increasing political multipolarity and with global economic integration. The U.S. state remains at this time the greatest threat to world peace, the command center of the carnage that is global capitalism. Yet the United States is no longer the market of last resort, nor can it continue indefinitely to serve as the liquidity provider of last resort. The dollar, already eroded as the global reserve currency, has come under intense pressure since 2008 given the dollar denomination of much of the global financial system. At some point dollar-denomination of the global economy would have to give way to some new global currency regime that could potentially help reactivation by freeing transnational investment from the dollar or dollar denomination and from the political control this dollarization affords U.S. policymakers. The prevailing distribution of formal decision-making power among states in the post-WWII international order does not reflect radical changes in recent decades in the relative weight of states in the international system, and especially the rise of China. Wars as military affairs are outcomes of other causes. As Clausewitz said, war is politics by other means. But politics is political economy by other means. It is the political economy of global capitalism in crisis that generates pressures for wars, as I will discuss in Chapter 5.

4 | Collapse of the Biosphere

The Infinite Character of Capital in a Finite Biosphere

Science fiction writer Kim Stanley Robinson opens his best-selling 2020 novel, *The Ministry of the Future*, with a wet-bulb heat wave event in India that took the lives of millions of people in a matter of hours.[1] While the novel was a work of fiction, the event it describes is within the realm of the possible, indeed most likely the probable. Wet-bulb temperatures produce the kind of heat from which our organism cannot cool down. It is estimated to be about 35 °C (95 °F) with a relative humidity approaching 100 percent.[2] Putting aside the structural, social, and political dimensions of crisis that we discussed in the previous chapters, even in the best-case scenario for global capitalism, in which digitally driven restructuring unleashes a new round of productive expansion and international stability, the ecological crisis makes it very questionable that capitalism can continue to reproduce itself as a global system.

Each major crisis of world capitalism has involved predictions that the system would collapse in on itself in the face of intractable contradictions. Yet capitalism has repeatedly proved to be more resilient and adaptable than its doomsday forecasters. A number of social scientists have predicted that capitalism will not last into the second half of the twenty-first century. But capitalism as a world system has proved remarkably resilient even as it has faced one crisis after another in its centuries-long existence, emerging renewed after each major crisis. It would be foolish to assume we are in the end game of global

---

[1] Kim Stanley Robinson, *The Ministry of the Future* (New York: Orbit, 2020).
[2] Fady Jameel, "Wet-Bulk Heat is Cooler than You Think," *Abdul Latif Jameel*, April 6, 2021, https://alj.com/en/spotlight-by-fady-jameel/deadly-heat-is-cooler-than-you-think-the-chilling-science-of-wet-bulb-temperatures/. See also Jeff Goodell's popular journalistic account, *The Heat Will Kill You First: Life and Death on a Scorched Planet* (Boston: Little, Brown and Company, 2023).

capitalism. While the outcome is entirely contingent on how class struggles and politics play out, it appears nonetheless that capitalism cannot last into the twenty-second century.

What makes this crisis different than previous ones that shook the world? Controversies over capitalist crises in the early twentieth century, sometimes called "collapse controversies," as I discussed in Chapter 1, as well as those of the 1970s, did not take into account the ecological dimension of capitalist reproduction and its implications for the endless accumulation of capital. The pioneering work of James O'Connor may be an exception. Although ecology was not its main focus, O'Connor argued in his 1984 book, *Accumulation Crisis*, that Marxist theorists of crisis did not take into account "external barriers" to capitalist accumulation in the form of either "limits to growth" or the "availability of natural resources."[3] In the 1990s, O'Connor identified what he termed capitalism's "second contradiction": If the first is between capital and labor, the second is between capitalism and the ecosystem.[4]

While I will discuss the limits of this perspective momentarily, it did open the way for the development of what O'Connor referred to as an ecological Marxism and pointed to what I wish to highlight in this chapter: Capitalism's war on nature, which includes its war on the proletariat, produces the destruction of the very ecosystem that it requires for its reproduction. Never before has crisis and collapse involved such matters as human-induced climate emergencies and mass extinction. An uninhabitable earth, as I will argue in this chapter, is not a place where capital can continue to accumulate. Capitalism is an extinction force. Will the planetary ecosystem collapse before the collapse of capitalism, or will capitalism be overthrown while it is still possible to salvage the planetary ecosystem?

Readers will object, hasn't capitalism been able to overcome its socio-ecological limits in the past? Capital must expand and must conquer the rest of nature along with the conquest of human beings. This process of capitalist expansion is historically finite. For capital there can never be a "final frontier" if crisis is to be displaced in time and space on an ongoing basis by extensive and intensive enlargement.

---

[3] James O'Connor, *Accumulation Crisis* (New York: Basil Blackwell, 1984), p. 6.
[4] James O'Connor, *Natural Causes: Essays in Ecological Marxism* (New York: The Guilford Press, 1997).

However, this is the rub: The infinite character of capitalist accumulation runs up against the finite character of the biosphere. As I discussed in Chapter 2, human beings as producers of surplus value have to be reproduced in order for capital to continue accumulating, whereas the rest of nature has not had to be reproduced up until now, for capital's reproduction, so long as the system continued its outward expansion, continued to crack open new "virgin" frontiers of accumulation, and to appropriate more and more of nature, both human and extra-human.

A new wave of appropriation and commodification of nature has been central to capitalism's globalization boom, and it will also be to any renewed round of worldwide accumulation. At a certain point there is not enough extra-human nature to appropriate; people can no longer reproduce themselves – and as I have suggested, capital, even if by some newfound generosity it wanted to, cannot manage their reproduction. As we saw in Chapter 2, humans are not necessarily needed when quantities or supplies of active and reserve labor as a commodity already suffice and when masses of surplus humanity are on the move and knocking on capital's door. We can conjecture a certain point at which the crisis in value caves the system in. The limits to nature – human and extra-human – mark the limits to capital. It is entirely true that human beings transform the rest of nature at the same time that extra-human nature transforms us, and that the natural limits to capitalist expansion are not predefined or static. Nonetheless, there are limits coming into focus to the indefinite expansion of capital revolving around the exhaustion of the conditions of extra-human nature required for capital's reproduction that we will discuss in this chapter. That said, we want to distinguish from the outset the "limits to growth" ideology that identifies resource scarcity rather than capitalist relations of production as the root problem.

The collapse of global capitalism, even if not by socialist revolution, would not necessarily be a bad thing for a majority of the world's people, especially in the worldwide peripheries. Recall that the collapse of the Roman empire, as Faulkner reminds us, dramatically improved the lot of the former slaves, peasants, and proletarians.[5] David Harvey has argued that the majority of the world's people are now so integrated

---

[5] Neil Faulkner, *Rome: Empire of the Eagles, 753 BC AD 476* (New York: Routledge, 2009).

into the worldwide circuits of capital and therefore so dependent on capital that capitalism is "too big to fail."[6] But he misses the point: Even if we put aside that the reproduction and expansion of global capitalism represents escalating misery, exploitation, and carnage for the global proletariat and surplus humanity, it cannot but fail as it destroys and exhausts its very life support system. The open-ended question – open-ended because the answer depends on collective agency and contingency – is if a world in which capitalist civilization has collapsed is left so ecologically devastated that the remaining humans are unable to pick up life again on a new and improved basis.

Anthropocene or Capitalocene?

The study of ecology has shown that natural and social history, always a dialectical unity, are converging in unprecedented ways. The new epoch in planetary history commonly called the *Anthropocene* highlights what Marx referred to as a *metabolic rift* between human society and natural systems. Capitalist production, said Marx, "disturbs the metabolic interaction between man and earth," or the equilibrium of exchanges, the "metabolism" between human society and natural systems. In the words of Marxist ecological theorist John Foster and his colleagues, there is "a potentially fatal ecological rift emanating from the conflicts and contradictions of the modern capitalist society."[7] Building on Marx's notion of a metabolic rift, Foster and his colleagues warn that "the planet is now dominated by a technologically potent but alienated humanity – alienated from both nature and from itself; and hence ultimately destructive of everything around it."[8]

---

[6] See David Harvey, "Global Unrest," in Harvey (edited by Jordan T. Camp and Chris Caruso), *The Anti-Capitalist Chronicles* (London: Pluto, 2020): discussion in Raju J. Das, "The Good and the Bad in David Harvey's Popular Marxism," *Critical Sociology*, 9, 7/8: 2022, https://journals.sagepub.com/doi/full/10.1177/08969205221137765. To be fair, Harvey observes:

> A socialist and anti-capitalist program will have to negotiate a knife-edge path between preserving that which services the world's population and which appears too big and foundational to fail while confronting the fact that it is becoming too monstrous to survive without sparking geopolitical conflicts that will likely turn the innumerable small wars and internal struggles already raging across the planet into a global conflagration. p. 11.

[7] John Bellamy Foster, Brett Clark, and Richard York, *The Ecological Rift: Capitalism's War on the Earth* (New York: Monthly Review Press, 2010), p. 14.

[8] Foster, Clark, and York, *The Ecological Rift*, 14, 35.

The "world-ecology" perspective developed by Jason Moore and his colleagues takes this unity of natural and social history one crucial step further in their effort to synthesize the theory of accumulation crisis and the study of environmental crisis. In *Capitalism in the Web of Life* that I want to focus on as an introduction to this chapter, Moore rejects the Cartesian dualism of nature and society put forth by the mainstream Anthropocene perspective that views nature as external to humanity. Our relationship to nature can be specified at two levels of abstraction – "humanity-in-nature" and "capitalism-in-nature." Capitalist social relations are not external to the environment but internal to the larger "web of life." They argue that a view of nature as external to humanity is not coincidental. It is an outcome of a capitalist epistemology that came out of the Enlightenment and that converted nature into an externality that can be exploited "to yield its 'free gifts' on the cheap." An ontological approach that identifies "humanity in nature" and "nature in humanity" moves beyond the dualism of "nature and society."[9] Nature/society is not the only dualism, says Moore, "but it is the originary [sic] dualism. The separation of the peasant from the land and the symbolic separation of Humans and Nature were a singular process."[10]

Up until the current crisis, "new technologies and organizations of power and production emerged after great systemic crises, and resolved the older crises by putting nature to work in powerful new ways." The turn toward capitalist globalization after the 1970s was the most recent example, but now it is increasingly difficult to get nature to yield those free gifts. "This indicates we may be not merely in a transition from one phase of capitalism to another, but something more epochal: the breakdown of the strategies and relations that have sustained capital accumulation over the past five centuries."[11] It is important to note that when Moore refers to putting nature to work, he is not just referring to extra-human nature but as well to humans as a part of nature. In his view, the process of primitive accumulation

---

[9] See the groundbreaking work by Jason W. Moore, *Capitalism in the Web of Life: Ecology and the Accumulation of Capital* (London: Verso, 2015), and for a conversation around the idea of the Capitalocene, see Moore (ed.), *Anthropocene or Capitalocene? Nature, History, and the Crisis of Capitalism* (Oakland: PM Press, 2016).
[10] Moore, *Capitalism in the Web of Life*, p. 48.
[11] Ibid., p. 1.

that separated the peasant from the land and "the symbolic separation of Humans and Nature" were a singular process. Capitalism commodifies both nature and labor (which is a natural activity) and therefore instrumentalizes both in function of accumulation. When we reference the violence inflicted on nature, we must recall that humans are part of nature, and when we reference the commodification of nature, we mean also the commodification of the labor (labor power) of *humans as nature*.

The world-ecology project seeks to displace the assumptions associated with the idea of the *Anthropocene* with that of the *Capitalocene*. The term Anthropocene was first coined by atmospheric chemist Paul Crutzen to mark the coming of a new epoch in planetary history that replaced the Holocene, which refers to the stable, interglacial geological epoch dating 10 to 12,000 years ago. Just as the term implies, humanity is seen as the chief driver of rapid changes in the earth system in a new epoch of geological-scale change that enters suddenly into human history itself. In this perspective, there has always been a complex coevolution of nature and human society (human production to be specific), or of "earth systems" and "world systems." At this time, however, the world system is a truly global system and the transformations in natural systems brought about by human activity have now begun, in the words of ecologist Peter Vitousek, to "alter the structure and function of Earth as a system."[12] The concept of the Anthropocene has played an important role in environmental consciousness since the late twentieth century, raising awareness that humanity cannot be separated from the rest of nature, that there is a singular life-pulse or metabolism to nature involving the unity of the reproduction of humanity and of extra-human nature, or, as Marx put it, the human labor process "mediates the metabolism between man and nature."[13]

The coupling or the idea of a coevolution of the earth system and the world system in the Anthropocene approach, even in many radical ecology approaches, underscores the dualism that Moore critiques, in which nature is something external that we act upon. This ontological approach has political consequences: capital remains

---

[12] As cited in John Bellamy Foster, Brett Clark, and Richard York, *The Ecological Rift: Capitalism's War on the Earth* (New York: Monthly Review Press, 2010), p. 35.

[13] Marx, *Capital*, Vol. I, p. 133.

unindicted. The Anthropocene framework involves a metatheory of humanity as a collective agent "without acknowledging the forces of capital and empire that have cohered modern world history."[14] Is anthropogenic destruction of nature the fault of humanity itself or humanity in capitalism? "Accumulation is reckoned as a social process with environmental consequences, rather than a way of bundling human and extra-human nature" in their dialectical unity, insists Moore. "The radical critique of capitalism since 2008 has proceeded in terms entirely agreeable to the Cartesian sorting out of crisis tendencies. One can now add 'climate' or 'ecology' to the proliferating list of significant fractures in twenty-first century capitalism .... but concrete historical wholes – such as capitalism – cannot be constructed by 'adding up' the Social and the Environmental parts."[15] The binary "obscures, more than it illuminates, humanity's place in the web of life," insists Moore. "'Nature plus Society' appears especially unsuited to dealing with today's proliferating crisis – not least those linked to climate change and financialization – and also with the origins and development of these crisis tendencies over the broad sweep of modern world history."[16]

Moore and others who critique the concept of the Anthropocene draw on Neil Smith's pioneering work on the "production of nature," which in turn draws on the Henri Lefevre's classic study, *The Production of Space*.[17] Nature is not something external to the social; the relationship between human and extra-human nature is produced by the dynamics of capital accumulation. This binary "Nature/Society is directly implicated in the colossal violence, inequality, and oppression of the modern world; and that the view of Nature as external is a fundamental condition of capital accumulation." It is not just that humans are natural forces, a part of nature, but so too are human productions – families, empires, corporations, markets, and all the rest are natural forces, as if capitalism acts upon a nature that operates independently of humanity. The Anthropocene approach places humans in one category, nature in another, and the feedbacks between them

---

[14] Moore, *Capitalism in the Web of Life*, p. 171.
[15] Ibid., p. 40.
[16] Ibid., p. 34.
[17] Neil Smith, *Uneven Development: Nature, Capital, and the Production of Space* (Atlanta: University of Georgia Press, 2008, third ed.); Henri Lefebvre, *The Production of Space* (Hoboken: Wiley Blackwell, 1992).

identified. "'*The* economy' and '*the* environment' are not independent of each other." Capitalism is not just an economic or a social system in the Capitalocene approach. It is "*a way of organizing nature*" [emphasis in original],[18] that is, capitalism develops less as an external force acting upon nature than as one operating in and through the web of life. The Anthropocene approach to the metabolic rift remains "captive to the logic of human exceptionalism," says Moore, whereby "relations between humans are regarded as ontologically prior to relations of nature, a meta-theoretical procedure that allows one to speak of modernity as a set of social relations that act upon, rather than develop through, the web of life."[19]

At least as it has become popularized in the media, politics, and the environmental movement itself, the Anthropocene sees the problem not as humanity in capitalism but as humanity itself. Environmentalists operating within its logic date the environmental crisis to the new age of coal and steam inaugurated in the mid eighteenth century with the industrial revolution. Yet urban planner and ecologist Romain Felli, who shares Moore's critique of the lack of class and capital in the Anthropocene concept, observes that the replacement of earlier renewable energy sources such as wind and water by coal at the beginning of the industrial revolution did not owe simply to some technological advantage but rather gave an advantage to emerging capitalists and states in subjecting uprooted peasants to industrial production for the market.[20] "The driving force behind coal and steam?" asks Moore. "Not class. Not capital. Not imperialism. Not even culture.... you guessed it: the Anthropos: Humanity as an undifferentiated whole."[21] The Capitalocene, in contrast, sees the contemporary historic era as shaped not by an abstract Anthropos but by relations that privilege the endless accumulation of capital.

---

[18] Moore, *Capitalism in the Web of Life*, p. 2.
[19] Ibid., p. 77.
[20] Romain Felli, *The Great Adaptation: Climate, Capitalism and Catastrophe* (London: Verso, 2021). The relationship between the control and exploitation of workers on the one hand, and the development of the fossil fuels industry in the twentieth century, is discussed also by Timothy Mitchell, *Carbon Democracy: Political Power in the Age of Oil* (London: Verso, 2011), and by Andreas Malm in *Fossil Capital: The Rise of Steam Power and the Roots of Global Warming* (London: Verso, 2016).
[21] Moore, *Capitalism in the Web of Life*, p. 170.

This debate between the Anthropocene and the Capitalocene approaches is far from arcane insofar as our concern is to analyze the epochal crisis of global capitalism and also to contribute toward a theory of capitalist exhaustion. The Anthropocene approach obstructs our ability to identify capitalist production relations – more generally, the value relation – at the core of the ecological holocaust. It is hard to disagree with Moore on this matter. For capital, nature is an obstacle to accumulation that must be overcome and also a bounty that must be seized and converted into the value form so as to accumulate. Human beings have fundamentally shaped life on earth for thousands of years, as alluded to by the term Anthropocene, whereas Capitalocene hones in on the power relations of capitalism. There has been an important debate among Marxist ecologists, most publicly between Moore as representative of the Capitalocene approach and ecologist John Foster, who defends the Anthropocene approach (as well, Moore has been criticized for his failure to identify the specificity of human relative to extra-human nature and the role of consciousness in that specificity).[22] I cannot delve here into that debate – and we need not relative to the focus here on the epochal crisis – other than to note that Moore wants to identify the specificity of capitalism and its epistemology, the Capitalocene, distinct from humanity in nature more generally, that is, humanity in nature and capitalism in nature.[23]

As I discussed in Chapter 1, it is in our very species being to cooperate with one another in the collective labor process to transform (extra-human) nature in order to supply ourselves with the necessities of life. We do not undertake our interaction with one another outside of our interaction with the rest of nature, and we transform extra-human nature through our social interactions with one another, in the process transforming ourselves as well. But the particular way in which we transform extra-human nature depends on how we interact with one another, on the complex of social relations and the social structures we build, that is, on the relations of production. That particular way under capitalism is precisely the value relation, the drive to accumulate, which commodifies labor as our very species being and

---

[22] See Foster, Clark, and York, *The Ecological Rift*. On the debate, see inter-alia, Moore (ed.), *Anthropocene or Capitalocene? Nature, History, and the Crisis of Capitalism*.
[23] For a conversation around the idea of the Capitalocene, see Moore (ed.), *Anthropocene or Capitalocene?*

all the rest of nature. We cannot reproduce ourselves indefinitely by destroying the rest of nature. Our survival depends on establishing a new relationship with one another – new relations of production – *in order to* establish a new relationship with the rest of nature. This is to say that in order to change our relationship with the rest of nature, we must change the relationship among ourselves. A different collective relation to the rest of nature is predicated on a different set of production/reproduction relations.

We return again, now on a more expansive footing, to Marx's insistence that the limits to capitalism are not its external constraints but its internal contradictions. Those social relations go beyond the capital–labor relation that generates surplus value yet are structured by it, which is why Moore insists that we must distinguish between the value form pertaining to the production of surplus value and value relations that more broadly structure humans' relations among themselves and to the rest of nature. The crux of the argument here is that the expansion of commodity relations, or exploitation, requires an even greater expansion of the frontier of unpaid labor or appropriation of nature (human and extra-human). If we accept this proposition, it follows that each wave of expansion inevitably intensifies the crisis of social reproduction analyzed in Chapter 2. The crisis of social reproduction is more than one of expulsion and the redundancy of billions of people: The exhaustion of humanity and of extra-human nature form a singular process.

Accumulation crises can be offset by countervailing tendencies, as I discussed in Chapter 1, above all by an intensive and/or extensive expansion of the frontiers of capital. In order for this expansion to continue, however, there must be a greater appropriation of nature (human and extra-human) than of commodification of nature, an expansion of the "ecological surplus," representing the gap between appropriated and capitalized nature. In other words, there has been an accumulation of socio-ecological contradictions that, in my view, have reached the point where the resolution of these contradictions can only take place by superseding capitalism. From the standpoint of nature as a whole, entropy may be reversible and cyclical, but from the standpoint of humans as nature, this is not necessarily so. Many have cautioned against the tendency toward a catastrophic view of the crisis because it is politically disempowering. However so that may be, we cannot deny that the internal contradictions of capitalism are *indeed leading to catastrophe.*

Ecological Holocaust

We know that the effects of climate change and environmental degradation are not shared equally, with the traditional periphery and the poor everywhere disproportionately impacted, overwhelmingly so. My analytical focus here, however, is whether global capitalism can survive a collapse of the biosphere. Climate change is a meta-disaster, a threat of an entirely different category and scale, that makes the crisis of global capitalism existential. It lays bare capitalism's rupture with the metabolic processes of nature. The worldwide wave of capitalist expansion through globalization over the past half century has resulted in cascading environmental degradation, exacerbating the multiple dimensions of the ecological crisis. Human-induced climate change is "already affecting many weather and climate extremes in every region across the globe," warned the United Nations' Intergovernmental Panel on Climate Change (IPCC), made up of the world's leading climate scientists, in its 2021 report, including extreme heatwaves and uncontrollable fire events; heavy precipitation and deluge-level floods; megadroughts; tropical cyclones; melting polar ice and glaciers; deforestation and desertification; water scarcity; land, air, and sea pollution; a rapid rise in sea levels; and ocean acidification.[24]

The IPCC released its final assessment report two years later, in 2023, warning that devastation has *already* been inflicted on vast swathes of the world. Extreme weather caused by climate change is continuous and on an ever more severe scale. There are increasing deaths from intensifying heat waves in all regions, millions of lives and homes destroyed in droughts and floods, millions of people facing hunger, and "increasingly irreversible losses" in vital ecosystems. Half of the global population experienced severe water scarcity in 2023. In many places, the limits of adaptation have already been reached.[25] One British government study found that under current trends, fully one-third of the planet's landmass will be desert by 2100, while up to half the land surface will suffer drought. The study also predicted that

---

[24] IPCC, Working Group, "Climate Change 2021: The Physical Science Basis," www.ipcc.ch/report/ar6/wg1/downloads/report/IPCC_AR6_WGI_Full_Report.pdf.

[25] Fiona Harvey, Scientists Deliver 'Final Warning' on Climate Crisis: Act Now or It's Too Late," *The Guardian*, March 20, 2023, www.theguardian.com/environment/2023/mar/20/ipcc-climate-crisis-report-delivers-final-warning-on-15c.

during the same period the proportion of land in "extreme drought" will increase from the current 3 percent to 30 percent.[26]

Climate change may have received the most attention, but it is far from the only threat to humanity and all life on our planet. Environmental scientists have identified nine "planetary boundaries" crucial to maintaining an environment in which humans can exist: climate change, ocean acidification, stratospheric ozone depletion, the nitrogen and the phosphorus cycles, global freshwater use, change in land use, biodiversity loss, atmospheric aerosol loading, and chemical pollution. Four of these are already experiencing the onset of irreversible environmental degradation and three of them, climate change, the nitrogen cycle, and biodiversity loss, are at "tipping points," meaning that these processes have already crossed their planetary boundaries.[27] Biodiversity loss is accelerating at an alarming rate. From the 1970s to 2022, wildlife populations plummeted by 69 percent.[28] More than 75 percent of global food crops depend on pollination by animals. The narrow range of plant and animal species that humans eat depends on a much greater diversity of animals, plants, and bacteria. Writing in the journal *Nature*, Barnosky and his colleagues reported in 2011 that 90 percent of all known species were headed toward extinction and millions have already gone extinct.[29] Even short of a mass extinction, which would be the sixth in planetary history (all but one involved climate change produced by greenhouse gas), the loss of biodiversity threatens to undermine the fragile ecosystems needed for agriculture and animal husbandry on a scale needed to feed billions of people. The world lost one-third of its arable land in the forty years from 1975 to 2015 due to erosion or pollution.[30]

We are currently adding carbon to the atmosphere at a rate up to ten times faster than the rate that brought about the Permian

---

[26] As cited in Christina Parenti, *Tropic of Chaos: Climate Change and the New Geography of Violence*. See p. 47 for the British government report.

[27] As reported by Foster, Clark, and York, *The Ecological Rift*. The nine are: climate change, ocean acidification, stratospheric ozone depletion, the nitrogen and the phosphorus cycles, global freshwater use, change in land use, biodiversity loss, atmospheric aerosol loading, and chemical pollution.

[28] R. E. A. Almond, M. Grooten, Juffe D. Bignoli, and T. Petersen (eds.) "Living Planet Report 2022" (Gland, Switzerland, WWF, 2022).

[29] Anthony D. Barnosky et al., "Has the Earth's Sixth Mass Extinction Already Arrived?" *Nature*, 471(2011), pp. 51–57.

[30] Oliver Milman, "Earth Has Lost a Third of Arable Land in Past 40 Years, Scientists Say," *The Guardian*, December 2, 2015, www.theguardian.com/environment/2015/dec/02/arable-land-soil-food-security-shortage.

extinction, which wiped out 90 percent of all species. The rate is 100 times faster than at any point in human history before the beginning of industrialization.[31] The collapse of world agriculture together with climate change that makes major portions of the world uninhabitable would lead to mass death on a scale unprecedented in human history. Climate- and weather-related disasters surged five-fold from 1971 to 2021, while 90 percent of climate deaths were in poor countries.[32] Fossil fuel air pollution is responsible for one in five deaths worldwide, taking nearly nine million lives each year, according to a Harvard University study.[33] Maps of the world's hottest places consistently show a belt from India and Pakistan through Central Asia to the Middle East and North Africa. The same crisis affects sections of sub-Saharan Africa. One 2018 study estimated that an additional 150 million people would die from air pollution alone in a 2-degree warmer world, while that same year the IPCC reported that in the gap between 1.5 and 2.0 degrees, hundreds of millions of lives were at stake.[34]

The transnational elite has touted the alleged success of the landmark 2015 Paris agreement to keep a global temperature rise in the current century to below 2 °C above preindustrial levels. But it did not include any binding measures to reduce greenhouse gas emissions, which have steadily increased under the Paris accord. Climate scientists now predict a minimum increase by century's end of at least 3 °C, which itself will be catastrophic, and many believe that figure will be much higher, especially given an acceleration of warming due to secondary factors beyond an increase in carbon emissions, such as the release of vast quantities of methane gas due to the melting of permafrost and the increase in warming caused when ice

---

[31] David Wallace-Wells, *The Uninhabitable Earth: Life after Warming* (New York: Tim Duggan Books, 2019), p. 4.
[32] UN News, "Climate and Weather-Related Disasters Surge Five-Fold over 50 years – But Early Warning Saves Lives – WMO Report," United Nations, September 1, 2021, https://news.un.org/en/story/2021/09/1098662.
[33] Karn Vohra et al., "Global Mortality from Outdoor Fine Particle Pollution Generated by Fossil Fuel Combustion: Results from GEOS-Chem," *Environmental Research*, vol. 195, April 2021, www.sciencedirect.com/science/article/abs/pii/S0013935121000487.
[34] Drew Shindell, Greg Faluvegi, Karl Seltzer, and Cary Shindell, "Quantified, Localized Health Benefits of Accelerated Carbon Dioxide Emissions Reductions," *Nature Climate Change*, 8(4), 2018, www.ncbi.nlm.nih.gov/pmc/articles/PMC5880221/; IPCC, "Global Warming of 1.5 °C," 2018, www.ipcc.ch/site/assets/uploads/sites/2/2022/06/SR15_Full_Report_HR.pdf.

sheets melt and therefore do not reflect sunlight back into space. The current benchmark of three degrees Celsius of warming would make parts of the planet unlivable for humans by the end of the century. Yet, notes Wallace-Wells in his best-seller *The Uninhabitable Earth*, four degrees *or more* is possible, even probable according to some estimates. Four degrees "would mean that whole regions of Africa and Australia and the United States, parts of South America north of Patagonia, and Asia south of Siberia would be rendered effectively uninhabitable by direct heat, desertification, and flooding," he warns, adding that "this is not our worst-case scenario. It is closer to our itinerary, our baseline."[35] A 2020 study estimated that by 2070, upward to three billion people will be living in regions experiencing unbearable heat.[36]

So great is this threat to the biosphere and to life itself that even some among the mainstream have come to call out capitalism. A 2021 report published by seventeen prominent scientists from around the world did not mince words. "The scale of the threat to the biosphere and all its lifeforms – including humanity – is in fact so great that it is difficult to grasp for even well-informed experts." The report went on to warn that "the gravity of the situation requires fundamental changes to global capitalism," including "the abolition of perpetual economic growth, properly pricing externalities, a rapid exit from fossil-fuel use, strict regulation of markets and property acquisition,

---

[35] David Wallace-Wells, *The Uninhabitable Earth: Life after Warming* (New York: Tim Duggan Books, 2019), p. 6. The Paris accords of 2015 warned against any increase above 1.5 degrees, yet there seems to be little chance of achieving that goal. Wallace-Wells warns that

> recent research into the deep history of the planet suggests that our current climate models may be underestimating the amount of warming we are due for in 2100 by as much as half. In other words, temperatures could rise, ultimately, by as much as double what the IPCC predicts. Hit our Paris emissions targets and we may still get four degrees of warming, meaning a green Sahara and the planet's tropical forests transformed into fire-dominated savanna (p. 13).

[36] Timothy A. Kohler, Timothy M. Lenton, and Marten Scheffer, "Future of the Human Climate Niche," *PNAS*, 117(21), 2020, www.pnas.org/doi/full/10.1073/pnas.1910114117. The report did not specify if "unbearable" meant unsurvivable, leading to some controversy over the meaning of its findings. See the discussion in Climate Feedback website, undated, https://climatefeedback.org/evaluation/article-in-business-insider-accurately-describes-results-from-a-study-estimating-up-to-3-billion-people-could-live-in-much-warmer-temperatures-by-2070/.

reigning in corporate lobbying, and the empowerment of women."[37] Perhaps the scientists were unaware that the abolition of perpetual growth they call for is *tantamount to* the abolition of capitalism.

As I mentioned in Chapter 2, the United Nations High Commission on Refugees warned in 2021 that more than 20 million people are forced each year to leave their homes due to extreme weather events.[38] A 2020 study by the U.S. National Academy of Sciences predicted that for every additional one-degree centigrade rise in the average global climate, a billion people will be forced to abandon their locations and to endure insufferable heat. The report warned that areas that are home to one-third of the world's population will experience the same temperature as the hottest parts of the Sahara within fifty years.[39] Drawing on UN data, a widely cited 2021 report by the Institute for Economics and Peace estimates that people living in 151 countries face exposure to destabilizing ecological threats, and that 1.2 billion people living in thirty-one high-risk countries, largely in South Asia, Sub-Saharan Africa, and the Middle East and North Africa, could become climate refugees by 2050 as the climate crisis generates water and food shortages, greater exposure to natural disasters, and temperatures too hot for human existence.[40]

However, we must specify that "climate refugees" can be a misleading characterization absent a critique of the larger conditions of capitalist development, including patterns of landownership, state violence, and market pressures that undermine resilience, uproot people, and force them into migrant streams. Class power relations determine how groups experience climate-related disasters, and such power relations will determine whether we are able to weather the climate crisis

---

[37] Corey J. A. Bradshaw, et al., "Underestimating the Challenges of Avoiding a Ghastly Future," *Frontiers in Conservation Science*, January 13, 2021, www.frontiersin.org/articles/10.3389/fcosc.2020.615419/full.

[38] See UNHCR, "Climate Change and Disaster Displacement," www.unhcr.org/en-us/climate-change-and-disasters.html, no specific date indicated, accessed on June 1, 2024.

[39] Chi Xu, Timothy A. Kohler, Timothy M. Lenton, Jens-Christian Svenning, and Marten Scheffer, "Future of the Human Climate Niche," Proceedings of the National Academy of Sciences, May 26, 2020, www.pnas.org/content/117/21/11350.

[40] Institute for Economics and Peace, "Ecological Threat Report 2021: Understanding Ecological Threats, Resilience and Peace, Sydney, October 2021, www.visionofhumanity.org/wp-content/uploads/2021/10/ETR-2021-web.pdf.

(no pun intended) or succumb to it. Our concern here is not one of environmental determinism but rather how the climate emergency and other threats to the biosphere and humanity in nature are enmeshed in the dynamics of a predatory global capitalism in crisis and whether capitalism can continue to reproduce itself as these threats escalate.

Capital's "Green" Strategy

The ruling groups are approaching the ecological crisis with a multipronged strategy that seeks, beyond minimizing the extent of the threat, to turn the ecological holocaust into vast new opportunities for appropriation and accumulation – all in the name of protecting the environment. This "green capitalism" approach is a response by capital to the economic challenge of opening up new outlets for accumulation and the political challenge of facing increasingly radical demands from the environmental movement for fundamental restructuring of the global economy away from fossil fuels and other environmentally destructive accumulation processes. As youth-led environmental activism has spread, it has begun to explicitly identify capitalism as the cause of environmental devastation and to call for fundamental system change. The TCC's cynical green strategy has been to co-opt the burgeoning international efforts to address the environmental crisis in order to deflect attention away from capital as the source of this crisis by redirecting it toward the poor themselves, and then go on to make the fantastical claim that new waves of expansion and expropriation by the TCC would actually be the savior of the environment.

The Poor Are to Blame

The first step in capital's strategy – and in this they merely echo bourgeois environmentalism – is to place the blame on the "carbon footprint" of each person in the world, a Malthusian argument that inevitably blames the poor masses who are the most numerous. The argument is made more credible by the assumption in the Anthropocene approach that the problem is humanity rather than the particular social form. Yet according to one report among many that have been published in recent years, the consumption of the richest one percent of humanity, who live in climate-insulated built environments and make up 77 million people – the so-called "polluter elite" – is responsible for more carbon emission than the poorest 66 percent of humanity.[41] Another report found that in 2015 the 10 percent most affluent households in the world emitted 49 percent of global CO_2, while the 50 percent of the global population in the lowest income brackets accounted for just 7 percent.[42] The Malthusian "environmental footprint" narrative – first popularized by the fossil fuel industry itself[43] – may be empirically flawed, but it serves to ideologically legitimize the ruling class's effort to promote capitalist expansion in the name of environmentalism, as we shall see momentarily.

A 2022 study by Oxfam factored in the carbon footprint of the investments made by the world's billionaires. "Extreme inequality and wealth concentration undermine the ability of humanity to stop climate breakdown," it warned. The ultra-rich "emit huge and unsustainable amounts of carbon and have an outsized influence over our economy." They hold extensive stakes in many of the largest and most powerful corporations in the world – large enough stakes to influence the actions taken by these corporations. Unlike ordinary people, 50 to 70 percent of the emissions of the world's richest people are the result of their investments. The study estimated that each billionaire emits an average of 3.1 million tons of carbon, including individual consumption and investment-related emissions, over a million times higher than the average emissions for someone in the bottom 90 percent of humanity.[44]

Such studies are useful in belying the idea that the poor place the greatest stress on the environment, but their limitations should be obvious.[45] The problem is not capitalism, according to this approach, but

---

[41] Jonathan Watts, "Richest 1% Account for More Carbon Emissions than Poorest 66%, Report Says," *The Guardian*, November 19, 2023, www.theguardian.com/environment/2023/nov/20/richest-1-account-for-more-carbon-emissions-than-poorest-66-report-says.

[42] Helena Horton, "'Carbon Footprint Gap' Between Rich and Poor Expanding, Study Finds," *The Guardian*, February 4, 2022, www.theguardian.com/environment/2022/feb/04/carbon-footprint-gap-between-rich-poor-expanding-study.

[43] Matthew T. Huber, *Climate Change as Class War* (London: Verso, 2022), p. 13.

[44] Oxfam, "Carbon Billionaires: The Investment Emissions of the World's Richest People" (London: Oxfam, 2022), https://oxfamilibrary.openrepository.com/bitstream/handle/10546/621446/bn-carbon-billlionaires-071122-en.pdf;jsessionid=C857642AB9D9348BC82A554064BB3327?sequence=14.

[45] As has been amply discussed in the ecology literature. See, inter-alia, discussion in Huber, *Climate Change as Class War*.

human consumption, and the solution is to scale back on consumption even though the poor majority of humanity *under-consumes the necessities of life*, so much so that their survival is at risk, as we saw in Chapter 2. Moreover, the vast majority of humanity is now integrated into the circuits of global capitalism. In order to survive, they have no choice but to acquire the commodities whose production is controlled by the TCC in function of accumulation. The rich could theoretically reduce or eliminate their luxury consumption, and affluent strata could eliminate all unnecessary purchases, but capital cannot, by definition, stop seeking its endless self-expansion. The problem is not consumption but the *logic of capitalist consumption* as the *realization phase of the accumulation of capital*. The irony is that in the logic of capital, the scaling back of consumerism, no matter how urgently required to address the threat to the biosphere, will only deepen the structural crisis of overaccumulation.

Waste, discard, planned obsolescence, and needless packaging – all must be engineered into mass production and mass consumption. Capitalist reproduction requires the endless sale of commodities, whether necessary or not. Powerful mass propaganda ("marketing") campaigns that manipulate reason and emotion, wants and desires, must be permanently waged for this purpose. Capitalism must inculcate consumerism and generate a permanent stream of waste at every phase of global production, distribution, and consumption. This waste is built into the accumulation imperative, irrational from any social or environmental logic yet impeccable in its accumulation logic. "Mass production is profitable only if its rhythm can be maintained — that is if it can continue to sell its product in steady or increasing quantity," explained Edward Bernays in his classic 1928 booklet, *Propaganda*, written to council the political and economic elite of the early twentieth century on how to pursue modern methods of mass psychological manipulation to secure the interests of the ruling elite and the capitalist system. "Today supply must actively seek to create its corresponding demand … [and] cannot afford to wait until the public asks for its product; it must maintain constant touch, through advertising and propaganda, to assure itself the continuous demand which alone will make its costly plant profitable."[46]

---

[46] Edward Bernays, *Propaganda* (New York: IG Publishing, 2005 [1928]), p. 84. See Kerryn Higgs excellent book, *Collision Course: Endless Growth on a Finite Planet* (Cambridge: MIT Press, 2016), for discussion on the

From the very birth in the early twentieth century of mass marketing, notions of organizing an economic system to meet everyone's needs with an adequate level of production of basic necessities did not feature into the logic of capitalist consumption. The prospect of ever-extendable consumer desire, characterized as "progress," promised a new way forward for modern manufacture, a means to perpetuate economic growth. Progress was about the endless replacement of old needs with new, old products with new ones. "Our enormously productive economy demands that we make consumption our way of life, that we convert the buying and use of goods into rituals, that we seek our spiritual satisfaction, our ego satisfaction, in consumption," counseled the marketing consultant Victor Lebow in 1955. "We need things consumed, burned up, replaced and discarded at an ever-accelerating rate."[47]

Digital technologies may operate in cyberspace, but they are not "clean" because they must be grounded in the industrial production of commodities and their operation requires vast amount of energy that at this time comes predominantly from fossil fuel. The renewed wave of worldwide capitalist expansion driven by the new digital technologies that I have anticipated in the previous chapters must also involve an expansion of energy production and of electronic hardware as both producer and consumer goods. Electronic and digital devices, especially given their short lifespan, end up in the waste stream. Every year, the world discharges almost 50 million tons of e-waste. Most of the waste ends up in landfills, where heavy metals such as lead, mercury, cadmium, and other toxins leak into the ground and contaminate the groundwater and the food chain. Recycling and scavenging at these sites take place in precarious conditions and through crude and highly toxic methods, including smashing, open burning, and bathing electronics in acids, to collect small scraps of precious materials that can be sold.

The flip side of wasteful mass consumption is mass deprivation, as we have already discussed. Yet the more inequality rises, the more the consumer market contracts, which undermines capital's effort to promote

---

development by capital of consumerism throughout the twentieth century. See also the two modern classics: Vance Packard, *The Waste Makers* (New York: IG Publishing, 2011 [1960]); John Kenneth Galbraith, *The Affluent Society* (Boston: Mariner Books, 1998 [1958]).

[47] Victor Lebow, "Price Competition in 1955," *Journal of Retailing*, Spring 1955, reprinted here: https://notbuyinganything.blogspot.com/p/price-competition-in-1955-victor-lebow_27.html.

ceaseless consumption. At the same time, global communications allow transnational capital to inundate virtually every community in the world with mass advertising, projecting images of the consumptive good life and generating wants and desires that will never be satisfied – and could never be satisfied without producing a complete collapse of the biosphere. Sublimating mass social anxiety into consumerist fantasy is not a viable economic or social control strategy for the TCC with regard to disposable people who do not provide a mass market and whose condition propels them to rebel. What awaits them is less seduction by consumer fantasies than a global police state to contain the escalating conflicts resulting from the impacts of environmental breakdown. Pentagon planners have called climate change a "threat multiplier" as extreme weather and water scarcity inflame and escalate existing social conflicts, leading to "militarized management of civilization's violent disintegration."[48]

So too the fury of the global police state awaits the environmental justice movement. The climate crisis is radicalizing youth. "Tech savvy and globally connected, Gen Z and Millennial activists are becoming increasingly militant as runaway fossil fuel development destroys their future," observed one journalistic report. "The kids are not alright. They are very, very scared.... Researchers collected over 10,000 responses across 10 countries and found young people felt anxious and 'betrayed by their governments.' Helplessness and anger permeate Gen Z and Millennials from Nigeria to Portugal, from the Philippines to the United States." As youth across the world "have surged into environmental groups from the mainstream to the militant," they "have scaled up to demand deep systemic change," explicitly identifying capitalism as the root source of the climate breakdown.[49] The

---

[48] As cited in Parenti, *Tropic of Chaos: Climate Change and the New Geography of Violence*, p. 47. The Pentagon itself is said to be the single worst emitter worldwide of greenhouse gases. See Neta C. Crawford, *The Pentagon, Climate Change, and War: Charting the Rise and Fall of U.S. Military Emissions* (Cambridge: MIT Press, 2022).

[49] The portion cited directly is in Nicholas Powers, "As Climate Crisis Grows, Youth Environmental Movements are Radicalizing," *Truthout*, April 22, 2024, https://truthout.org/articles/as-climate-crisis-grows-youth-environmental-movements-are-radicalizing/. On the movement identifying capitalism as the cause of the climate emergency, see Ben Martin, "How the Youth Climate Movement has Evolved from School Strikes to Systemic Change," The Green Economic Tracker, March 3, 2023, www.greeneconomycoalition.org/news-and-resources/from-school-strikes-to-systemic-change-how-the-youth-climate-movement-has-evolved.

movement has placed what it calls *ecocide*, the wanton destruction of nature, at the forefront of environmental activism, combining mass action with legal efforts to have governments declare ecocide a crime.

In 2021, a panel of criminal and environmental attorneys from around the world created a legal definition of ecocide as a crime under the Rome Statute of the International Criminal Course, an unprecedented step in pushing to criminalize mass damage and destruction of ecosystems. The legal panel defined ecocide as "unlawful or wanton acts committed with knowledge that there is a substantial likelihood of severe and either widespread or long-term damage to the environment being caused by those acts."[50] The transnational elite has taken notice. The World Economic Forum cautioned in 2021 that legislation had been passed in eleven countries as of 2021 to make ecocide a crime, and pressure from environmental activists and mass protests has led other countries to consider doing so. If ecocide were to be enlisted as a crime at the International Criminal Court, warned the WEF, "this would create an arrestable offence for anyone committing ecocide, and would make individuals responsible for acts or decisions that cause severe damage to the environment liable for criminal prosecution."[51]

The escalation worldwide of an environmental consciousness and of an increasingly radical and assertive environmental justice movement has led governments to ramp up the criminalization of collective action associated with the environmental protest activities. In the United States, for instance, mass protest in 2016 and 2017 to block the construction of the Dakota Access oil pipeline that traverses indigenous lands in the state of North Dakota as it transports shale oil from Canada to the Gulf of Mexico led state legislators to introduce a spate of antiprotest bills. Forty-one of these bills had passed by 2024, and hundreds more were being debated. Some of these laws made it a felony to engage in protest on or near energy infrastructure. While much of this legislation was originally introduced in response to the Dakota

---

[50] "Top International Lawyers Unveil Definition of Ecocide," Press Release, *Stop Ecocide International*, 2021 (no day given), www.stopecocide.earth/press-releases-summary/top-international-lawyers-unveil-definition-of-ecocide.
[51] Center for Nature and Climate, "What is Ecocide and Which Countries Recognize it in Law," *World Economic Forum*, August 30 2021, www.weforum.org/agenda/2021/08/ecocide-environmental-harm-international-crime/.

protest, the bills criminalized or proposed to criminalize a wide range of longstanding protest tactics by oppositional movements, such as blocking traffic and trespassing or obstructing access to public lands, in some cases making these protests an act of "domestic terrorism."[52] Worldwide, nearly 200 environmental defenders were killed in 2023, from campaigners against environmentally destructive mining to indigenous communities targeted by organized crime groups.[53]

Alice in Wonderland: The TCC Will Save the Planet

The class character of the ruling groups' explanation for ecological crisis – the environment is overwhelmed by the stress that the poor place on it – provided the political-ideological scaffolding for TCC's class solution to ecological holocaust: liberating capital from any restrictions on global accumulation through the appropriation and commodification of more and more of nature. They set about from the very start of modern environmental consciousness and diplomacy in the 1970s to assure that it would serve the ends of capitalist globalization. The TCC's two-track strategy was, on to the one hand, to prevent or eliminate environmental regulations that could obstruct the freedom to appropriate nature and expand accumulation, and second, to convert the calls for resolving the environmental crisis into concrete new opportunities for profit-making.

The 1987 Brundtland Report, *Our Common Future*, commissioned by the United Nations, coined the concept of "sustainable development" and defined it as "meeting the needs of the present without compromising the ability of future generations to meet their own needs."[54] The report, named after Norwegian prime minister Gro Harlem Brundtland who chaired the Commission, took up where the 1972 report, *The Limits to Growth*, left off. Coming

---

[52] Adam Federman, "The War on Protest is Here," *In These Times*, April 17, 2024, https://inthesetimes.com/article/war-protest-standing-rock-cop-city-repression-criminalize-dissent-political-rights-first-amendment.

[53] Patrick Greenfield, "Almost 200 People Killed Last Year Trying to Defend the Environment, Report Finds," *The Guardian*, September 9, 2024, www.theguardian.com/environment/article/2024/sep/09/almost-200-people-killed-last-year-trying-to-defend-the-environment-report-finds-aoe.

[54] UNEP, *Our Common Future* (Oxford: Oxford University Press, 1987), https://sustainabledevelopment.un.org/content/documents/5987our-common-future.pdf.

in the early years of global environmental consciousness (the first Earth Day was in 1970), *The Limits to Growth* fretted over the ability of capitalism to survive alleged overpopulation and resource exhaustion in the context of that decade's great crisis and reflected the fear among emerging transnational and corporate elites that environmental concerns could undermine capital's freedom and flexibility or raise the cost of doing business at a time when capital was about to go global. The two reports combined firmly established the neo-Malthusian approach to the global environmental crisis that seeks control of the poor and unfettered access to global resources based on the claim that environmental degradation stems from the poor and their poverty. (The Malthusian narrative, we must add, often leads to racist and xenophobic hysteria over poor barbarian hordes invading civilization, providing neofascists and ultranationalists with a convenient scapegoat for recruiting among those experiencing rising insecurity and social anxiety in the face of capitalist crisis.)

The Brundtland Report stated that global environmental problems were primarily the result of the poverty of the Global South and could be tackled by bringing about "development," which in turn would come about by increased growth achieved through "freeing up" markets. The series of high-profile UN-sponsored intergovernmental meetings, starting with a summit held in Rio de Janeiro in 1992 and that have since become annual affairs known as the Conference of Parties (COP), thus legitimated the "market solution" to ecological holocaust, promoting global "carbon markets" that by 2010 were worth over $100 billion. Hijacked at birth by the TCC, the annual UN-sponsored climate talks have become opportunities for oil, coal, auto, and chemical corporations to lobby the international community and assure that any agreements will not curtail market freedom or challenge the prerogatives of transnational capital to continue carbon-based accumulation.[55] Far from any reduction in emissions, under the carbon markets regime, carbon emissions have in fact steadily increased, from 26 billion tons of CO_2 in 1995, when the first COP was held, to 34 billion

---

[55] For accounts of how the TCC hijacked the talks from the start, see: Kenny Bruno and Joshua Karliner, *Earthsummit.Biz: The Corporate Takeover of Sustainable Development* (Oakland: Food First Books, 2002); Matthew T. Huber, *Climate Change as Class War: Building Socialism on a Warming Planet* (London: Verso, 2022).

in 2010, 37 billion in 2018, and over 40 billion in 2023.[56] Capital's "polluter pays" approach does nothing to reduce emissions because it is intended not to do so but to extend market relations.

The TCC is salivating over a vast new round of appropriation and capitalization of nature, what in capitalist lexicon is termed "natural capital," in the name of "conservation" and "sustainability." A glimpse into this new "gold rush" was provided in 2021, when the Malaysian state of Sabah signed an agreement with the Singapore shell company Hoch Standard, giving the company title to the management and marketing of two million hectares of forest for "natural capital/ecosystem services" for 100 to 200 years, with an estimated revenue stream of $80 billion. The deal, brokered by an Australian consulting firm specializing in the financialization of natural capital, gives commercial rights to Hoch Standard and allows it to sell its rights without government permission. The agreement was backed by undisclosed multibillion-dollar private equity investors whose identity remains a secret, although an exposé by sociologist John Bellamy Foster identified the involvement of major global financial conglomerates, among them Credit Suisse, HSBC, and major Singapore banks. It is impossible to exaggerate the extent of this "natural capital" rush promoted by global speculative finance to acquire real assets in the physical environment and turn them into financial instruments. Foster refers to this financialization of nature as a "new ecological regime." This "transmutation of so-called natural capital into tradable exchange value over the last decade is seen in the almost unlimited opportunities for corporations and money managers."[57]

A more mind-boggling glimpse into the juggernaut of land grabs in the name of conservancy comes from what has been called the "new scramble for Africa." Emblematic of this scramble is a hitherto unknown corporation from the United Arab Emirates (UAE), Blue

---

[56] For data up until 2023, see Statista, "Annual Carbon Emissions Worldwide," www.statista.com/statistics/276629/global-co2-emissions/. For 2023, see Stanford University, School of Sustainability, "Global Carbon Emissions from Fossil Fuel Reached Record High in 2023," December 5, 2023, https://sustainability.stanford.edu/news/global-carbon-emissions-fossil-fuels-reached-record-high-2023.

[57] John Bellamy Foster, "The Defense of Nature: Resisting the Financialization of the Earth," *Monthly Review*, April 1, 2022, https://monthlyreview.org/2022/04/01/the-defense-of-nature-resisting-the-financializaton-of-the-earth/.

Carbon, owned by Sheikh Ahmed al-Maktoum, a member of Dubai's ruling family. Deals signed by Blue Carbon with a number of African governments promised the company's control over vast tracts of land as carbon offsets, including 10 percent of the land mass in Liberia, Zambia, and Tanzania, and 20 percent in Zimbabwe. In response to condemnation by environmentalists, Blue Carbon insisted in late 2023 that these deals were only in the exploratory state. However, by late 2023 the indigenous Ogiek people in eastern Kenya had already been driven from their lands as part of negotiations between Blue Carbon and the Kenyan government. Numerous studies have shown that carbon offsets do not reduce carbon emissions and are little more than greenwashing to legitimate the expansion of transnational finance through the new wave of commodification of nature. The TCC has leveraged the unprecedented debt crisis in Africa to expand these carbon markets. The formation in 2022 under United Nations auspices of the African Carbon Markets Initiative (ACMI), which brings together African governments, corporate investors and foundations, and international organizations. "The emergence of carbon credits as a new product allows for the monetization of Africa's large natural capital endowment, while enhancing it," declares ACMI's founding document.[58]

The Corporate Ecoforum, founded in 2008 as an invitation-only forum of the CEOs of leading global corporations from finance and industry to "demonstrate a serious commitment to sustainability as core to business strategy,"[59] captured the spirit of this new wave of worldwide plunder specifically through a strategy of greenwashing – that is, presenting corporate plunder as good for the environment. It called in a 2012 report it co-published with Nature Conservatory for a sweeping new round of appropriation, commodification, and financialization of nature:

Each year, our planet's complex land and water systems produce an estimated $72 trillion worth of "free" goods and services essential to a well-functioning global economy. Because these benefits aren't bartered and

---

[58] For all these details and further sources, see Adam Hanieh, "Laundering Carbon – The Gulf's 'New Scramble for Africa'," MERIP, No. 311, 2024, https://merip.org/2024/07/laundering-carbon-the-gulfs-new-scramble-for-africa/.

[59] See the Corporate Ecoforum home page at https://corporateecoforum.com/about/.

sold in the marketplace, their value is exceedingly hard to monetize on corporate or government financial statements. As a result, this value has largely been left unaccounted for in business decisions and market transactions. [Now] top executives at some of the world's biggest companies are awakening to the profound business value of Earth's natural resources. Without healthy ecosystems, water and raw materials that were once cheap and abundant can become so costly they erase profits and threaten entire business models.[60]

Without a hint of shame, the TCC statement went on to explain that such approaches are urgent in order to undercut "impending regulatory changes that could limit product or production choices, avoid fines, suspensions, lawsuits or other liabilities due to over-exploitation or contamination of natural systems," and "avoid damage to corporate reputation and brand," "exploit opportunities to educate consumers about high-performance sustainable products to increase demand and create new market segments," and "leverage emerging 'natural capital' markets such as water-quality trading, wetland banking and threatened species banking, and natural carbon sequestration."[61]

Spatial mapping of "natural capital" by the United Nations Environment Program (UNEP) indicates that "terrestrial ecosystem assets" are highly concentrated in equatorial regions, particularly in the Brazilian Amazon and Congo Basin, while marine ecosystems are concentrated in Southeast Asia and along coastlines, often among indigenous populations whose resistance stands in the way of appropriation.[62] Sub-Saharan Africa has been singled out since an estimated 90 percent of land is "untitled," or held on the basis of customary rights – that is, as part of the global commons – making them primary targets for expropriation and conversion into marketable "natural capital."[63] Once unbundled from the rest of nature, these so-called

---

[60] Corporate Ecoforum and Nature Conservatory, *The New Business Imperative: Valuing Natural Capital*, 2012, www.truevaluemetrics.org/DBpdfs/Metrics/NaturalCapital/The-New-Business-Imperative-Valuing-Natural-Capital-2012.pdf.

[61] Ibid.

[62] United Nations Environmental Program, "Towards a Global Map of Natural Capital: Key Ecosystem Assets," 2014, pp. 30–31, https://digitallibrary.un.org/record/779213.

[63] Foster, "The Defense of Nature."

ecosystem services can then be rebundled as financial assets to be marketed. "In today's carbon market, focusing on offsets, financial interests purchase credits in large numbers from suppliers so as to 'bundle' them," shows Foster, "combining various tranches of derivatives and gathering these together in portfolios, consisting of carbon and offsets associated with widely different forms of natural capital."[64]

We find in the Indian state of Andhra Pradesh a revealing case study in the mechanisms of capitalist expansion, dispossession, and death through financialization in the name of adaptation to climate change. In the 2010s, the state became a prime destination for global capital flows in the form of microcredit pushed on hundreds of thousands of local farmers facing drought. The need to pay back the loans forced the peasant borrowers to turn to commercial crops for the market in place of food crops for family and local consumption. The intensification of production this involved stretched the local ecology to its ecological limits in the face of water scarcity. Pushed into bankruptcy when they were unable to pay back their loans, peasant borrowers then lost their land to agribusiness and finance, converted into impoverished proletarians, many of whom ended up committing suicide.[65]

Transnational finance capital in this way was able to transfer the risks associated with climate change to local communities and to extend its reach in the process. "Apart from the common psychological defenses against what is often called 'catastrophism,' the financialization of transnational capital has put in place systemic barriers to taking into account the medium- and long-term risks of climate change," observes Michael Gordy.

In recent years the financial markets have gained the ability to respond very quickly to short-term profit-making opportunities, and this focus has made it more difficult for them to pay attention to longer-term liabilities or systemic risks. This is because the expectation of many financial investors now is that they will only spend a short time with any particular investment, buying and selling their holdings quickly and exposing themselves to risks only in the short run.[66]

[64] Foster, "The Defense of Nature."
[65] For discussion on the case of Andhra Pradesh, see Felli, *The Great Adaptation*, pp. 100–103.
[66] Michael Gordy, *Disaster Risk Reduction and the Global System: Ruminations on a Way Forward* (New York: Springer, 2016), p. 64.

The Climate Emergency Is Good for Business

The ruling elite and their organic intellectuals have already accepted the inevitability of major climate change impacts and the need to "adjust" to them. It would not be an overstatement to note that the climate emergency opens up all sorts of new profit-making opportunities for a wide range of capitalist sectors led by finance and revolving around diverse mechanisms for the financialization of nature. An "adaptation market" has expanded in lockstep with the climate crisis, ranging from climate risk insurance and the seizure of nature reserves in the name of "conservation," as discussed earlier, to the outsourcing to private capital of natural disaster prevention and relief services. "Wherever there is a climate problem there are climate capitalists looking for solutions," note Lovins and Cohen.[67]

"Green capitalism" involves converting the crisis into new opportunities for accumulation through alternative energy production, technological fixes such as "carbon capture" and geoengineering schemes, global "carbon markets," and new appropriations of natural reserves in the name of "protecting the environment."[68] Capital's technological fetish seeks to modify the forces of production in response to the ecological crisis without affecting the capitalist relations of production. The buzzwords of green capitalism are "sustainability," "adaptation and mitigation," and "conservation." So-called green technologies are based as much as "dirty" technologies on a radical expansion of capital into extra-human nature, for instance, in the search for new sources of lithium, cobalt, and rare earth minerals used in the production of "green" commodities. More than 500 environmental groups in the United States and Canada signed a petition in 2021 urging their governments to "abandon the dirty, dangerous myth of CCS," or carbon capture and storage technological fixes, as "a dangerous distraction driven by the same big polluters who created the climate emergency,"[69] in reference to carbon energy companies that themselves are

---

[67] Hunter Lovins and Boyd Cohen, *Climate Capitalism: Capitalism in the Age of Climate Change* (New York: Hill and Wang, 2011), pp. 260, 265.
[68] See, inter-alia, Richard Smith, *Green Capitalism: The God that Failed* (Bristol: World Economics Association, 2015).
[69] Jessica Corbett, "'A False Solution': 500+ Groups Urge US, Canadian Leaders to Reject Carbon Capture," *Common Dreams*, July 19, 2021, www.commondreams.org/news/2021/07/19/false-solution-500-groups-urge-us-canadian-leaders-reject-carbon-capture.

pushing the carbon capture industry as a new source of accumulation. In 2018 the journal *Nature* dismissed all scenarios for reversing global warming based on carbon capture as "magical thinking."[70]

The TCC and capitalist states will propose nothing that challenges the fundamental logic of capital accumulation, but they may attempt to intervene in markets to redirect accumulation toward less environmentally destructive energy production and industrial processes under the illusion that these measures will be sufficient to avert disaster. Yet green capitalists are just as dependent as are fossil and other capitalists on the global police state to open up access to resources and to repress popular resistance to capitalist displacement and exploitation. They are just as much as other capitalist sectors dependent on and integrated with transnational tech and financial capital. Green capitalism is therefore not any more benign to the proletariat and surplus humanity just because it claims to be environmentally friendly. Equally as important, it is no more capable of resolving the crisis of global capitalism, much less the ecological crisis, than is the rest of capitalism.

The electric car brings home capital's "ecological modernization" strategy as a weapon for the TCC to undertake new rounds of appropriation and, in the process, to sharpen the global police state. The car itself, and all the ancillary industries involved in the commodity chain – lithium extraction for batteries being only one – offer vast new opportunities for accumulation. Billionaire Tesla electric car CEO Elon Musk epitomizes TCC salivation over the profits to be made. "I would really like to encourage, once again, entrepreneurs to enter the lithium refining business," he said in 2022. "It's basically like minting money right now. You can't lose!"[71] The transition to "green" energy is driven by the application of new digital technologies dependent on lithium, cobalt, rare earth, and other minerals that require a predatory seizure by the TCC of resources around the world. Gelderloos and Dunlap note that "green energy" is tied into some of the biggest colonial land grabs in the twenty-first century. In 2020, Musk referred to the 2019 coup d'état that overthrew the democratically elected government of Evo Morales in Bolivia, a country in the process of developing its vast lithium reserves.

---

[70] As Cited in Wallace-Wells, *The Uninhabitable Earth: Life after Warming*, p. 50.
[71] Business Insider, "Must to Entrepreneurs: Lithium Refining is 'Like Minting Money'," July 21, 2022, www.businessinsider.com/elon-musk-entrepreneur-advice-lithium-refining-like-minting-money-2022-7.

In reply to a tweet that condemned Musk and the United States for tacitly supporting the coup, Musk quipped: "We will coup whoever we want! Deal with it."[72] Moreover, the green marketing propaganda around the electric car, as Gelderloos and Dunlap point out, shifts the responsibility for the climate crisis away from capital and toward "the ecologically-conscious consumer and the governments that strive to incentivize 'smart choices' by investors and consumers alike."[73]

What Felli calls the "Great Adaptation" seeks to respond to the climate crisis with further steps to integrate populations, ecosystems, and institutions into capital accumulation. It is "part of the extension of the market and – on that basis – of the primitive accumulation of capital."[74] The strategy of adaptation, defined as "learning to live with climate change," is aimed at redirecting calls for more radical responses to the climate emergency into schemes for global capitalism to adjust to changing climate conditions. There would be no need to curtail the market because society could adapt as the environment changes, and capital can provide the adaptative programs and technologies. "Adaptation" has thus become a discourse to counter the demand for a reduction in emissions by state intervention and public policy. "The shock of global warming is being used to extend market mechanisms and to increase the integration of marginal populations into the global market," according to Felli. Yet adaptation is a fantasy, he observes, because climate change does not involve arriving at a new state of equilibrium around which the world can adapt. It will get worse over time as long as greenhouse gas is produced. Wallace-Wells similarly notes that "the experience of life in a climate transformed by human activities is not just a matter of stepping from one stable ecosystem into another no matter how degraded or destructive the transformed climate is."[75] The evidence suggests, to the contrary, that change is not

---

[72] Vijay Prashad and Alejandro Bejarano, "'We Will Coup Whoever We want': Elon Musk and the Overthrow of Democracy in Bolivia," *Counterpunch*, July 29, 2020, accessed on December 5, 2020 at www.counterpunch.org/2020/07/29/we-will-coup-whoever-we-want-elon-musk-and-the-overthrow-of-democracy-in-bolivia/.
[73] Peter Gelderloos and Alexander Dunlap 2023. "'The Poisons Are Already in Here with Us:' Framing for Ecological Revolutions from Below." *Globalizations*, 21(4), 2023, pp. 758–775, citations from p. 763, https://doi.org/10.1080/14747731.2023.2225306.
[74] Fell, *The Great Adaptation*, pp. 12, 94.
[75] Wallace-Wells, *The Uninhabitable Earth: Life after Warming*, p. 21.

just cumulative, but as impacts accumulate, the pace of change will accelerate; it will become too abrupt for capital to set up new accumulation activities.

The ecological crisis is inseparable from the other dimensions of global crisis. The escalation of social and political conflicts around the world in the face of the effects of climate change, especially water scarcity and drought, severe strain on agriculture and herding, resource depletion, and extreme weather storms, has been the focus of numerous studies in recent years.[76] Escalating "climate wars" may be the most visible social manifestation of ecological holocaust. Climate is not the sole cause of escalating wars and conflicts "but the spark igniting a complex bundling of social kindling," observes Wallace-Wells.[77] Extreme weather events further destabilize social order and generate violent conflict, adding fuel to the fires of global crisis. Eight hundred million people in South Asia alone, according to the World Bank, will see their living conditions sharply diminished by 2050 as a result of climate change,[78] aggravating the crisis of social reproduction.

The Final Frontier and the Specter of Collapse

I agree with the critique of the Anthropocene concept put forth by Moore, Felli, and others insofar as it indicts humanity rather than the particular social form of capitalism. We want to recall, however, that capitalism is not the first system that thrust humanity into devastating contradiction with extra-human nature. Precapitalist and ancient civilizations collapsed under the impact of their social forms on environmental changes. The domination of some human beings over others in class societies, whether capitalist or precapitalist, has historically

---

[76] See, inter-alia: Christian Parenti, *Tropic of Chaos: Climate Change and the New Geography of Violence* (New York: Nation Books, 2012); Gwynne Dyer, *Climate Wars: The Fight for Survival as the World Overheats* (Oxford: OneWorld Publications, 2010); Harald Welzer, *Climate Wars: Why People Will Be Killed in the 21st Century* (Oxford: Polity Press, 2017); Michael E. Mann, *The New Climate War: The Fight to Take Back Our Planet* (New York: Public Affairs, 2022).
[77] Wallace-Wells, *The Uninhabitable Earth*, p. 140.
[78] Mani Muthukumara, Sushenjit Bandyopadhyay, Shun Chonabayashi, Anil Markandya, and Thomas Mosier, "South Asia's Hotspots: The Impact of Temperature and Precipitation Changes on Living Standards" (Washington, DC: World Bank, 2018), https://openknowledge.worldbank.org/server/api/core/bitstreams/15c3d2db-33f2-50a9-a011-3db01e57437d/content.

been coupled with human domination over the rest of nature in a way that renders civilization unsustainable. The ruling elites of the Mayan city-states, the Khmer empire, the late Bronze Age empires of the Mediterranean, and the very first known civilizations, the Sumerian and Akkadian empires, among others, could not separate their imperative of domination from the destruction that their systems of domination and exploitation wrought on the environment, thus undermining the capacity of these societies for social reproduction. Debate has continued on the nature of historical civilizational crises and long-established narratives that reduce collapse to "ecosuicide," as in the case of Easter Island, have of late become complicated by new evidence and hypotheses.[79]

Regardless of the causal explanations in each specific case of collapse, there remain many historical episodes of such collapse when civilizations are unable to resolve the internal contradictions that tear them apart.[80] When no social or political force is able to prevail and impose a stable system of domination, demise has been the outcome, from Sumer and the Mayan states already mentioned to the collapse of the Roman and several Chinese dynasties. These civilizations have all been class societies, suggesting that the contradictions located in a mode of production torn apart by class are what brought them down. Specifically, the impulse to extract as much surplus as possible from the laboring masses undermines the capacity for adaptation in class societies, whether capitalist or precapitalist. It seems clear that social and political crises in these ancient civilizations combined with their contradictions with extra-human nature, especially when climate changes destabilized the delicate internal cohesion that held together exploitative modes of production with their extra-human environs, so that ecological constraints played a role in their collapse. However, we must avoid an environmental determinism that makes causal climate change, whether natural or human induced, in place of the dialectical unity of social form and environmental stress.

---

[79] See Terry Hunt and Carl Lipo, *The Statues that Walked: Unraveling the Mystery of Easter Island* (Berkeley: Counterpoint, 2012).

[80] See, for example, Jared Diamond, *Collapse: How Societies Choose to Fail or Succeed* (New York: Penguin, 2005); Paul Cooper, *Fall of Civilizations: Stories of Greatness and Decline* (New York: Hanover Square Press, 2024). For my earlier discussion on the matter, see William I. Robinson, *Global Capitalism and the Crisis of Humanity* (New York: Cambridge University Press, 2014).

Civilizations based on class antagonisms have left in their stead, according to sociologist Sing Chew, "recurrent dark ages" in world history, including mass dying, political chaos, and a regression in levels of social organization and productive forces as civilizations decompose.[81] "Dark Ages (as historical events and as a theoretical concept) are critical crises periods in world history over the course of the last five thousand years when environmental conditions have played a significant part in determining how societies, kingdoms, empires, and civilizations are reorganized and organized." While it is difficult to generalize to all cases of collapse, during these Dark Ages, he notes, more advanced technologies and material skills, even the written language, disappeared for generations, crafts and the arts declined, trade and commerce collapsed, disease spread, food production and living conditions plummeted, and population declined drastically. "As the world system evolved over time, the occurrence of Dark Ages extending over wider and wider geographic space revealed the interconnectivity of socioeconomic and political relationships."[82] Any new Dark Ages would encompass all of humanity. What sets ecological crisis under capitalism apart from earlier crises of humans-in-nature is the commodification of nature, the unprecedented *velocity* of environmental degradation and destruction, and, above all, that ecological crisis under capitalism is *global* in scope.

The more the ruling groups pursue their multipronged strategy to address environmental problems, the more they aggravate the underlying contradictions that generate crisis. At best, they are buying time. The capitalist pursuit of endless extensive enlargement, involving ongoing appropriation and commodification of nature, is doomed to fail in the long run. We are reaching the limits of nature as "tap" (nutrient and resource depletion) and nature as "sink" (a dump for waste and toxins). At some point the cumulative impacts of environmental

---

[81] Sing C. Chew, *World Ecological Degradation: Accumulation, Urbanization, and Deforestation* (Lanham: AltaMira Press/Rowman and Littlefield Publishers, 2001), and *The Recurring Dark Ages: Ecological Stress, Climate Changes, and System Transformation*.

[82] Chew, *The Recurring Dark Ages: Ecological Stress, Climate Changes, and System Transformation*, 170. As I noted earlier with regard to the collapse of the Roman empire, such "dark ages" are not necessarily a bad thing from the viewpoint of the exploited classes, who may be freed from the control exercised by their exploiters. That said, a collapse of global capitalism may be so cataclysmic that the exploited classes may not survive such an outcome.

collapse will impede the global circuits of accumulation – supply lines, transportation systems, energy infrastructure, and the reproduction of labor power. It will cripple labor productivity, undermine growth, make it too difficult to access resources, and displace and disrupt too swiftly for capital to adapt and to reproduce itself. Any new arrangement will not have enough time to stabilize.

As whole regions become too hot for habitation, outdoor work will be severely impeded. Capital will continue to throw desperate workers into outdoor work conditions that will kill. The 2022 World Cup held in Qatar gives us a window into the killing fields of work for global capital in conditions of extreme heat. More than 6,500 migrant workers from India, Pakistan, Nepal, Bangladesh, and Sri Lanka died in Qatar constructing stadiums and other facilities in the lead-up to the 2022 World Cup – a figure that does not include the deaths of workers imported from other countries, such as Kenya and the Philippines.[83] Hundreds of thousands of migrant workers toiled in temperatures of up to 45 °C (113 °F) for up to ten hours a day under conditions akin to modern slavery. A third of these workers, according to one study, experienced dangerously high body temperatures.[84] Capital has no hesitation in throwing millions of workers into such deadly outdoor conditions – heat, and also extreme air pollution – but at some point these conditions will undermine the ability to accumulate, that is, to continue to pump out surplus value from masses of workers who are unable to perform outdoor work.

When outdoor work becomes impossible, agribusiness plantations cannot be worked, infrastructure cannot be maintained, and often cannot withstand scorching conditions (asphalt melts, for instance). When fisheries become exhausted, capital will lose marine resources worth billions. Zones that become uninhabitable for human beings are zones where capital cannot mobilize labor power and pump out surplus value. They become inhospitable to accumulation. To the

---

[83] Pete Pattisson, et al., "Revealed: 6,500 Migrant Workers Have Died since World Cup Awarded," *The Guardian*, February 23, 2021, www.theguardian.com/global-development/2021/feb/23/revealed-migrant-worker-deaths-qatar-fifa-world-cup-2022.

[84] International Labor Organization, "Assessment of Occupational Heat Strain and Mitigation Strategies in Qatar," jointly published by the ILO and the FAME Laboratory, Department of Exercise Science, University of Thessaly, 2019, www.ilo.org/wcmsp5/groups/public/---arabstates/---ro-beirut/documents/publication/wcms_723545.pdf.

extent that these zones are centers for global agribusiness and extractive industries, their collapse represents a crisis for capitalism as a whole. An uninhabitable earth is not a place where capital can freely accumulate. We are reaching what Moore defines as *negative value*: "the emergence of historic natures that are incrementally hostile to capital accumulation."[85]

The turnover time of capital must continuously accelerate, whereas the "turnover" (reproduction) time of human and extra-human nature remains for the most part constant. The renewal time of soil, forests, oceans, and so on cannot on their own accelerate. Capitalist efforts to accelerate them through industrial and high-tech applications such as chemical fertilizers and pesticides, GMOs, and fish farming can only speed up environmental devastation. As one report puts it, the more capital "tames" natural processes, the more they spin out of control, provoking new and more aggressive taming measures with increasingly calamitous outcomes.[86] For centuries, the possibility of moving to new frontiers created the mirage of suspending the most problematic aspects of the taming cycle. But as frontiers of appropriation close, the very dynamism of the system intensifies the evolutionary response so that "extra human natures are evolving faster than the controls imposed on them."[87]

Notwithstanding momentary spurts of growth, as we saw in Chapter 1, the global economy has been mired in long-term stagnation for close to half a century. The destabilization of the biospheric conditions necessary for sustained growth makes it difficult to imagine a sustained recovery of high growth rates. It is estimated that every degree Celsius of warming reduces growth on average by about one percentage point. Similarly, it is predicted that warming of just 3.7 °C will cause unfathomable economic damages of $551 trillion, some six times the value of the current entire global economy.[88] These types of losses are beyond depression levels.

Accumulation at all cost, the Salvage Collective insists, is "accumulation by extinction." The ecological emergency is without doubt a social

---

[85] Moore, *Capitalism in the Web of Life*, p. 98.
[86] Food and Water Watch, Superweeds: How Biotech Crops Bolster the Pesticide Industry (Washington, DC: Food and Water Watch, 2013), https://seedsoffreedom.info/doc/superweeds.pdf.
[87] Moore, *Capitalism in the Web of Life*, p. 274.
[88] Wallace-Wells, *The Uninhabitable Earth: Life after Warming*, p. 128.

emergency for the exploited classes and also an emergency for capital insofar as it destroys capital's capacity to reproduce. There can be no resolution of the "metabolic rift" from within the system of global capitalism because by its very nature it is a form of social organization that *can never be stationary*.[89] A global reformism or neo-Keynesianism, even if it could bring some temporary alleviation to the sharpest social contradictions of neoliberal globalization, is not viable because any project that seeks to resolve the crisis from within the logic of capital accumulation must by definition seek continued growth, that is, the continued expansion of the system (the endless self-expansion of capital). The depletion of resources, the destruction of the biosphere, and the impending collapse of agriculture make impossible a further expansion of the system, at least if we want to avoid a mass dying. Implosion will be the eventual outcome to the drive for further expansion.

It is important not to get swept up into catastrophism and the political fatalism it engenders. Yet it cannot be denied, to reiterate, that the planetary ecosystem on which human civilization is based is breaking down under the impact of global capital accumulation, suggesting that any new phase of global capitalist expansion would be catastrophic in itself. The abolition of perpetual economic growth that is necessary to avoid environmental disaster can only be achieved by the abolition of capitalism, since, by definition, capitalism is based on the endless accumulation of capital. At some point it will become impossible for the system to reproduce itself as the biosphere collapses. The crisis of global capitalism, hence, is existential for humanity *and* for capitalism.

In the long run, the only solution is to replace global capitalism as a system organized for private accumulation with one based on rational planning, resource allocation according to basic social needs, and a radical reduction in waste and frivolous consumption along the lines of an ecosocialism, or what Huber, in his study *Climate Change as Class War*, calls a "proletarian ecology."[90] Huber's calls for a

---

[89] Among many studies I have found invaluable from the "Marxist ecology" perspective, and from a deeper historical, world system and earth system perspective, Sing C. Chew, *The Recurring Dark Ages: Ecological Stress, Climate Changes, and System Transformation* (Lanham: AltaMira Press, 2006).

[90] Huber, *Climate Change as Class War*. There is a very considerable literature now on ecosocialism. I found useful, inter-alia, the short book by Michael Lowy, *Ecosocialism: A Radical Alternative to Capitalist Catastrophe*

radicalized Green New Deal, the "degrowth" movement advanced by Jason Hickel in his bestselling book, *Less is More*, the critique of "the imperial mode of living" put forth by Brand and Wissen, all propose radical reforms to mitigate the crisis and a "just transition" to an ecological and postcapitalist future. These and other critiques of capitalism's accumulation imperative make important contributions to a rising worldwide anti-capitalist environmental consciousness and to an ecosocialist vision.[91]

As humanity fights for its survival, it has no choice but to replace a system based on the imperative of accumulation with one based on social need and in harmony with the rest of nature (which is to also say, in harmony among ourselves). However, *the tempos of economic crisis and ecological collapse diverge* insofar as a collapse of the planetary ecosystem may take decades or centuries, should it not be averted by mass action and revolution against capitalism, whereas ongoing economic turbulence and more financial collapses such as that of 2008 followed by new rounds of expansion are likely to occur in the next years or decades. Periods of recovery, therefore, should not be confused with the resolution of the epochal crisis. In order for global capitalism to resolve the current structural crisis of overaccumulation, it must undergo new rounds of expansion, each one more catastrophic for the planetary ecosystem, each one throwing more people into the ranks of surplus humanity, aggravating the political and military dimensions of the crisis. The capitalist class and privileged strata of humanity may be able to survive collapse for decades to come, but there is eventually a terminal point as mass extinction and the radical alteration of the natural environment make life for our species and most others impossible. Sustainable capitalism is an oxymoron.

(Chicago: Haymarket, 2015). For a recent summary of the discussion and literature around ecosocialism, see Patrick Bond, "The Case for Ecosocialism in the Face of the Worsening Climate Crisis," *Science & Society*, 86(4), 2022, pp. 485–515.

[91] See Jason Hickel, *Less Is More: How Degrowth Will Save the World* (London: Windmill Books, 2021); Ulrich Brand and Markus Wissen, *The Imperial Mode of Living: Everyday Life and the Ecological Crisis of Capitalism* (London: Verso, 2021).

5 | Into the Vortex

Systemic Crisis

In recent years a number of studies have been published on the end of capitalism.[1] There is no doubt that global capitalism is in decay. In times of rapid social change, variables that help us make sense of things are most fluid and great uncertainty hangs in the balance. What is certain is that the existing state of affairs cannot be sustained. Radical change is coming, but exactly what that change will involve is not clear. We can identify structural contradictions with more certainty than we can predict how they play out in political conjunctures, given the role of the subjective and of contingency. Each wave of historic expansion has given capitalism a new lease on life, yet each wave has been more sweeping and destructive, each amplifying the underlying contradictions that we have explored in the previous chapters. The most fundamental of those contradictions is that between private profit and social need. Capitalism cannot reproduce itself without reproducing human and extra-human nature, yet this reproduction has natural limits. In Chapter 1 I observed that there are two types of capitalist crises, cyclical and structural. We can identify a third type, *systemic*, by which I mean a crisis that cannot be resolved within the capitalist system. Its resolution requires a supersession to another social order.

We are, I believe, facing a systemic crisis, but this does not mean that capitalism will collapse automatically. It is certainly possible that global capitalism will suffer an internal collapse, as Henrique

---

[1] See, inter-alia, Wolfgang Streeck, *How Will Capitalism End?* (London: Verso, 2016); J. K. Gibson-Graham, *The End of Capitalism (As We Knew It)* (Minneapolis: University of Minnesota Press, 2006); Minqi Li, *The Rise of China and the Demise of the Capitalist World Economy* (New York: Monthly Review Press, 2009); Ulrike Hermann, *The End of Capitalism: Why Growth and Climate Protection Are Incompatible – and How We Will Live in the Future* (New York: Scribe, 2025).

Grossman argued, or a breakdown because there are no longer new colonial frontiers to conquer, as Rosa Luxemburg insisted. More likely, however, global capitalism will experience an ongoing disintegration as the conditions that allow for its continued reproduction and expansion become exhausted, like a fire turning into embers rather than a revolutionary bucket of water or a sudden cataclysmic implosion that extinguishes its flame all at once. It will be among these embers that the new may become clear. It would be a fruitless exercise to try to predict exactly *how* the end of capitalism plays out. I believe Wolfgang Streeck[2] struck the right metaphor by suggesting that it will "die by a thousand cuts" (a phrase first used in China to describe a medieval torture technique for the slow, painful death of the victim), punctuated by trauma wounds such as devastating wars, depressions, local revolutions, political turmoil, and regional collapses, like the slow bleeding to death of an exhausted beast.

There are numerous scenarios that may cut short the life of global capitalism before the system extinguishes itself. I do not rule out anticapitalist revolution that would resolve the global crisis nor a world war that would destroy us all. However, more likely than world revolution are revolutions in coming years and decades in individual countries. No matter how politically cynical it appears, nonetheless, I contend that no revolution in a single country can withstand the pressure from global capital. There would need to be a cascade of revolutions along the lines of what Leon Trotsky referred to as a permanent revolution. More to the point, the end of capitalism will be the result not of a single factor – earlier I discussed the problem of monocausal explanations of capitalist crises – but of the accumulation of conditions and limitations for reproduction and renewal, more a crumbling than a collapse, pockmarked by what systems theorists refer to as cascading systems failures. The next question is *how* will this great crumbling take place? I suggest, on the one hand, that it is *already* taking place. On the other hand, speculating on specific scenarios is foolish. Instead, we return to the matter of the relationship between theory and history. I concur with Mandel insofar as "inability to re-unite theory with history inevitably leads to inability to re-unite theory and practice."[3]

---

[2] Wolfgang Streeck, *How Will Capitalism End?* (London: Verso, 2016).
[3] "As soon as 'laws of development' come to be regarded as so abstract that they can no longer explain the actual process of concrete history, then the discovery of such tendencies of development ceases to be an instrument for

Hence, the present study is considerably less ambitious than a claim to settle the matter of the demise of global capitalism. Rather, it is an attempt to serve as notes for, or as a point of departure, *towards a theory of global capitalism's exhaustion*. In this concluding chapter I analyze the critical historic moment as we enter the second quarter of the twenty-first century and leave open the possibility of any number of futures. The only future I rule out is the long-term stabilization of global capitalism. If we manage to avoid annihilation in a world war, the most likely scenario in the next years and decades is a new round of capitalist expansion, as I suggested previously, punctuated by conflicts and upheavals everywhere, through the digital transformation of global circuits of accumulation that opens up productive outlets for unloading surplus accumulated capital and momentarily restores growth and profit rates. Such a transformation would have to be coupled with a global Keynesian-style program of transnational taxation, redistribution, and regulation in order to offset extreme levels of social polarization, expand markets, and mediate intra-capitalist competition and inter-state conflict. Should reform of such a radical nature actually occur, it may prolong the life of capitalism for years and even decades.

In the early years of globalization, many observers turned to the notion of a double movement put forth by Karl Polanyi in his famed study, *The Great Transformation*.[4] Polanyi argued that as capitalism emerged, it disembedded the market from society (the first movement), wreaking havoc on people and nature. This liberation of the market from any social constraint led to mass upheavals in which society forced capital to become reembedded through the welfare and regulatory state (the second movement). Those that followed Polanyi suggested that capitalist globalization disembedded global society from the global economy and that the second movement, presumably the global justice movement, would reembed it through the return to some sort of a neo-Keynesian welfare state involving transnational redistribution and regulation of global markets.

---

the revolutionary transformation of this [capitalist] process," noted Mandel in reflecting on the limitations of the monocausal explanations for crisis that abstract from the actually history of world capitalism. Ernest Mandel, *Late Capitalism* (London: Verso, 1975 [1972]), p. 20.

[4] Karl Polanyi, *The Great Transformation: The Political and Economic Origins of Our Time* (New York: Beacon, 1967 [1944]).

Into the Vortex 183

This is indeed what the reformist elements among the transnational elite have been calling for.⁵ The more far-sighted organic intellectuals and political managers of global capitalism in the World Economic Forum (WEF), the Trilateral Commission, and other elite enclaves have been searching for a model beyond neoliberalism that could revitalize global capitalism. The WEF launched its "global governance" initiative in the early 2000s in an attempt to strengthen policy coordination among leading national states,⁶ followed by its "stakeholder capitalism" initiative in 2020.⁷ Stakeholder capitalism, in the WEF view, must be the new "global organizing principle for business." Corporations should work with states and international institutions – essentially, with transnational state apparatuses – to subordinate short-term profit-making to the imperatives of long-term global capitalist stabilization involving a measure of transnational regulation and social welfare.⁸

Along parallel tracks, the report of the Trilateral Commission Task Force on Global Capitalism in Transition, released in 2022, claimed that capitalism is now in the midst of a fifth transition. The first, mercantilism, lasted for some 300 years. This was followed in the nineteenth century by "liberal industrial capitalism," and then in the twentieth century by "managed" capitalism, what I have referred to as nation-state redistributive, or Fordist-Keynesian capitalism. The fourth, neoliberal capitalism, is now fracturing. A new, fifth stage whose contours are not yet in focus must address the three great challenges of climate change, the disruptions triggered by the digital revolution, and rising inequalities.⁹ Yet another initiative along very similar lines was the

---

⁵ On the aspirations of this reformist elite, see William I. Robinson, *Can Global Capitalism Endure?* (Atlanta: Clarity Press, 2022).
⁶ World Economic Forum, "Global Governance Initiative: Executive Summary, 2004."
⁷ World Economic Forum, "Measuring Stakeholder Capitalism: Towards Common Metrics and Consistent Reporting of Sustainable Value Creation," White Paper, September 2020, www.weforum.org/stakeholdercapitalism/about/.
⁸ World Economic Forum, "What is Stakeholder Capitalism?", January 22, 2021, www.weforum.org/agenda/2021/01/klaus-schwab-on-what-is-stakeholder-capitalism-history-relevance/.
⁹ The Trilateral Commission, "Report on the Task Force of Global Capitalism in Transition," Cambridge, MA, June 2022, https://acrobat.adobe.com/link/track?uri=urn%3Aaaid%3Ascds%3AUS%3A36b64e0b-a325-35f0-a6c8-2420e7a748b4.

creation in 2020 by 550 reformist-oriented transnational corporate executives and their organic intellectuals from around the world of the Council for Inclusive Capitalism, a term that seems to be substitutable with "stakeholder capitalism."[10]

Some among these reformist elites have turned for inspiration to the Chinese model of capitalism, which they see as an alternative to neoliberalism that goes beyond neo-Keynesianism. China, according to WEF founder and executive chairman Klaus Schwab "is a role model for many countries" and an exemplar of stakeholder capitalism.[11] China registered double-digit growth rates from 1980 to 2008. It is unlikely, however, notwithstanding WEF expectations, that the Chinese model of state capitalism I discussed earlier can offer a long-term solution to the structural crisis of overaccumulation. China is subject to the same contradictions internal to capitalism as the rest of the global economy. As elsewhere, the 2008 crisis marked a turning point for China in which growth rates experienced a secular decline, dropping to the 5 percent range by the end of the 2010s and remaining there into the next decade.[12] Chinese capitalism began to show many of the telltale structural signs of crisis: A hypertrophied financial sector, including banking assets that ballooned to some $50 trillion in 2021, not including shadow finance; a runaway spiral of household and corporate debt that went from 178 percent of GDP in 2010 to 287 percent in 2021; overcapacity; a slowdown in growth rates; and social polarization.[13] But even as China has served as the anchor of globalization in recent decades, the generalization of its model cannot be accomplished by China or any one set of national state managers, even if they wished to do so, for reasons we already discussed in Chapter 3.

---

[10] See the Council's website: www.inclusivecapitalism.com/.

[11] As cited in Bradford Betz, "World Economic Forum Chair Klaus Schwab Declare on Chinese State TV: 'China is a Model for Many Nations'," *Fox News*, November 23, 2022, www.foxnews.com/world/world-economic-forum-chair-klaus-schwab-declares-chinese-state-tv-china-model-many-nations/. See also discussion in Michael Rectenwald, *The Great Reset: Unraveling the Global Agenda* (Nashville: World Encounter Institute/New English Review Press, 2023).

[12] See World Bank, "GDP Growth (Annual%) – China," accessed on December 10, 2021 at https://data.worldbank.org/indicator/NY.GDP.MKTP.KD.ZG?locations=CN.

[13] For these figures, see The Economist, "Bail-Outs and Bedlam," *The Economist*, September 25, 2021, p. 12.

If a global neo-Keynesianism or the globalization of the Chinese model could be achieved, for at least two reasons it would at best buy the system time. First, a new regime of global accumulation that manages to resolve the crisis of overaccumulation and attenuate social polarization would not automatically translate into political stabilization. Historically, wars have pulled the capitalist system out of accumulation crisis, while they serve to deflect attention from political tensions and problems of legitimacy. The immediate danger we face is the threat of geopolitical conflict escalating into a world war. Given the magnitude and the widespread availability of the means of violence and destruction, it is difficult to see how humanity would survive the type of large-scale conflicts and world wars that were associated with hegemonic decline and international chaos in the past. The gravest danger is that international conflagration escalates into nuclear confrontation in the face of a renewed global conventional and nuclear arms race that is already underway. The Bulletin of the Atomic Scientists, founded in 1945 by Albert Einstein and other scientists who had been involved in the Manhattan Project, has been continuously publishing since 1947 its annual Doomsday Clock warnings. Its 2024 Clock warned that climate change and the risk of nuclear war placed the hands at "90 seconds to midnight" – the closest the hands have ever been to the symbolic Armageddon.[14]

Second, even assuming a military conflagration of cataclysmic proportions can be averted, any new round of expansion will be catastrophic to the planetary ecosystem. The type of statis required to avert a collapse of the biosphere is not an option for capitalism. Expansion is an imperative of the system's reproduction, requiring a never-ending appropriation of new natures that are finite. At some point in the coming decades, the self-expansion of capital must cease in order for us to survive on a habitable planet. We will reach a point by the next century in which we either overthrow capitalism or we perish. The alternative to superseding capitalism with a system that puts an end to exploitation, alienation, and war with nature, which is also to say war with ourselves, as we are a part of nature, is the calamitous collapse of civilization and quite possibly of much life on the planet.

The TCC and its political allies are aware of the severity of the global crisis. The WEF's annual "Global Risk Report" for 2023 I discussed

---

[14] Bulletin of the Atomic Scientists, "A Moment of Historic Danger: It is Still 90 Seconds to Midnight," January 23, 2024, https://thebulletin.org/doomsday-clock/current-time/.

in the Introduction warned of a runaway "polycrisis."[15] But the ruling groups appeared clueless as to how to maintain their grip on power beyond violence and repression as they moved to permanent crisis management. They are unable to reestablish hegemony as the global capitalist consensus they managed to construct at the height of neoliberalism continues to disintegrate in the face of economic turmoil, geopolitical confrontation, environmental degradation, and the worldwide revolt of the working and popular classes. Instead, the crisis is leading the world toward war and fascism. We are headed for an extremely violent and widespread devaluation and destruction of capital. Another major financial crisis is on the horizon. That is absolutely anticipated. However, when it will hit and what will be its outcome cannot be predicted with precision. It may already be underway by the time this book is in the reader's hands, and just as possible is a significant reactivation of the global economy in the immediate future, whether through the digital restructuring now underway or through escalating wars that, in all the perversity of capitalism, constitute crucial economic stimuli.

Capitalism's Extermination Impulse

Genocide: The Gaza Option

As global capitalism descends into decadence, its extermination impulse rises to the surface. Gaza gives us a ghastly window into this impulse, a case study in how conjunctures play out in time and space in the context of global capitalist crisis. As I set about to write this final chapter in mid 2024, the world watched in horror the genocidal Israeli assault on the Palestinians of Gaza, live-streamed by the victims themselves through cellphones and social media. In January 2024, the International Court of Justice found the charge of genocide that South Africa had brought before it to be plausible and issued a preliminary injunction that Israel ignored. The genocide set off an unprecedented global intifada of solidarity with Palestine. In the United States, Europe, and elsewhere, students set up protest encampments to demand that their universities divest from companies doing business in Israel, pushing a campaign of boycott, divestment, and sanctions, known as BDS,

---

[15] World Economic Forum, "The Global Risks Report 2023," Geneva, 2023, www3.weforum.org/docs/WEF_Global_Risks_Report_2023.pdf.

that decades earlier proved successful in placing international pressure on South Africa to end apartheid. The campus protests were met with violent police repression. The CEO of Palantir, Alex Karp, made clear the very high stakes that the TCC believed were at play in the protests. Palantir, a multi-billion-dollar high-technology corporation based in Silicon Valley, signed an agreement in 2024 with the Israeli Ministry of Defense to supply the Israeli Defense Forces with artificial intelligence and other digital technologies that were used in the siege on Gaza. "College campus protests are not a sideshow. They *are* the show," said Karp. "If we lose the intellectual battle, we will not be able to deploy any army in the West, ever."[16]

Yet it would be a mistake to reduce the project of genocide in Palestine to Israel and to the Western states that gave it steadfast support. Gaza is a global space through which we see all the features and contradictions of a global capitalism in crisis, and thus it tells us a much larger story than meets the eyes. Individual capitalist states and transnational elites outside of the West condemned the genocide and withdrew political support for Israel, but they were not – and could not be – against the imperatives of global capital accumulation that undergirds the extermination impulse. To the contrary, political opposition to genocide by the BRICS countries (Brazil, Russia, India, China, South Africa, and several other more recent members) simultaneous to the promotion of worldwide capitalist expansion is a contradiction internal to the managers of global capitalism. Indeed, even in the midst of the genocide in 2024, Russia remained the number one supplier of coal to Israel and South Africa the number two supplier. India provided military equipment to Israel for use in Gaza, the West Bank, and Lebanon. Such weapons were unloaded at Israel's main port, Haifa, which had already been privatized to the Shanghai International Port Group and the India-based Adani group, while China–Israeli trade in 2023 hit a record $20 billion.[17] The Chinese state-owned high-tech

---

[16] Karp made these comments in an interview published by CNBC in mid-May 2024 (no exact date given) as a Youtube here: www.youtube.com/watch?v=E1schQrqJFU. See also Palantir's own X (formerly Twitter) post: https://x.com/PalantirTech/status/1788316740847276358.

[17] For these details, see Patrick Bond, "'The Blessing' for Genocide: Nearly all BRICS+ Regimes Nurture Israel, Economically," *Counterpunch*, October 3, 2024, www.counterpunch.org/2024/10/03/the-blessing-for-genocide-nearly-all-brics-regimes-nurture-israel-economically/.

company Hikvision supplied facial recognition technology to Israel for use in the occupied Palestinian territories.[18]

This contradiction is brought home in the Middle East. Globalization in the region began in the 1980s and accelerated with the 2003 U.S. invasion and occupation of Iraq that followed the establishment in 1997 of the Middle East Free Trade Area and a host of related bilateral and multilateral regional and extra-regional free trade agreements and structural adjustment programs. This integration unleashed a cascade of transnational corporate and financial investment in finance, energy, high-tech, construction, infrastructure, luxury consumption, tourism, and other services. It brought Gulf capital, including trillions of dollars in sovereign wealth funds, together with capital from all around the world, involving the EU, North and Latin America, and Asia, inextricably enmeshing them all in global circuits of accumulation.[19] China became the region's principal trading partner and an important investor in Israel, including in high-tech military and security.[20] The Middle East-Asia corridor had become by the 2020s a major conduit for global capital flows.[21] The genocide in Gaza could not be separated from the global networks that enabled it. The framework of "Western imperialism" against the Middle East entirely missed the larger picture.

This globalization of the Middle East fundamentally changed regional politics. For much of the post-WWII period, the world understood the region through the frame of the "Arab-Israeli conflict." The Arab countries withheld diplomatic recognition of Israel and boycotted it economically. This Arab–Israeli conflict corresponded to an earlier historical period, especially from 1948 to 1967, in the context of decolonization, the spread of pan-Arab nationalism and socialism,

---

[18] Amnesty International, "Automated Apartheid: How Facial Recognition Fragments, Segregates and Controls Palestinians in the OPT," 2023, pp. 9, 62, 76, https://banthescan.amnesty.org/opt/wp-assets/Automated_Apartheid.pdf.

[19] Dinesh Nair, Anthony Di Paola, and Ben Bartenstein, "BP-Adnoc's Landmark Israel Gas Bid in Flux as Conflict Escalates," *Bloomberg*, October 11, 2023, www.bloomberg.com/news/articles/2023-10-11/bp-adnoc-s-landmark-israel-gas-bid-in-flux-as-conflict-escalates.

[20] Giulia Interesse, "China-Israel Bilateral Trade and Investment Outlook, *China Briefing*, October 11, 2023, www.china-briefing.com/news/china-israel-investments-trade-outlook-belt-and-road-initiative/.

[21] HSBC, "Middle East-Asia Corridor – A New Conduit for Global Capital," September 4, 2023, www.gbm.hsbc.com/en-gb/insights/financing/middle-east-asia-corridor-a-new-conduit-for-global-capital.

and the development of postcolonial national bourgeoisies. As globalization arrived, it integrated Israeli-based capital with capitals throughout the region. The "Arab-Israeli conflict" as a political frame proved to be an anachronism, a backward political-diplomatic dispensation out of sync with the emerging global capitalist economic structure and the replacement of nationally oriented with transnationally oriented Arab bourgeoisies, starting with the 1970s oil diplomacy that integrated these bourgeoisies into global financial circuits, and continuing through neoliberal structural adjustment, free trade, and the transnationalization of Arab capital. The Israeli and Arab bourgeoisies developed common class interests that came to trump historical political differences over Palestine.

A new political-diplomatic dispensation was needed. Already Egypt had normalized relations with Israel in 1980, followed by Jordan in 1994. In 2020 the UAE and several other Gulf countries signed the Abraham Accords that normalized relations between the Israeli state and the Arab signatories. Soon hundreds of thousands of Israeli tourists were filling hotels in Dubai and elsewhere, while Gulf investment groups poured hundreds of millions into the Israeli economy.[22] The clincher in this process was to be Saudi–Israeli normalization that had been scheduled for late 2023. This normalization was to be not just a matter of economic integration; it was to have cemented the region-wide oppressive political and social order. However, normalization was placed on hold by the October 7, 2023 Hamas attack on Israel and the subsequent Israeli siege. Just weeks into the Gaza war, the global corporate and financial elite meeting in Riyadh for their annual "Davos in the Desert" conclave fretted over how the Gaza war had escalated geopolitical tensions and financial instability and strategized over how they could place back on track a project of global capitalist expansion in the region.[23]

The Palestinians, in effect, stood in the way of a new round of accumulation. The 1948 Nakba that established the Israeli state involved

---

[22] *The Economist*, "Can Israeli-Emirati Business Ties Survive the Gaza War?", November 2, 2023, www.economist.com/business/2023/11/02/can-israeli-emirati-business-ties-survive-the-gaza-war.

[23] Hadeel Al Sayegh and Rachna Uppal, "As Israel-Hamas War Rages, Global Finance Chiefs in Saudi Sound Gloomy Note," *Reuters*, October 24, 2023, www.reuters.com/world/middle-east/israel-hamas-war-rages-finance-chiefs-meeting-saudi-pessimistic-2023-10-24/.

the violent expulsion of the Palestinians and the expropriation of their land but also the subordinate incorporation of hundreds of thousands of Palestinian laborers to work on Israeli farms, construction sites, industries, caregiving, and other service jobs and the conversion of the West Bank into a captive market for Israeli capitalists. Up until globalization took off in the late twentieth century, the relationship of Israel to the Palestinians reflected classical colonialism, in which the colonial power had usurped the land and resources of the colonized and then exploited their labor. But Middle Eastern integration into the global economy and society on the basis of neoliberal economic restructuring, trade liberalization, and IMF-supervised austerity helped spark the spread of mass worker and social movements and grassroots democratization pressures, reflected in the Palestinian intifadas, the labor movement across North Africa, mounting social unrest, and most visibly in the 2011 Arab Spring uprisings.

The Palestinian intifadas aggravated the historic tension that Israel faced between the drive to ethnically cleanse the Jewish state and the need it had for cheap, ethnically demarcated labor. Starting in the 1990s, Israel began to resolve this tension between dispossession/super-exploitation and dispossession/expulsion in favor of the latter. The Israeli economy began to draw on transnational migrant labor from Africa, Asia, and elsewhere as globalization displaced millions in former Third World regions and made them available as transient labor that is disenfranchised and easy to control. Transnational migrant workers in Israel need not be subjected to the apartheid system imposed on Palestinians because their temporary migrant status achieves their social control and disenfranchisement more effectively, and because they are not demanding the return of occupied lands and do not have a political claim to a state. While this transient migrant labor system is a worldwide phenomenon, it became a particularly attractive option for Israel because it does away with the need for politically troublesome Palestinian labor. By the 2010s, hundreds of thousands of migrant workers – by some estimates up to 600,000 – from Thailand, China, Nepal, Sri Lanka, India, Eastern Europe, the Philippines, Kenya, and elsewhere came to form the predominant labor force in Israeli agribusiness and increasingly in other sectors of the economy, under the same precarious conditions of super-exploitation and discrimination that migrant workers face around the world. In the wake of the 2023 Hamas attack, Israel deported the remaining 10,000

Gazan Palestinian workers back to Gaza. In early 2024, even in the midst of war, thousands of Indian and other foreign workers were pouring into Israel to replace them.[24]

As the Palestinians went from cheap labor to surplus humanity, the siege of Gaza and the West Bank appeared to be a form of primitive accumulation. In the midst of Israeli bombardments in Gaza, the Israeli government set about granting licenses to transnational energy companies for gas and oil exploration off the Mediterranean coast, part of its plan to become a major regional gas producer and energy hub as well as an alternative to Russian gas for Western Europe.[25] Israeli real estate companies advertised for the construction of luxury homes in bombed-out Gaza neighborhoods, while others spoke of resuscitating the Ben Gurion Canal Project that has been dormant since it was originally proposed in the 1960s. The project involved building an alternative to the Egyptian-run Suez Canal that would run from the Gulf of Aqaba across the Negev desert and Gaza out to the Mediterranean. The only thing stopping the newly revised Canal project was the presence of Palestinians in Gaza.[26]

If these are the particular historical circumstances that constitute the background to the Gaza war, they also help us understand how the world-historic conjuncture of globalization and crisis can activate the always-latent potential for extermination. Gaza became an

---

[24] For these details and for further discussion, see William I. Robinson, "Palestine and Global Crisis: Why Genocide? Why Now," *Journal of World-Systems Research*, 30(1), 2024, https://jwsr.pitt.edu/ojs/jwsr/article/view/1264/1651.

[25] See, inter-alia: Rachel Donald, "Everybody Wants Gaza's Gas." Planet: Critical. October 31, 2023, www.planetcritical.com/p/everybody-wants-gazas-gas; Kate Arnoff, "Don't Expect Gas Companies to Pause Business on Gaza's Behalf." The New Republic, November 14, 2023, https://newrepublic.com/article/176917/fossil-fuel-companies-plowing-ahead-profit-israeli-gas; United Nations Conference on Trade and Development (UNCTAD, "The Economic Costs of the Israeli Occupation for the Palestinian People: The Unrealized Oil and Natural Gas Potential," Geneva, 2019, https://unctad.org/system/files/official-document/gdsapp2019d1_en.pdf.

[26] Yvonne Ridley, "An Alternative to the Suez Canal is Central to Israel's Genocide of the Palestinians." *Middle East Monitor*, November 5, 2023, www.middleeastmonitor.com/20231105-an-alternative-to-the-suez-canal-is-central-to-israels-genocide-of-the-palestinians/; Bret Wilkins, "Cashing in on Genocide: Israeli Firm Pitches Beachfront Real Estate in Leveled Gaza." *Common Dreams*, December 19, 2023, www.commondreams.org/news/israel-settlements-gaza.

exemplary space for experimentation with how the ruling groups may choose to resolve the problem of surplus humanity, a site for the exercise of new forms of absolute despotic power that has no need for political legitimacy. The ruling classes fear mass uprisings in the face of ongoing and growing popular protest around the world against a wide range of social and economic injustices and other capitalist pathologies, such as the climate emergency, racism, and the persecution of immigrants. Palestine is more than old-fashioned settler colonialism. It shows us the past and the future, a redux of the dark history of European colonialism that reached its zenith in the nineteenth and early twentieth centuries, and also a horrifying glimpse into the future. The Gaza genocide was a microcosm and extreme manifestation of the fate that awaits the working classes and surplus humanity as the global order hardens into ever more virulent and violent forms of domination, symbolizing a radical new stage in ruling class modalities of control, the creation of new geographies of containment and butchery.

Locking In, Locking Out, and Locking Up Surplus Humanity

Gaza as a giant open-air concentration camp locking up the disposable Palestinian proletariat may be an extreme case of managing surplus humanity, yet such mega-prison geographies are spreading around the world. In 2023, the Salvadoran government inaugurated its draconian mega-prison, Center for the Confinement of Terrorism, the largest in the world, locking up 40,000 prisoners, virtually all of them young, unemployed, and impoverished. Salvadoran president Nayib Bukele enjoyed overwhelming popular support for this "get tough" program of mega-imprisonment without trial. If Gaza shows us the extermination option, El Salvador provided a model of control over surplus labor based on manipulating insecurity and inducing fear in the face of crime and social violence, themselves the consequence of chronic poverty, unemployment, and deprivation. A similar strategy was pursued in Ecuador. There, the government of far-right president Daniel Noboa, after coming to power in 2023, allowed violent criminal groups to operate with impunity as they established control in numerous poor communities. Only after the population became desperate for safety from the lawlessness and violence of these mafias did the government step in, this time to declare a state of emergency in 2024 and deploy the army throughout the country. But rather than targeting the criminal gangs, the army turned on the indigenous-led popular protest mobilizations while at the same time the government implemented new IMF-mandated austerity measures under cover of the country's military emergency.[27]

Mega prisons as a method of containing surplus humanity have spread very rapidly around the world. After the Salvadoran prison was opened, Brazil, China, Turkey, Thailand, the Philippines, and India, among other countries, announced similar plans for prisons holding tens of thousands of people. Between 2016 and 2021, construction began in Turkey on no less than 121 new prisons. In Sri Lanka the government announced in 2021 plans to build a 200-acre prison complex that would allow 100,000 people to be detained across the country – more than three times the prison population in that year. Egypt announced that year it would soon open a new prison to lock up 30,000 people. Prisons are increasing not just in scale but in geographic remoteness – the better to keep surplus labor far away from the centers of power and wealth. While there were already some 200 private for-profit prisons around the world, many of those under construction were to be "public-private partnerships," with corporations contracted to build and run prisons – for a handsome profit, of course. In Kazakhstan, the government entered into such private corporate deals to build no less than forty new prisons by 2025.[28] Virtual cities warehousing surplus labor point to new forms of spatial control over a mass of dispossessed humanity, part of a larger movement toward authoritarian, dictatorial, and even fascist systems to legitimate and develop the global police state as an "iron dome" of global capitalism.

Paramilitary insurgencies and multinational military deployments have displaced upward of seven million people in the Congo in recent years, most of them in the Eastern provinces, with the aim of opening

---

[27] Pablo Dávalos, "De la Demolición Institucional a la Doctrina del Shock," *Rebelión*, January 13, 2024, https://rebelion.org/de-la-demolicion-institucional-a-la-doctrina-del-shock/, and "La Doctrina del Shock para Asegurar el Retorno del FMI a Ecuador," *Rebelión*, January 22, 2024, https://rebelion.org/la-doctrina-del-shock-para-asegurar-el-retorno-del-fmi-a-ecuador/.

[28] For all these details, see Penal Reform International, "Global Prison Trends 2022: New Prisons, Planning and Location," www.penalreform.org/global-prison-trends-2022/new-prisons-planning-location/, and Penal Reform International, "Global Prison Trends 2023," https://cdn.penalreform.org/wp-content/uploads/2023/06/GPT-2023.pdf.

up access to the country's vast mineral resources, including abundant deposits of gold, diamonds, silver, cobalt, coltan, tin, oil, gas, and more.[29] Often reported as ethnic conflict or struggles among local factions for political control, these are proximate causes of transnational wars by capitalists and states to seize recourses in which twin dimensions of the global police state merge: militarized accumulation, or accumulating capital and seizing resources through war and conquest, and accumulation by repression, or accumulating capital by mass repression of the working and popular classes.[30] In some of these cases the playbook comes from the colonial era. Ethnic differences are fanned or simply created, so as to divide the victims of conquest and expulsion. Favored factions are given weapons and allowed to commandeer the crumbs that fall from capital's banquet table. The better to distribute weapons and let the oppressed cannibalize one another, allowing capital to seize resources in the stampede of confusion and proximate conjunctural explanations for humanitarian crises. This may become the pattern as whole regions, even states, collapse, in which political and economic mafias, paramilitary organizations, cartels, mercenaries, criminal gangs, and corrupt clicks fill power voids, as we have seen in Haiti and Sudan, or in parts of the Mexican and Colombian countryside, for instance, ruling by terror and extortion in consort with transnational capital.

Borders become less physical markers of territory than axes around which intensive control over those expelled is organized. They are ever more militarized. In the half century of capitalist globalization, no less than sixty-three border walls have been built worldwide to lock in or keep out surplus humanity.[31] Along with repression meted out by states, transnational migrants are subject to the predation of human traffickers, slavers, drug cartels, and other criminal gangs. Borders between national jurisdictions become war zones and zones of death. Palestine is one such death zone, the most egregious perhaps, because it is tied to occupation, apartheid, and ethnic cleansing. Yet tens of

---

[29] United Nations International Organization for Migration (IOM), "Record High Displacement in DRC of Nearly 7 Million," October 30, 2023, www.iom.int/news/record-high-displacement-drc-nearly-7-million.

[30] For extended discussion, see Robinson, *The Global Police State*.

[31] Ainhoa Ruiz Benedicto, Mark Akkerman, and Pere Brunet, "A Walled World: Towards a Global Apartheid," Transnatioan Institute, Amsterdam, 2020, file:///Users/user./Downloads/informe46_walledwolrd_centredelas_tni_stopwapenhandel_stopthewall_eng_def-1.pdf.

thousands have died along the U.S.–Mexico border and North Africa–Middle East-Europe corridors and in other borderlands between surplus humanity and zones of intense accumulation in the global economy. The U.S. border patrol reported more than 7,000 deaths at the Mexico/U.S. border from 1998 to 2023, likely a great underestimate since it does not take into account those whose bodies were not recovered or the many who have died making the long journey through Central America and Mexico. The figures for deaths in the Mediterranean are utterly shocking – more than 24,000 drowned or disappeared from 2014 to 2024.[32] As I pointed out in Chapter 2, just two months before the October 7, 2023 Hamas attack that sparked the Israeli genocide, it was reported that Saudi border guards opened fire without warning and in cold blood killed hundreds of Ethiopian migrants trying to join 750,000 of their countrymen already working in the Kingdom.[33]

The British government has taken the lead in introducing draconian new forms of surplus labor management. In 2023 it began to lock up asylum seekers on floating prisons off the country's coast, retrofitting a barge with cabins the size of prison cells.[34] The next year it began to deport refugees thousands of miles away, to the Central African country of Rwanda, known for its widespread human rights abuses, for the processing of asylum requests. Once the precedent was set, other EU countries announced they would follow suit and establish their own systems for the banishment of asylum applicants to distant lands where they can be removed from the public eye and silenced, in the process generating handsome profit for the private corporations involved in transporting and processing the deportees. The price tag to deport the first 300 asylum seekers from Britain was an astounding $665 million,

---

[32] *Democracy Now!*, "Dozens of Asylum Seekers Drown in Shipwrecks Near Tunisia and Libya Attempting to Reach Europe," January 3, 2025, www.democracynow.org/2025/1/3/headlines/dozens_of_asylum_seekers_drown_in_shipwrecks_near_tunisia_and_libya_attempting_to_reach_europe. The report cites International Organization for Migration data.

[33] Human Rights Watch, "They Fired on Us Like Rain: Saudi Arabian Mass Killings of Ethiopian Migrants at the Yemen-Saudi Border," August 21, 2023, www.hrw.org/report/2023/08/21/they-fired-us-rain/saudi-arabian-mass-killings-ethiopian-migrants-yemen-saudi.

[34] Amelia Gentleman, "'Cabins Slightly Larger Than a Prison Cell': Life Aboard the UK's Barge for Asylum Seekers," *The Guardian*, July 21, 2023, www.theguardian.com/uk-news/2023/jul/21/life-aboard-bibby-stockholm-asylum-seeker-barge-home-office-tour.

or $2.2 million per person, a small fortune explainable only by the profit to be made by the private corporations contracted.[35] With millions fleeing conflicts around the world, noted the 2024 annual report of Amnesty International, migration management and border enforcement relied on the proliferation of abusive technologies, including digital alternatives to detention, border externalization technologies, data software, biometrics, and algorithmic decision-making systems.

Gaza, the Congo, and other hellscapes are real-time alarm bells that genocide may become a powerful tool in the decades to come for resolving capital's intractable contradiction between surplus capital and surplus humanity. Political chaos and chronic instability can create conditions quite favorable for capital. Working-class populations abandoned by states and parties that claim to represent them turn to ethnonationalist ideologies and charismatic politicians as the global police state ratchets up surveillance and repression with sophisticated new digital technologies of social control and as communities continue to be pillaged, their environments poisoned and ravaged, rendering the planet increasingly uninhabitable for vast swathes of the world's population. The 2024 Amnesty International report warned of an unprecedented collapse of human rights, "a harvest of terrifying consequences from escalating conflict and the near breakdown of international law, a dismal picture of alarming human rights repression and prolific international rule-breaking, all in the midst of deepening global inequality, superpowers vying for supremacy and an escalating climate crisis." It is worth quoting the report at length:

> Lawlessness, discrimination and impunity in conflicts and elsewhere have been enabled by unchecked use of new and familiar technologies which are now routinely weaponized by military, political and corporate actors. Big Tech's platforms have stoked conflict. Spyware and mass surveillance tools are used to encroach on fundamental rights and freedoms, while governments are deploying automated tools targeting the most marginalized groups in society. Israel's flagrant disregard for international law is compounded by the failures of its allies to stop the indescribable civilian bloodshed meted out in Gaza. Many of those allies were the very architects of that post-World War Two system of law. Alongside Russia's ongoing aggression against Ukraine... [there are a] growing number of armed conflicts, and

---

[35] Aljazeera, "UK Passes Law to Send Asylum Seekers to Rwanda after Months of Wrangling," April 23, 2024, www.aljazeera.com/news/2024/4/23/uk-law-to-send-asylum-seekers-to-rwanda-passed-after-months-of-wrangling.

massive human rights violations witnessed, for example, in Sudan, Ethiopia and Myanmar. The global rule-based order is at risk of decimation.... Political actors in many parts of the world are ramping up their attacks on women, LGBTI people and marginalized communities who have historically been scapegoated for political or electoral gains. New and existing technologies have increasingly been weaponized to aid and abet these repressive political forces to spread disinformation, pit communities against each other and attack minorities.... States including Argentina, Brazil, Indian and the UK have increasingly turned to facial recognition technologies to police public protests and sporting events and discriminate against marginalized communities – particularly migrants and refugees.[36]

Death and Destruction: "Fit Quite Nicely with Our Portfolio"

Historically wars have provided critical economic stimulus and pulled the capitalist system out of accumulation crises, as I noted previously, while they serve to deflect attention from political tensions and problems of legitimacy. But there is something qualitatively new going on now with the rise of the global police state. The limits to growth must be overcome with new technologies of death and destruction. Barbarism appears as the face of capitalist crisis. Each new conflict around the world opens up fresh profit-making possibilities to counteract stagnation. Endless rounds of destruction followed by reconstruction have ripple effects. They fuel profit-making not just for the arms industry, but for engineering, construction, and related supply firms, high-tech, energy, and numerous other sectors, all integrated with the transnational financial and investment management conglomerates at the center of the global economy. These are the gales of creative destruction, to be followed by booms of reconstruction.

Death, destruction, and mayhem, even genocide, provide perverse lifelines for a transnational capitalism in crisis to the extent that they are inextricably linked to opening up new opportunities for

---

[36] Amnesty International, "The State of the World's Human Rights," Annual Report 2023/24. These quotes are from the executive summary, dated April 24, here: www.amnesty.org/en/latest/news/2024/04/amnesty-international-sounds-alarm-international-law-flagrant-rule-breaking-governments-corporate-actors/. The full report in English is available here: file:///Users/user./Downloads/POL1072002024ENGLISH.pdf.

accumulation through violence. The 2022 Russian invasion of Ukraine and Israel's genocidal war in Gaza launched the following year paved the way for a more sweeping militarization of what was already a global war economy. U.S. officials were keenly aware that the drive to expand NATO to Russian borders would eventually push Moscow into a military conflict. The RAND corporation, a Pentagon-affiliated think tank, explained U.S. goals in a 2019 study: "We examine a wide range of nonviolent measures that could exploit Russia's actual vulnerabilities and anxieties as a way of stressing Russia's military and economy and the regime's political standing at home and abroad."[37]

Beyond the United States, war stocks around the world, in Europe, India, China, and elsewhere experienced surges following the Russian invasion in expectation of an exponential rise in global military spending.[38] As one giddy consultant to Boeing, General Dynamics, Lockheed Martin, and Raytheon Technologies explained in the wake of the Russian invasion: "For the defense industry, happy days are here again."[39] U.S. senator Lindsey Graham was even more to the point. The war in Ukraine "is all about making money" and U.S. official should "cut deals" for access to Ukraine's rare earth minerals in

---

[37] The report added: "The steps we examine would not have either defense or deterrence as their prime purpose. Rather, these steps are conceived of as elements in a campaign designed to unbalance the adversary, leading Russia to compete in domains or regions where the United States has a competitive advantage, and causing Russia to overextend itself militarily or economically." James Dobbins, et al., "Extending Russia: Competing from Advantageous Ground," The Rand Corporation, 2019, www.rand.org/pubs/research_reports/RR3063.html. This summary page provides a link to the full report.

[38] Sergei Kiebnikov, "War Stocks Are Surging As Russia-Ukraine Conflicts Rages On: Lockheed Martin, Northrop Up 20%," *Forbes*, March 4, 2022, accessed on March 12, 2022 at www.forbes.com/sites/sergeiklebnikov/2022/03/04/war-stocks-are-surging-as-russia-ukraine-conflict-rages-on-lockheed-martin-northrop-up-20/?sh=26fe902c43f0; Asit Manohar, "Russia-Ukraine War: Defence Spending to Surge. Experts Bullish on These Stocks," *Mint*, March 2, 2022, accessed on March 12, 2022 at www.livemint.com/market/stock-market-news/russiaukraine-war-defence-spending-to-surge-experts-bullish-on-these-stocks-11646209657963.html; Edward Helmore, "Defense and Cybersecurity Stocks Climb Amid Russia's Invasion of Ukraine," *The Guardian*, February 28, 2022, accessed on March 12, 2022 at www.theguardian.com/business/2022/feb/28/defense-cybersecurity-stocks-russia-ukraine-eu.

[39] Lee Hudson and Connor O'Brien, "Russia Threat Sets Off Mad Dash for Defense Dollars," *Politico*, March 28, 2022, www.politico.com/news/2022/03/28/russia-ukraine-defense-dollars-00020590.

order to "enrich ourselves."[40] A year after the Russian invasion, the Gaza war provided fresh stimulus for militarized accumulation, with billions flowing to Israel from the U.S. and other Western governments and international arms dealers. Orders at many of the world's biggest arms companies were near record highs within weeks of the October 7, 2023, Hamas attack.[41] The siege of Gaza, as one Morgan Stanley executive put it, "seems to fit quite nicely with [our] portfolio."[42] In 2023 there were more armed conflicts around the world than any other year since World War II.[43]

Such bursts of militarized accumulation help offset the overaccumulation crisis further into the future. It took World War II to finally lift world capitalism out of the Great Depression. The Cold War legitimated a half century of expanding military budgets, followed by the so-called "war on terror" that helped keep the economy sputtering along in the face of chronic stagnation in the first two decades of the century. It is estimated that from 2001 to 2021 the "war on terror" cost $21 trillion.[44] The Russian invasion of Ukraine accelerated but did not originate the ongoing surge in military spending around the world. It is notable that state military spending worldwide skyrocketed in the wake of the 2008 global financial collapse, even beyond the post-September 11, 2001, spending hike, rising from about $1.5 trillion in 2008 to over $2.3 trillion in 2023 – coinciding perfectly with continued stagnation in the global economy following the Great Recession, and suggesting that the heightened militarization of the global economy is

---

[40] Stavroula Pabst, "Gleeful Graham: Ukraine War All 'About Money'," *Responsible Statecraft*, November 25, 2024, https://responsiblestatecraft.org/lindsey-graham-ukraine/.

[41] Brett Wilkins, "Business of War Is Booming as Orders Surge at Top Global Arms Firms," *Common Dreams*, December 28, 2023, www.commondreams.org/news/arms-trade-2666819054.

[42] Eli Clifton, "Hamas Has Created Additional Demand: Wall Street Eyes Big Profits," *The Guardian*, October 30, 2023, www.theguardian.com/world/2023/oct/30/wall-street-morgan-stanley-td-bank-ukraine-israel-hamas-war.

[43] Siri Aas Rustad, "Conflict Trends: A Global Overview, 1946–2023," Peace Research Institute Oslo (PRIO), PRIO Paper, Oslo, 2024, https://cdn.cloud.prio.org/files/92a7aad5-3572-4886-9e9c-8aa155f1d0f4/Conflict_Trends-2024_DIGITAL.pdf?inline=true.

[44] Tom O'Connor, "'War on Terror' Cost U.S $21 Trillion, Its Conflicts Killed Nearly One Million, Report Shows," *Newsweek*, September 2, 2021, www.newsweek.com/war-terror-cost-us-21-trillion-its-conflicts-killed-nearly-one-million-reports-show-1625114.

as much or more a response to this chronic stagnation than to perceived security threats.[45] If bursts of militarized accumulation such as that unleashed by the events of September 11, 2001, then by the 2008 financial collapse, and later on by the Russian invasion and the Israeli siege, help offset the overaccumulation crisis further into the future, they are also high-risk bets that heighten worldwide tensions and push the world dangerously toward all-out global conflagration.

The new digital technologies, with AI at their center, are widely deployed in these systems of warfare, social control, and repression. In its siege of Gaza, for instance, it was revealed that the Israeli military used at least three new advanced AI systems known as Lavender, Gospel, and Where's Daddy to autonomously generate thousands of potential targets for assassination based on facial recognition and other AI-collected surveillance data. As the Israeli commander of the military unit that deployed this technology explained, the system was used to get around "human bottlenecks for both locating the new targets and decision-making to approve the targets." AI-guided bombs were then used in attacks. "It's really like a data driven mass assassination factory," said the commander. "Once you go automatic target generation goes crazy."[46] Gaza thus became an artificial intelligence warfare testing ground and practice run for capitalist states around the world. "Other states are going to be watching and learning," said one White House official.[47] In 2024 there were 109 countries that are

---

[45] See Robinson, *The Global Police State*, for details. See also: Statista, "Global Defense Spending from FY 2008 to FY 2022," www.statista.com/statistics/859455/global-defense-spending/ (note: this site requires for full access that one open an account, which is free); Alex Irwin-Hunt, "Defence [sic] FDI and Military Spending Hits Record Highs," FDI Insights, March 20, 2024, www.fdiintelligence.com/content/news/defence-fdi-and-military-spending-hits-record-highs-83607?xnpe_tifc=4kH7xfes4IYdxfHDxkYZxjpsafeWaeiWhFW9RkeZVusDx.xlnk4vaf4LVjncauUlrFUuxILN4.zJOFe_OFblb.bT&utm_source=exponea&utm_campaign=fDi%20-%20Intelligence%3A%20Graph%20Time%20-%20Newsletter%20-%2020.3.24&utm_medium=email.

[46] Yuval Abraham, "'Lavender': The AI Machine Directing Israel's Bombing Spree in Gaza," +972 *Magazine*, April 3, 2024, www.972mag.com/lavender-ai-israeli-army-gaza/.

[47] Harry Davies, Bethan McKernan and Dan Sabbagh, "The Gospel: How Israel Uses AI to Select Bombing Targets in Gaza," *The Guardian*, December 1, 2023, www.theguardian.com/world/2023/dec/01/the-gospel-how-israel-uses-ai-to-select-bombing-targets.

either using or have approved the use of facial recognition technology for surveillance purposes.[48]

Beyond warfare, ubiquitous and all-invasive algorithmic digital and biometric surveillance allow a more despotic control over workers, a digital totalitarianism. *The Economist* reported in 2022, at a time when hundreds of millions of employees had moved to remote work due to the COVID-19 pandemic:

> Both the scope and the scale of corporate surveillance has ballooned. Global Demand for employee spying software more than doubled between April 2019 and April 2020. Within weeks of the first lockdown in March 2020, search queries for monitoring tools rose more than 18-fold. Surveillance software makers sales jumped. At Time Doctor, which records videos of users screens or periodically snaps photos to ensure they are at their computer, they suddenly trebled in April 2020, while those at Desktime more than quadrupled.... Employers can follow every keystroke or mouse movement, gain access to webcams, scan emails for gossip or take screenshots, leaving the surveilled worker none the wiser. Last year, Fujitsu, a Japanese technology group, unveiled AI software which promises to gauge employees' concentration based on their facial expression.[49]

But those engaged in remote and other screen-based office work are far from the sole targets of the new digital surveillance and exclusion. *Business Insider* revealed in 2020 that Amazon was monitoring its employees' social media posts for hints of union organizing efforts, while management in the Whole Foods stores it owns had begun deploying a heat map capable of detecting the physical congregation of workers for the same reason.[50] A global drive to implement digital central bank currencies, a move that would provide governments with an unprecedented degree of surveillance and control over their populations' consumption habits, is well under way.[51]

---

[48] UNCTAD Digital Economy Report 2021 (New York: United Nations Publications, 2021), p. 45.

[49] *The Economist*, "Welcome to the Era of the Hyper-Surveilled Office," May 14, 2022, www.economist.com/business/welcome-to-the-era-of-the-hyper-surveilled-office/21809219.

[50] David B. Feldman, "Against the Global Police State. Review of The Global Police State, by William I. Robinson," *New Politics*, February 17, 2021, https://newpol.org/against-the-global-police.

[51] Martha Muir, "Central Banks' Digital Currency Plans Face Public Backlash," *Financial Times*, March 12, 2023, www.ft.com/content/e0b7f134-c935-4cd6-bf27-460c37db1512.

New systems of biometric control defy the imagination. The Massachusetts Institute of Technology reported in 2019 that it developed a method of tattooing nanocrystals under the skin that can transmit a signal readable by a smartphone or computer for the purpose of biomedical identification and for access to vaccination history and other data.[52] Two years earlier, the Otsuka Pharmaceutical corporation announced that it had invented an ingestible pill, subsequently approved by the U.S. Food and Drug Administration, that contained a nanochip that could "send a wireless signal to relevant authorities," presumably to doctors when a medication is ingested.[53] Meanwhile, the U.S. military's research wing, DARPA, developed a similar technology called "hydrogel" that would be introduced into the body through a dispenser placed underneath the skin. Once developed, DARPA privatized the hydrogel technology to Profusa, which announced that it had prepared an injectable biochip with which "COVID could be detected."[54] While defenders of these invasive technologies claimed that they were intended to aid doctors in treating patients, we must recall that under capitalism, medical technologies and treatments are developed and administered not to treat or cure patients (although that may well be an outcome) but to generate profit, that is, to accumulate capital. But as we saw with the COVID contagion, such technologies are as much or more so deployed for purposes of tracking and control of those noncompliant with state edicts.

As states turn toward coercive and authoritarian forms of social control, many are also doubling down with a radically conservative social retrenchment, often veiled in religious mysticism. In the United States, abortion and other reproductive rights have been rolled back. In December 2022, the Indonesian government passed a new criminal code that outlawed sex outside of marriage, imposing severe jail terms for violators, and also made it illegal for Indonesians to abandon

---

[52] Anne Trafton, "Storing Medical Information Below the Skin's Surface," *MIT News*, accessed on November 14, 2022 at https://news.mit.edu/2019/storing-vaccine-history-skin-1218.

[53] *Associated Press*, "Video Shows Pfizer CEO at Davos in 2018 Talking about Another Company's Pill," May 23, 2022, accessed on November 14, 2022 at https://apnews.com/article/fact-check-Pfizer-CEO-Davos-256352183903.

[54] Profusa webpage, dated July 12, 2016, "Profusa, Inc. Awarded $7.5M DARPA Grant to Develop Tissue-integrated Biosensors for Continuous Monitoring of Multiple Body Chemistries," https://profusa.com/profusa-inc-awarded-7-5m-darpa-grant/.

their religion or to persuade anyone else to be a nonbeliever. In that same month, the Afghan government resumed public executions and ordered judges to adhere closely to sharia law, the interpretation of which included stoning adulterers. In Iran those who protested against the government during the 2022–2023 popular uprising in the wake of a Kurdish woman who died in police custody after being arrested for not wearing her veil properly were declared by the government to be committing an "act against God" punishable by death. In 2023, the Russian Supreme Court banned the "international LGBT movement" as "extremist."[55] In what may be the most extreme case, the Ugandan government passed an Anti-Homosexuality Act in 2023 that stipulated a lifetime prison sentence and even the death penalty for anyone engaged in homosexual relations.[56] Proliferating religious and other fundamentalisms – Christian, Hindu, Jewish, and Islamic – use the language and symbolism of earlier periods, but their emergence is a very modern and often neofascist response to capitalist globalization and crisis.

The emerging global capitalist pluralism may offer greater maneuvering room for popular struggles around the world, but a politically multipolar world does not mean that emerging poles of global capitalism are any less exploitative or oppressive than the established centers. The established West and new centers in the emerging polycentric world are converging around remarkably similar "Great Power" tropes, especially jingoistic – often ethnic – nationalism and nostalgia for a mythologized "glorious civilization" that must now be rejuvenated. The Spenglerian narratives differ from one country to another according to particular histories and cultures. In China, hypernationalism combines with Confucian obedience to authority, Han ethnic supremacy,[57] and a new Long March to recover great power

---

[55] Human Rights Watch, "Russia: Supreme Court Bans 'LGBT Movement' as 'Extremist'," November 30, 2023, www.hrw.org/news/2023/11/30/russia-supreme-court-bans-lgbt-movement-extremist.

[56] Human Rights Watch, "Uganda: Court Upholds Anti-Homosexuality Act," April 4, 2024, www.hrw.org/news/2024/04/04/uganda-court-upholds-anti-homosexuality-act.

[57] A new Chinese university textbook, reportedly required reading, claims that Han Chinese are a biological (bloodline) race going back two million years to a distinct hominid species, James Leibold, "New Textbook Reveals Xi Jinping's Doctrine of Han-Centric Nation-Building," China Brief, 24(11), May 24, 2024, https://jamestown.org/program/new-textbook-reveals-xi-jinpings-doctrine-of-han-centric-nation-building/.

status. For Russian President Vladimir Putin, it is the glory days of a "Great Russia" empire anchored in Eurasia, politically propped up by extreme patriarchal conservatism that Putin calls "traditional spiritual and moral values" embodying the "spiritual essence of the Russian nation over the decaying West." In the United States, it is the hyper-imperial bravado of a waning Pax Americana legitimated by the doctrine of "U.S. exceptionalism" and the bombast of "democracy and freedom," at whose fringe has always been white nationalism, now incarnated in a rising fascist movement as "replacement theory." To these we could add pan-Ottomanism, Hindu nationalism, and other such quasi-fascist ideologies in this rising polycentric world.[58]

The Urgency of the Moment and the Centrality of the Political

We are in the midst of a global civil war, superimposed on which is escalating geopolitical and interstate conflict whose ultimate causes emanate from the class contradictions that are at the heart of global capitalism. This is a civil war not in the sense that there are two opposed armies in combat but, rather, class-based conflict is escalating as the global proletariat and popular classes are everywhere facing off against the ruling groups and the states that they control. Mass protest around the world has come in successive waves since the globalization boom of the 1990s. The turn of the century saw the rise of what has become known as a global justice movement and the formation in 2001 of the World Social Forum that brought together thousands of social movements of every stripe, anti-neoliberal insurgencies in much of Latin America, the second Intifada in Palestine, worldwide mobilizations against the U.S. invasion of Iraq, and much more. The burst of protest following the 2008 finance collapse produced such diverse popular insurgencies as the Occupy movement that started in the United States and spread to all continents, the Red Shirts movement in Thailand, the Arab Spring that shook the Middle East and North Africa, and mass uprisings against austerity from Europe to Asia to Africa, among many others. The late 2010s and early 2020s saw sustained rebellion

---

[58] For these details, see William I. Robinson, "The Travesty of 'Anti-Imperialism'," *Journal of World-Systems Research*, 29(2), 2003, https://jwsr.pitt.edu/ojs/jwsr/article/view/1221/1628.

across the globe, from mass strikes in Colombia, Ecuador, and elsewhere in Latin America, to the Yellow Vest movement in France, the Black Lives Matter insurrection in the United States, the Sudanese revolution, a second Arab Spring with protest breaking out in Tunisia, Jordan, Iraq, Lebanon, and elsewhere in the region, a prolonged strike and mass mobilization in Sri Lanka, two mass strikes in India involving hundreds of millions of workers and farmers, and so on.

Where the global revolt headed is not clear. Are we headed for a new period of reform, a worldwide fascist dictatorship, a revolutionary rupture with capitalism, or a collapse of global civilization – in the words of *The Communist Manifesto*, toward "the common ruin of the contending classes?" I do not have the answer to these questions precisely because the future depends on a host of political and subjective factors that make prediction difficult if not impossible. Outcomes will depend on the struggles among antagonistic social and class forces, the politics that come out of these struggles, and on contingent circumstances that present themselves in ways often hard to anticipate.

There is little doubt, however, that cataclysmic upheavals are on the horizon – indeed, are already unfolding – as global capitalism enters a stage of unrestrained predation. The capitalist form of global society cannot continue. The ultra-rich appear to have read the writing on the wall. They are preparing for a collapse by buying up islands, building luxury bunkers, and hiring private armies. In his book, *Survival of the Rich*, Douglas Rushkoff describes a meeting he had with a handful of tech billionaires. "The CEO of a brokerage house explained that he had nearly completed building his own underground bunker system, and asked: 'how do I maintain authority over my security force after the event? The event. That was their euphemism for the environmental collapse, social unrest, nuclear explosion, solar storm, unstoppable virus, or malicious computer hack that takes everything down." He concludes: "Their extreme wealth and privilege served only to make them obsessed with insulating themselves from the very real and present danger of climate change, rising sea levels, mass migrations, global pandemics, nativist panic and resource depletion. For them, the future of technology is about only one thing: escape from the rest of us."[59]

---

[59] Douglas Rushkoff, "The Super-Rich 'Preppers' Planning to Save Themselves from the Apocalypse," *The Guardian*, September 4, 2022, www.theguardian.com/news/2022/sep/04/super-rich-prepper-bunkers-apocalypse-survival-richest-rushkoff.

Welcome to Global Fortress, a world in which the global elite and a narrow stratum of highly skilled intellectual and technical workers may be able to survive, even flourish for a time being, behind the ironclad walls of a global police state, with tightly controlled flows of labor and resources from the mass of humanity to the privileged few. The global refugee crisis is a sign that this fortress world is already upon us. This fortress will depend on transient labor flows similar to the migrant labor system that has developed in the Gulf countries, where workers from far away locations are allowed in temporarily, their movements tightly controlled, and their labor, civil, and political rights denied under conditions tantamount to slavery. But most of surplus humanity will be locked out of the fortress and left to die by abandonment. Great suffering is already upon the world's poor majority, masses who do not have the power or the resources to protect themselves from war, climate change, and economic collapse. Their suffering will get worse. There will be mass dying. These are modern Victorian holocausts, in the same way as British colonialists in India during Victorian times simply allowed countless millions of redundant Indian subjects to die of starvation and disease as they syphoned resources out of the country.[60] However, this fortress world should not be counterposed to collapse because it could not be sustained indefinitely. Apart from massive widespread conflict that unprecedented inequalities and mass deprivation generate, the fortress can never be self-contained. It would sooner rather than later run up against what Rushkoff refers to as the "insulation equation." The collapse of agriculture, resource depletion, the inability to maintain industrial production and global supply lines, and so on, would not make the fortress sustainable.

The global expansion of capitalism has taken place through the dialectic of countervailing tendencies to the tendency toward crisis and breakdown. At their core, these tendencies and countertendencies are driven by class struggles played out in the economy, in the political system, and in the realms of culture and ideology. Mass class struggle in the early decades of the twentieth century forced the ruling groups to change course and thereby acted to renew world capitalism in the wake of the Great Depression. Mass struggles in the 1960s and 1970s

---

[60] The phrase is in reference to the book by Mike Davis, *Late Victorian Holocausts: El Niño Famines and the Making of the Third World* (London: Verso, 2002).

precipitated globalization as a response from above that renewed the worldwide circuits of capital accumulation. What are the possibilities now of a radical reform of global capitalism? Could resistance and struggle from below force the system into a substantial restructuring premised on a redistribution of wealth downward and some modicum of popular control over, or at least constraint on. the implacable process of capital accumulation?

The protest movements since the turn of the twenty-first century have fought against austerity, endemic corruption, authoritarianism and dictatorship, displacement, police violence, inequality, unemployment, corporate abuse, environmental degradation, and so on. The global revolt has spread unevenly and faces many challenges, including fragmentation, absorption by capitalist culture and, for the most part, the lack of a coherent left ideology and a vision of a transformative project beyond immediate demands. We do need to fight for radical reforms that could ameliorate the worst of the climate catastrophe, redistribute wealth downward, expand social welfare on a mass scale, impose some regulation on the global market, and reign in on capital's policy prerogatives. But the only hope of achieving such reform is not by appealing to the good sense of the powers that be but by sustained mass struggle that could leave those powers with no alternative but to take substantial reform measures. A radical reform would come about by militant struggle from below in the same way that social democracy, the welfare state, and regulated mid twentieth-century capitalism came about because trade unions, socialists, communists, and other mass struggles from below seeking a much more radical transformation forced the ruling groups to shift direction. The struggle for reform of a very substantial nature may push back the threat of descent into barbarism and create more favorable conditions for an accumulation of counter-hegemonic and anti-systemic forces. The project of a global socialist-oriented left, in my view, however, should not be a reform of global capitalism but its overthrow. As this study has made clear, in the long run radical reform can only attenuate the crisis. The question is, will capitalism's epochal crisis take humanity down with it before we are able to overthrow it?

Beyond reform, what are the possibilities of a revolution against capitalism? The Bolshevik leader Vladimir Lenin, described the *symptoms* of what he called a revolutionary situation: (1) when there is a crisis in the prevailing system and it is impossible for the ruling classes to rule in the old way; (2) when the want and suffering of the oppressed classes have grown more acute than usual; and (3) when as a consequence the masses increase their historical action. These symptoms are clearly upon us. We are at this time, however, very far from a revolution against global capitalism. If crises arise from the objective forces of capitalism, their outcome is dependent on subjective forces that develop through numerous political, cultural, and organizational mediations. Class consciousness develops at the level of these mediations. If capitalist crises are times of great upheavals and suffering for millions of people, they also shatter complacency and activate mass struggles, for there is little room for reified illusions when survival hangs on a thread. Crises thus mediate new forms of consciousness and organization that are requisite for any system change. But this requisite will not come automatically. How to break out of the habitus of capital and forge a counterhegemonic proletarian habitus under the new conditions of twenty-first century-global capitalism?

Why has the worldwide revolt not yet seriously challenged the power of global capital? I discussed this revolt and its quandaries in my 2022 book, *Global Civil War: Capitalism Post-Pandemic*.[61] There is a rapid political polarization in global society as the center collapses between poorly organized and ideologically inchoate counterhegemonic forces and an increasingly well-organized far-right. Where is the historic subject that could bring about a revolution against capitalism? Why has this historic subject not been able to overthrow capitalism, an act of revolution being in its own objective interests? The proletariat is now the biggest class in history, billions strong, at the same time that there has been a radical decline in recent decades in proletarian class consciousness, *despite sustained popular movements and protests*, attributable in part to capital's ideological offensive, to the atomization and fragmentation of labor and everyday life, including the effects of social media, and in part to a petty bourgeois politics of identity involving hostility to the language of class. Digital communications and social media, as many have observed, generate silos among distinct political communities that exacerbate the social atomization and alienation experienced under capitalism yet also make it possible for

---

[61] William I. Robinson, *Global Civil War: Capitalism Post-Pandemic* (Oakland: PM Press, 2022).

ruling groups to constitute new forms of hegemony based on emotive manipulation in which truth and fiction are ever more blurred.[62]

In his classic study, *History and Class Consciousness*, Georg Lukacs attributed the gap between actual and ascribed class consciousness to *reification*, that is, to a profound alienation in which the world appears in an inverted form. The reality we produce through our activity in it appears to us as having an objective existence outside of the world that we ourselves have created, as a force external to us and that rules over us. Writing in the 1920s, Lukacs discussed the rise of Fordism as an emerging form of alienation (his contemporary, the Italian revolutionary Antonio Gramsci, would refer to the human beings that Fordist capitalism sought to produce as "happy robots"). The Fordist industrial revolution changed not just production but consumption, culture, and consciousness, redefining what it meant to be human. The profound changes worldwide that have taken place through capitalist globalization, as discussed in the present study, have had a similar transformative effect on culture, social being and consciousness. "If the proletariat finds the economic inhumanity to which it is subjected easier to understand than the political, and the political easier than the cultural," argued Lukacs, "then all these separations point to the extent of the still unconquered power of capitalist forms of life in the proletariat itself."[63]

How to develop the subjective and organizational conditions that would allow the mass of oppressed humanity to take advantage of the objective reality of the epochal crisis of global capitalism to push forward anti-capitalist emancipatory projects? It would be hard to look back and discover any historic precedent for such a chasm as now

---

[62] Journalist Ron Suskind discussed his interview with a high-level official in the George W. Bush administration who dismissed as outdated what the official referred to as a "reality-based community," or those who base their judgements on facts. "That's not the way the world really works anymore," declared the official. "We're an empire now, and when we act, we create our own reality. And while you're studying that reality – judiciously, as you will – we'll act again, creating other new realities, which you can study too, and that's who things will sort out. We're history's actors...and you, all of you, will be left to just study what we do." Ron Suskind, "Faith, Certainty and the Presidency of George W. Bush," *The New York Times Magazine*, October 17, 2004, www.nytimes.com/2004/10/17/magazine/faith-certainty-and-the-presidency-of-george-w-bush.html. The official was alleged to be Karl Rove.

[63] Georg Lukács, *History and Class Consciousness* (London: Merlin Press, 1971 [1923]), pp. 76–77.

exists between a world objectively ripe for revolution and a subjective rift extending the distance between potential and actuality. The most remarkable, and despairing, aspect of the global revolt is the absence, for the most part, of organized left leadership that could amalgamate within and beyond borders the diverse movements into a program for confronting global capitalism with an emancipatory project of transformation. In previous moments of major crises, such as in the late 1800s, the 1930s, and the 1960s and early 1970s, for all their shortcomings and failures, there were mass socialist, communist, and other radical challenges to capitalism from below. Yet a socialist-oriented left that could give some direction to the mass revolts should not and could not be anything like the twentieth-century worldwide socialist left, with its debilitating top-down vanguardism and patriarchal authoritarianism. When the left has come to power, it has too often acted to contain popular struggles, as we have seen in the so-called Pink Tide, which refers to the turn to the left in Latin America in the early twenty-first century by institutional means. In power it has tended to accommodate itself to transnational capital by absorbing rebellion into the capitalist state and the hegemonic order, acting as transmission belts for the structural power of transnational capital and neutering the anti-systemic potential of one uprising after another.

This tragic situation in which a popular revulsion with the global capitalist status quo and mass rebellion from below is breaking out everywhere at a time when the organized socialist left is weak or even nonexistent in many countries opens space for authoritarian populists, fascists, and warmongers to manipulate the legitimate grievances among popular sectors facing despair. What a renewal of the left could or should involve is a discussion for elsewhere, although I believe we do need political organizations that cannot be collapsed into social movements as well as the inverse – mass social movements autonomous of political parties and independent of states. We have a lot to learn from such experiments as Rojava in the Kurdish region of the Middle East, with its model of Democracy Confederalism, the Zapatistas in Mexico, and other local emancipatory struggles that place bottom-up autonomy and the struggle against patriarchy at the front and center. But there is much to debate. Autonomy and popular power at the local level are of critical importance, but we cannot leave the macro levels and the states that dominate them free of anti-capitalist, anti-systemic challenges. What is the balance between developing local, autonomous popular power and challenging the capitalist state in its own space? Any renovated left would have to rethink the relationship between social movements, political parties, and states, and how it could play the role of articulating the struggles and demands of the popular classes, bringing them to the political arena without commandeering them, much less subordinating them to the institutions of the capitalist state. We cannot transform the world by simply occupying the capitalist state and expecting that this state can be used to overthrow the rule of capital and transform society from above. On the other hand, we cannot simply ignore the question of state power, yet in the larger picture, the only justification for occupying the capitalist state is to destabilize and dismantle it from within.

Long-term stagnation and constraints on the expansion of transnational capital limit the ruling groups' ability to co-opt the global proletariat, in particular, its ability to reproduce labor aristocracies that have historically tempered class struggle. These privileged layers among the proletariat, whether referred to as Fordist workers, white-collar workers, knowledge or cognitive workers, symbolic or immaterial labor, and more recently, as members of an alleged professional-managerial class, are often salaried and have historically enjoyed more autonomy and stability than their waged counterparts[64] while providing the technical expertise and ideologies to keep the capitalist system functioning smoothly. The earlier decades of capitalist globalization, as I discussed in Chapter 2, sharpened a bifurcation of the working classes into a mass of downwardly mobile and increasingly impoverished workers and a stratum of elite workers – high-skilled and high-paid professionals, managers, technicians, and cognitive workers. This stratum surely bought into and helped achieve the legitimacy of the global capitalist historic bloc that established its hegemony in the late twentieth and early twenty-first centuries. There is no doubt that, at least in the traditional core, with its material privilege, individualism, performative identitarianism, and petty bourgeois aspirations, this class group has

---

[64] The earliest iteration of the notion of a professional-managerial class, as far as I am aware, is Barbara and John Ehrenreich, "The New Left and the Professional-Managerial Class," *Radical America*, 11(3), 1977, pp. 7–24, available at https://files.libcom.org/files/Rad%20America%20V11%2013.pdf. See more recently Catherine Liu's short book, *Virtue Hoarders: The Case against the Professional Managerial Class* (Minneapolis: University of Minnesota Press, 2021).

exercised outsized political and ideological influence. It has been one important factor in the retardation of revolutionary class consciousness and politics.

Now, however, the rapid precariatization of this sector of the proletariat, as I discussed in Chapter 2, threatens to erode the system's social base and complicates the problem of legitimation. The subsumption by capital of previously independent professionals and small or independent businesses has further undermined the ability of capital to generate a social base among the traditional middle classes. "The more a dominant class is able to absorb the best people from the dominated classes, the more solid and dangerous is its rule," observed Marx.[65] Yet the prospects for new social contracts that could "buy" class peace are undermined by the deterioration of the conditions for capitalist renewal and as the crisis in value intensifies. The "professional-managerial class" in the historic core and the new middle and professional strata in the historic periphery may continue to operate as an ideological and political buffer for the ruling groups for some time but should the crisis continue its current trajectory and should the transformations in the labor process develop as I discussed in Chapter 2, it will undermine the structural basis for this class group's privilege. Meanwhile, as new opportunities for proletarian struggle open up, resistance strategies need to develop new conceptions of class struggle, taking into account that several billion members of the global proletariat are superfluous. Earlier revolutionary theory stressed paralyzing capital at the points of production, especially through withdrawing labor. This is still a critical element of any radical challenge to capitalism. But disrupting the ability of capital to function from outside of these points is ever more essential. The mass strike becomes equally as important as the industrial strike, as do struggles around social reproduction.

It is worth reiterating that, unable to continue to buy class peace, the ruling groups are turning to hyper-nationalism – in the United States, China, Russia, India, Turkey, and elsewhere. Nationalism has always been intended to obscure transnational class interests and fuel the competition among working classes of different countries. It is, as Rosa Luxemburg noted long ago, an instrument to betray the working class by fueling the competition among working classes of different countries and obscuring transnational class interests. Socialists have

---

[65] Marx, *Capital*, Vol. III, p. 736.

to combat this nationalism. Fascism is always founded on militaristic and chauvinistic nationalism and in response to capitalist crisis. Anti-capitalist struggles must be simultaneously anti-nationalist, in which the national and the global sites of struggle become organically interconnected spaces. Emancipatory struggles can only be transnational because they require the defeat of transnational capital. "Capitalism has already provided us with an integrated alternative to the nation-state," observes Indian scholar Tarang Saluja. "We must make it ours."[66] As the crisis intensifies, a socialist politics demands an uncompromising proletarian internationalism, or transnationalism, one that does not support one geopolitical bloc over another in place of supporting working- and popular-class struggles in each country and bloc.

Capitalism constitutes one giant humanitarian crisis for a majority of the world's people and also, given the ecological dimension of the global crisis, an extinction force. The question of whether capitalism can survive indefinitely – it cannot – or whether it is doomed to collapse should not be confused with the assumption that any collapse would necessarily lead to capitalism's replacement by a superior form of social organization rather than the disintegration of human civilization. Rosa Luxemburg famously warned on the eve of the fascist insurgency of the early twentieth century that the choice was between socialism and barbarism. While there is no doubt that we are now at a moment of barbarism, acknowledging that the crisis of global capitalism threatens to become an extinction-level event is not the same as falling into a politically debilitating "catastrophism" because there is nothing inevitable about such an outcome, at least at the time I write in 2024. The future is not predetermined, yet it is only class struggle against capitalism that can steer us toward a future of socialism rather than one involving our demise. Indeed, earlier theories of capitalist crises, notably those of both Luxemburg and Grossman that I discussed at the start of this study, based their arguments on the inevitability of collapse exclusively on the laws of motion of the capitalist system, leading to criticism that they did not make room for the contingency

---

[66] Tarang Saluja, "Understanding the Logic of Settler-Colonialism, Repression, and Necropolitics from the Perspective of Transnational Penetration: Changes in the Function of Land from National to Transnational Accumulation," 2024, unpublished manuscript provided to the author.

of class struggle and attendant political strategies in the outcome of crisis. Capitalism may face a profound crisis of its own reproduction, but without class struggle to overthrow it, the system may linger on for decades, at least until such time that the collapse of the biosphere and the breakdown of social reproduction on a mass scale make the reproduction of capital impossible. It is thus impossible to separate politics from the epochal crisis of global capitalism.

Select Bibliography

Books

Ulrich Brand and Markus Wissen, *The Imperial Mode of Living: Everyday Life and the Ecological Crisis of Capitalism* (London: Verso, 2021).

Manuel Castells and Alejandro Portes, eds., *The Informal Economy: Studies in Advanced and Less Developed Countries* (Baltimore: Johns Hopkins University Press, 1989).

Robert W. Cox, *Production, Power, and World Order: Social Forces in the Making of History* (New York: Columbia University Press, 1987).

Mike Davis, *Planet of Slums* (London: Verso, 2006).

Cédric Durand, *Fictitious Capital: How Finance Is Appropriating Our Future* (London: Verso, 2017).

John Bellamy Foster, Brett Clark, and Richard York, *The Ecological Rift: Capitalism's War on the Earth* (New York: Monthly Review Press, 2010).

Martha E. Gimenez, *Marx, Women and Capitalist Social Reproduction* (Chicago: Haymarket, 2019).

Henryk Grossmann, *The Law of Accumulation and Breakdown of the Capitalist System* (London: Pluto Press, 1992 [1929]).

Jason Hickel, *Less Is More: How Degrowth Will Save the World* (London: Windmill Books, 2021).

Kerryn Higgs, *Collision Course: Endless Growth on a Finite Planet* (Cambridge: Massachusetts Institute of Technology Press, 2016).

Matthew T. Huber, *Climate Change as Class War* (London: Verso, 2022).

Henri Lefebvre, *The Production of Space* (Hoboken: Wiley Blackwell, 1992).

Rosa Luxemburg, *The Accumulation of Capital* (Eastford: Martino Fine Books, 2015 [1913]).

Ernest Mandel, *Late Capitalism* (London: Verso, 1975 [1972]).

Karl Marx, *Capital*, Vol. I (New York: International Publishers, 1967 [1867]).

Karl Marx, *Capital*, Vol. II (New York: International Publishers, 1967 [1893]).

Karl Marx, *Capital*, Vol. III (London: Penguin, 1981).

Karl Marx, *Grundrisse* (London: Penguin Books, 1973).

Jason W. Moore, *Capitalism in the Web of Life: Ecology and the Accumulation of Capital* (London: Verso, 2015).
James O'Connor, *The Meaning of Crisis: A Theoretical Introduction* (New York: Basil Blackwell, 1987).
Peter Phillips, *Giants: The Global Power Elite* (New York: Seven Stories Press, 2018).
Peter Phillips, *Titans of Capital* (New York: Seven Stories Press, 2024).
Karl Polanyi, *The Great Transformation: The Political and Economic Origins of Our Time* (New York: Beacon, 1967 [1944]).
Nicos Poulantzs, *Political Power and Social Classes* (London: Verso, 1975).
Nicos Poulantzs, *State, Power, Socialism* (London: Verso, 2014 [1978]).
Michael Roberts, *The Long Depression: How It Happened, Why It Happened, and What Happens Next* (Chicago: Haymarket, 2016).
William I. Robinson, *Global Capitalism and the Crisis of Humanity* (New York: Cambridge University Press, 2014).
William I. Robinson, *Global Civil War: Capitalism Post-Pandemic* (Oakland: PM Press, 2022).
William I. Robinson, *The Global Police State* (London: Pluto Press, 2020).
William I. Robinson, *Latin America and Global Capitalism* (Baltimore: Johns Hopkins University Press, 2008).
William I. Robinson, *Promoting Polyarchy: Globalization, U.S. Intervention, Hegemony* (Cambridge: Cambridge University Press, 1996).
William I. Robinson, *A Theory of Global Capitalism* (Baltimore: Johns Hopkins University Press, 2004).
William I. Robinson, *Transnational Conflicts: Central America, Social Change, and Globalization* (London: Verso, 2003).
Neil Smith, *Uneven Development: Nature, Capital, and the Production of Space* (Atlanta: University of Georgia Press, 2008, 3rd ed.).
Nick Srnicek, *Platform Capitalism* (London: Polity Press, 2016).
Wolfgang Streeck, *How Will Capitalism End?* (London: Verso, 2016).
Lisa Vogel, *Marxism and the Oppression of Women* (Chicago: Haymarket, 2013 [1983]).
David Wallace-Wells, *The Uninhabitable Earth: Life after Warming* (New York: Tim Duggan Books, 2019).

Articles and Reports

Amnesty International, "The State of the World's Human Rights," Annual Report 2023/24.
Michael Chui et al., *The Economic Potential of Generative AI: The Next Productivity Frontier*, June 2023, McKinsey & Company, www.mckinsey.com/capabilities/mckinsey-digital/our-insights/the-economic-potential-of-generative-ai-the-next-productivity-frontier.

Ronald W. Cox, "The Crisis of Capitalism through Global Value Chains," *Class, Race and Corporate Power*, 7(1), 2019. https://class racecorporatepower.com/wp-content/uploads/2025/02/The-Crisis-of-Capitalism-Through-Global-Value-Chains.pdf

Richard Freeman, "The Great Doubling: The Challenge of the New Global Labor Market," *The Globalist* online magazine, March 5, 2010, www.theglobalist.com/StoryId.aspx?StoryId=4542.

International Labor Organization, United Nations, *World Employment and Social Outlook*, various years.

James Manyika, "Playing to Win: The New Global Competition for Corporate Profits," McKinsey Global Institute, October 20, 2015, www.mckinsey.com/mgi/overview/in-the-news/playing-to-win-the-new-global-competition-for-corporate-profits.

Oxfam (London), *Wealth: Having It All and Wanting More*, online report accessed on March 4, 2018 at the Oxfam website, http://policy-practice.oxfam.org.uk/publications/wealth-having-it-all-and-wanting-more-338125.

William I. Robinson, "The Travesty of 'Anti-Imperialism'," *Journal of World-Systems Research*, 29(2), 2023, 587–601. https://jwsr.pitt.edu/ojs/jwsr/article/view/1221/1628.

Manfred Steger and Paul James, "Disjunctive Globalization in the Era of the Great Unsettling," *Theory, Culture, and Society*, 37(7–8), 2020, 187–203.

The Trilateral Commission, "Report on the Task Force of Global Capitalism in Transition," Cambridge, MA, June 2022, https://acrobat.adobe.com/link/track?uri=urn%3Aaaid%3Ascds%3AUS%3A36b64e0b-a325-35f0-a6c8-2420e7a748b4.

United Nations Conference on Trade and Development (UNCTAD), *Digital Economy Report*, various years.

Kees van der Pijl, *Transnational Classes and International Relations* (New York: Routledge, 1998).

World Economic Forum, "The Global Risks Report 2023," Geneva, 2023, www3.weforum.org/docs/WEF_Global_Risks_Report_2023.pdf.

World Economic Forum, "What Is Stakeholder Capitalism?," January 22, 2021, www.weforum.org/agenda/2021/01/klaus-schwab-on-what-is-stakeholder-capitalism-history-relevance/.

Index

3-D printing, 40, 89

absolute surplus value, 22–30, 43, 46–53
accumulation by repression, 38
Accumulation Crisis (O'Connor), 144
The Accumulation of Capital (Luxemburg), 18
Adani group, 187
Adorno, T. W., 44
African Carbon Markets Initiative (ACMI), 167
agribusiness, 17, 78–81, 90
AI. *See* artificial intelligence (AI)
AIG, 127
air pollution, 155, 176
Alibaba, 41
Althusser, L., 117
Amazon, 41, 201
Amnesty International, 196
Anthropic's, 46
Anthropocene, 146–152, 158
Anti-Homosexuality Act, 203
Apple, 41, 42, 50, 127, 138
Arab Spring, 190, 204, 205
Arab-Israeli conflict, 189
Arrighi, G., 134
artificial intelligence (AI), 40, 41, 44, 45, 51, 93, 94, 96–98, 100, 200
chatbot, 45
augmented reality, 40
authoritarianism, 7, 67, 113, 114, 207, 210
automation, 40, 43–46, 50, 51, 84–93
of services, 94–102

Baidu, 41
Balenciaga, 76
Bales, K., 92
Bangladesh, 60, 176

Bank of America, 127
Bank of China, 127
barbarism, 197, 207, 213
Barclays, 127
Barnosky, A. D., 154
Basu, D., 28
Belts and Roads Initiative, 121
Ben Gurion Canal Project, 191
Berkshire Hathaway, 43
Bernays, E., 160
big data, 40
biodiversity loss, 154
Black Lives Matter, 205
BlackRock, 43, 127
Blackstone, 127
Blue Carbon, 167
BNP Paribas, 127
Boeing, 198
Bolsonaro, J., 115
Brand, U., 179
Brazil, 79, 115, 139, 193, 197
Bretton Woods institutions, 104
Brundtland Report, 164, 165
Budd, A., 65, 73
Business Insider, 201

Capital (Marx), 10, 19, 21, 35, 86
capital accumulation, 5, 6, 16, 20, 27, 28, 39, 55, 57, 65, 71, 80, 82, 86, 89
Capital Vol. III (Marx), 28
capitalism, 1–3, 7, 8, 51, 52, 59, 104, 108, 111, 129, 132, 135, 140, 143, 144, 148–153, 160, 175, 178, 180, 206, 213, 214
development of, 47, 122, 131
social reproduction, 64–67
Capitalism in the Web of Life (Moore), 147
capitalist exhaustion, 8

Index 219

capitalist globalization, 40, 65, 69, 73, 87, 104, 122, 132, 134, 147, 164, 182, 194, 203, 209, 211
   history of, 30
   process of, 12
Capitalocene, 146–152
carbon capture, 170, 171
carbon emissions, 155, 159, 165, 167
carbon markets, 165, 167, 169, 170
Castillo, P., 141
catastrophism, 169, 178, 213
Center for the Confinement of Terrorism, 62, 192
ceteris paribus, 49, 52, 88, 93
ChatGPT, 45, 46, 96
Chew, S., 175
China, 5, 16, 23, 50, 58, 62, 79, 83, 89, 108, 120–126, 129–134, 138, 139, 141, 142, 181, 184, 188, 190, 193, 198, 203, 212
   electronic devices in, 50
China Communications Construction Corporate, 127
China Construction Bank, 127
China Engineering General Corporation, 127
China Investment Corporation, 43
China Life Insurance, 127
China National Coal Group Corporation, 90
China Pacific Insurance, 127
China Rail Construction Corporation, 127
China Telecommunications, 127
CIT. *See* computer, information and related technologies (CIT)
CITIC, 127
Citigroup, 76, 127
class struggles, 43–46
Claude, 46
climate change, 6, 7, 59, 149, 153–155, 162, 169, 170–174, 183, 185, 205, 206
Climate Change as Class War (Huber), 178
cloud computing, 40
cobalt, 64, 92, 138, 170, 171, 194
Coca-Cola, 127
Cohen, B., 170
Cold War, 6, 112, 124, 129, 199

colonialism, 16, 30, 84, 86, 136, 139, 190, 192
commodities markets, 35
The Communist Manifesto (Marx and Engels), 12, 205
computer, information and related technologies (CIT), 25, 26, 34, 40, 41
Conference on Parties (COP), 165
consciousness, 109, 148, 163–165, 179, 208, 209, 212
constant capital, 26–28, 33, 45, 56
Cook, T., 43
Corporate Ecoforum, 167
Council for Inclusive Capitalism, 184
Covid-19 pandemic, 41, 44, 48, 117, 201, 202
Cox, R., 129, 133
creative destruction, 39
Credit Suisse, 166
crisis management, 108, 186
crisis of value, 52
crisis theory, 8, 11
Crutzen, P., 148
cryptocurrency, 35
currency markets, 35
cyclical crises, 8, 12

DARPA, 202
debt-driven growth, 34
deep learning, 45, 46
deforestation, 79, 153
desertification, 153, 156
Deutsch Bank, 127
Dialectic of Enlightenment (Adorno and Horkheimer), 44
digitalization, 1, 11, 40, 43, 44, 46, 51–53, 94
   automation, 84–87
   super-exploitation, 84–87
Disneyland, 96
Disneyworld, 96
Disposable People (Bales), 92
DJI, 125
drought, 153, 169, 173
Dunlap, A., 171

ecological crisis, 143, 153, 158, 164, 170, 171, 173, 175
ecological holocaust, 151, 153–158, 164, 165, 173

ecological modernization, 171
economic globalization, 3
The Economist, 92, 125, 201
ecosocialism, 178
education, 17, 67, 73–75
Einstein, A., 185
Embark Trucks, 95
Engels, F., 12
environmental degradation, 70, 153, 154, 165, 175, 186, 207
European Union (EU), 79, 104, 115, 120, 123, 141, 188, 195
exploitation, 13, 15, 16, 20, 22, 24, 31, 49, 55, 59, 61, 64, 66
  oppressive conditions of, 48
extensive enlargement, 16, 20
Exxon Mobile, 42

Facebook, 42
fascism, 7, 67, 109, 113–116, 186, 213
Faulkner, N., 10, 145
FEDEX, 95
Felli, R., 150, 172, 173
female reproductive labor, 67–72
Fernandez, R., 127
fictitious capital, 35, 36
financial speculation, 33–35, 39, 67
Financial Times, 27
financialization, 1, 11, 34, 37, 40, 80, 134, 149, 166, 167, 169, 170
Fordist-Keynesian capitalism, 31, 86, 106, 183
fossil fuels, 78, 156, 158, 159, 161, 162
Foster, J. B., 146, 151, 166
fourth industrial revolution, 40, 99
Foxconn, 49
futures markets, 35

G20, 104
Gaza, 6, 63, 103
  death and destruction, 197–204
  genocide in, 186–192
  surplus humanity, 192–197
GDP, 4, 33, 42, 71, 184
Gelderloos, P., 171
General Dynamics, 198
generative artificial intelligence (AI), 44–46, 49, 96, 98

Ghost Work (Gray and Suri), 99
Glencore, 127
global capitalism, 1, 4, 5, 7, 9, 10, 53, 57, 59, 62, 63, 91, 103, 105, 107–110, 112–115, 121, 129, 133, 135, 137, 142, 143, 145, 146, 151, 153, 156, 158, 160, 171, 172, 178–183, 186, 187, 193, 203–205, 207, 209, 213, 214
  crisis of, 12–18
Global Civil War: Capitalism Post-Pandemic (Robinson), 111, 208
The Global Police State (Robinson), 38, 111
Global Risk Report (2023), 6
globalization, 1, 3–6, 11, 16, 19, 22–26, 29–31, 40, 47, 48, 67, 72, 83, 85, 88, 89, 104–107, 110, 114, 117–120, 130, 139, 145, 153, 178, 182, 184, 188, 190, 191, 204, 207
  capitalist accumulation in, 54–57
  economic, 109
Goldman Sachs, 96
Google, 41
Gordy, M., 80, 169
GPT-4, 46
Gramsci, A., 112, 131
Gray, M. L., 112, 131
Great Adaptation, 172
Great Depression, 3, 30, 31, 104, 199, 206
Great Recession, 6, 36, 111, 199
The Great Transformation (Polanyi), 182
green capitalism, 158–164
  climate emergency, 170–173
  TCC, 164–169
Green New Deal, 179
Grossman, H., 18–22, 181
The Grundrisse (Marx), 44, 97
Gucci, 76

Habermas, J., 107
Hamas attack, 189, 190, 195, 199
Harvey, D., 145
health care, 27
Hendrikse, R., 127
Hermes, 76

Hikvision, 188
History and Class Consciousness (Lukacs), 209
Hoch Standard, 166
homelessness, 60, 96
Horkheimer, M., 44
HSBC, 127, 166
Huber, M. T., 178
humiliation, 60
hydrogel technology, 202

ICSB, 127
ILO. *See* International Labor Organization (ILO)
IMF, 190, 193
imperialism, 16, 18, 30, 84, 86, 135–142
Imperialism: The Highest Stage of Capitalism (Lenin), 137
impoverishment, 6
incarceration, 60, 62
India, 23, 58, 60–62, 90, 114, 138–140, 143, 155, 176, 187, 190, 193, 197, 198, 205, 206, 212
inequality, 6, 69, 73, 81, 84, 86, 106–108, 114, 149, 159, 161, 196, 207
insecurity, 6, 107, 114, 165, 192
food, 74, 75, 96
Institute for Economics and Peace, 78, 157
Intel, 41, 124
intensive enlargement, 16–18, 20
Intergovernmental Panel on Climate Change (IPCC), 153, 155
inter-imperialist rivalry, 30, 135, 141
International Court of Justice, 186
International Labor Organization (ILO), 61, 77, 91, 93, 100
International Organization on Migration, 77
Internet of Things (IoT), 40, 93, 94
Invesco, 127
IoT. *See* Internet of Things (IoT)
iPhones, 138
Israel, 63, 103, 114, 186–190, 195, 196, 198–200

James, P., 119
Japan, 3, 33, 51, 89

Johnson & Johnson, 127
JP Morgan, 127

Karp, A., 187
Kenya, 60, 167, 176, 190
Kering corporation, 76
Kondratieff, N., 39
Kuwait Investment Authority, 43

land grabs, 35
Land Inequality Coalition, 81
land pollution, 153
large language model (LLM), 46
late capitalism, 5
Late Capitalism (Mandel), 5
The Law of Accumulation and the Breakdown of the Capitalist System (Grossman), 19
Lefebvre, H., 24, 149
Lenin, V., 13, 207
leverages, 35
Levinson, A., 43
LGBT movement, 203
lithium, 170, 171
LLM. *See* large language model (LLM)
Lockheed Martin and Raytheon Technologies, 198
Louis Vuitton, 76
Lovins, H., 170
Lukacs, G., 209
Luxemburg, R., 18–22, 38, 181, 212, 213
LVMH, 76

machine learning, 45
malnutrition, 60
Mandel, E., 5, 20
Manhattan Project, 185
Marini, R. M., 47, 48
Marx, K., 10, 12–14, 18–22, 24–28, 33–35, 42–44, 47, 48, 55–57, 59, 68, 86, 88, 97, 109, 146, 148, 152, 212
Marxism, 10, 144
Marxist-feminist theory, 69
mass struggles, 2, 30, 31, 58, 63, 86
Massachusetts Institute of Technology, 202
McKinsey & Company, 46, 49, 52, 91, 95, 98

mercantilism, 5, 183
Meta, 41
Mexico, 83, 120, 121, 139, 195, 210
Microsoft, 41, 42
Middle East Free Trade Area, 188
migration, 60, 81, 196, 205
militarized accumulation, 34, 38, 39
mining, 78, 80, 81, 88, 90–92, 115, 126, 138, 140, 164
The Ministry of the Future (Stanley), 143
MMG, 140
Moore, J., 71, 147–152, 173, 177
Morgan Stanley, 127, 199
Motorola, 127
Musk, E., 171

Nakba, 189
nano- and biotechnology, 40
National Association of Manufacturers, 123
National Retail Federation, 123
nationalism, 6, 107–109, 114, 188, 203, 204, 212
NATO, 198
Nature (journal), 154, 171
neo-Keynesianism, 178, 182, 184, 185
neoliberal capitalism, 183
neoliberalism, 5, 6, 65, 67, 103, 114, 183, 184, 186
neo-Malthusian approach, 165
Nepal, 176, 190
New Deal capitalism, 31
New International Economic Order, 3
News Corp, 127
Nike, 89
Nixon, R., 2
Noboa, D., 192
North American Free Trade Area (NAFTA), 120
Nvidia, 41, 124

O'Connor, J., 144
ocean acidification, 153, 154
Offe, C., 107
OpenAI, 46
oppression, 15, 59, 68, 69, 108, 141, 149
Organization of Economic Cooperation and Development (OECD), 27, 118

Otsuka Pharmaceutical corporation, 202
overaccumulation crisis, 28, 30, 36, 40, 53, 93, 97, 103, 109, 160, 179, 184, 185, 199, 200

Pakistan, 155, 176
Palantir, 187
Peronism, 106
PetroChina, 127
Philippines, 62, 162, 176, 190, 193
Phillips, P., 42
Polanyi, K., 182
Pollock, F., 44
polycrisis, 6, 186
post-WWII, 5, 6, 24, 27, 28, 31, 32, 38, 39, 86, 103, 106, 141, 142, 188
Poulantzas, N., 106, 116
poverty, 29, 60, 61, 69, 72–75, 81, 96, 97
Powell, L., 1–3
  Memorandum, 2, 5
privatization, 17, 66, 67, 107, 115, 132
The Production of Space (Lefebvre), 24, 149
Production, Power, and World Order: Social Forces in the Making of History (Robert), 129
profitability, 18, 21, 26–28, 31, 65
Propaganda (Bernays), 160
public debt, 34
Putin, V., 204

Qatar, 176
Qatari Investment Authority, 126
Qualcomm, 124
quantum computing, 41, 93

racism, 60, 108, 114, 192
radical political economy, 9–11, 54
RAND corporation, 198
Reagan, R., 65
real estate, 35, 80, 191
Red Shirts movement, 204
relative autonomy, 116
relative surplus value, 22–30, 43, 46–53
repression, 38, 39, 48, 110–113, 115, 121, 186, 187, 194, 196, 200

Index

reproduction, 13, 14, 19, 27, 35, 38
  of capital, 14, 16
  social, 6, 8, 11
Richemont, 76
Robinson, K. S., 143
robots, 48, 50, 90, 94, 101
Rockefeller, D., 3
Rolls Royce, 76
Rosneft, 126
Rushkoff, D., 205
Russia, 60, 125, 131, 187, 196, 198, 212
Russian invasion of Ukraine, 103, 125, 126, 141, 198, 199

Saluja, T., 213
Saudi Arabia, 79, 140, 189, 195
Schumpeter, J., 38
sea pollution, 153
Shanghai International Port Group, 187
Silicon Valley, 126, 187
SINOPEC, 127
Smith, N., 149
social control, 38, 48, 62, 105, 111–113, 162, 190, 200, 202
social exclusion, 60, 87
social polarization, 29, 30, 53
social reproduction, 6, 8, 11, 40, 48, 53, 85, 103, 113, 174, 212, 214
  capitalism, 64–67
  crisis of, 72, 83, 84, 89, 91, 93, 97, 100, 101, 108, 152, 173
  definition of, 54–57
  female reproductive labor, 67–72
  surplus humanity, 57–64
  surplus labor, 67–72
social violence, 60, 62, 114, 192
South Africa, 79, 186, 187
South Korea, 33, 51, 89
Sri Lanka, 176, 190, 193, 205
stakeholder capitalism, 183, 184
State Street, 127
state violence, 60
state-owned enterprises (SOEs), 127
Steger, M., 119
stock markets, 35
stratospheric ozone depletion, 154
Streeck, W., 181

structural crisis, 2, 5, 6, 8, 11, 12, 30, 31, 39, 53
Suez Canal, 117, 191
super-exploitation, 47, 48, 50, 57, 82, 84–93
Suri, S., 99, 101
surplus humanity, 57–64
  Gaza, 192–197
surplus labor, 56–59, 67–72
surplus value, 13–16, 19–22, 41–43, 49
  absolute, 22–30
  relative, 22–30
Survival of the Rich (Rushkoff), 205
sustainable development, 164
synthetic biology, 40

Tata, 138
Temasek Holdings Limited, 43
Tencent, 41
tendency for the rate of profit to fall (TRPF), 19, 27, 28
Thailand, 51, 62, 190, 193, 204
third industrial revolution, 40
Tiffany, 76
TNS. *See* transnational state (TNS)
tourism, 78–81
trade liberalization, 190
transnational capitalist class (TCC), 3, 4, 6, 7, 16, 23, 24, 26, 29, 31, 34, 35, 39, 40, 43, 46–48, 52, 58, 62, 65, 66, 79, 85, 88, 90, 99, 104, 107, 110, 115, 129, 132, 137, 158, 160, 162, 185, 187
  economic, 116–128
  green capitalism, 164–169
  political, 116–128
transnational corporations (TNCs), 118
transnational finance capital, 37, 38, 80
transnational state (TNS), 104, 105
transnationalization, 23, 24, 26, 103, 121, 135, 189
  of the production process, 4
Trilateral Commission, 3, 104, 183
Trotsky, L., 181
TRPF. *See* tendency for the rate of profit to fall (TRPF)

Trump, D., 115, 120, 122, 125
TSMC, 41
Turkey, 62, 139, 193, 212

U.S. Food and Drug Administration, 202
U.S. National Academy of Sciences, 78, 157
Uber, 41, 98
UBS, 127
Ukraine, 6, 125, 129, 196, 198
unemployment, 26, 45, 58, 60, 65, 74, 81, 98, 192, 207
UNHCR. *See* United Nations High Commission for Refugees (UNHCR)
The Uninhabitable Earth: Life After Warming (Wallace-Wells), 156
United Arab Emirates (UAE), 166, 189
United Kingdom (UK), 87, 138
United Nations (UN), 77, 104, 153, 157, 164, 165, 167
United Nations Conference on Trade and Development (UNCTAD), 128
United Nations Development Program, 73, 87
United Nations Environment Program (UNEP), 168
United Nations High Commission for Refugees (UNHCR), 77, 78
United States, 2, 3, 33, 46, 47, 60, 62, 63, 74, 83, 87, 88, 96, 97, 100, 115, 120–124, 126, 127, 129, 133–136, 138–142, 156, 162, 163, 170, 172, 186, 195, 198, 202, 204, 212
    exceptionalism, 204
    imperialism, 141
    invasion of Iraq, 204
UPS, 95
US Chamber of Commerce, 123

Vale, 138
van der Pijl, K., 129–131
Vanguard Group, 43, 127
variable capital, 19, 26–28, 56, 92, 93
Vietnam, 51, 89, 120, 140
virtual reality, 40
Visa, 127
Vitousek, P., 148
Volcker, P., 3

Wallace-Wells, D., 156, 172, 173
war on terror, 199
water scarcity, 153, 162, 169, 173
water supply, 17
WEF. *See* World Economic Forum (WEF)
West Bank, 187, 190, 191
Williams, J., 43
Wissen, M., 179
Wolfe, A., 107
World Bank, 73, 74
World Economic Forum (WEF), 3, 6, 104, 122, 163, 183, 184
    Global Risk Report, 185
World Social Forum, 204
World Trade Organization, 104, 105
World War II, 31, 199

xenophobia, 6, 60, 114, 122, 165

Yellow Vest movement, 205

For EU product safety concerns, contact us at Calle de José Abascal, 56–1°,
28003 Madrid, Spain or eugpsr@cambridge.org.

www.ingramcontent.com/pod-product-compliance
Lightning Source LLC
LaVergne TN
LVHW020344260326
834688LV00045B/1524